PRAISE FOR

Spring Training for the Major Leagues of Government

"The public at large has no real insight into what goes on inside government agencies. This includes newly appointed officials, including Brian, the central character in *Spring Training for the Major Leagues of Government*.

Just as spring training readies rookies for the regular season, Brian will benefit from the array of topics contained in this work. Learning the fundamentals in this case means understanding the relationships with all the participants in government: Congress, contractors, lobbyists, superiors, subordinates, etc. Knowing how to successfully navigate the rocks and shoals that will inevitably appear is vital to a successful career. Frank McDonough has been on both sides of the table; he has been there and done that. Now he offers his advice to Brian in this book."

—TOM ROLSTON,

Former IBM executive and author of two books, *Fifty Years before Crack*, and *Faith or Duty*?

"Frank McDonough is a well-traveled veteran from the halls of the Washington establishment. This book reflects his unique perspective and historical background that can benefit everyone who seeks a successful career in the service of their country."

—JOHN SINDELAR

Member of the Federal Senior Executive Service, and Principal, Sindelar Group, LLC, *a Public Sector Consulting Service*.

"Frank McDonough, a long-time career federal executive has the experience to write *Spring Training for the Major Leagues of Government* to help high-level officials to survive and thrive in high-level government jobs. Frank led a large, complex organization where he saw the government from a government-wide perspective. With regulatory and policy authority, he managed many critical programs in government to ensure that the federal civil and military agencies acquired, managed and used information technology successfully to meet the many and varied missions of government. His deep experience domestically and internationally is reflected with insights, anecdotes, and advice in the 44 chapters in *Spring Training for the Major Leagues of Government*."

—MARTHA DORRIS,

Member of the Senior Executive Service, and awardee of Presidential Rank, Service to America Medals (SAMMIE), Government Computer News' (GCN) Civilian Executive of the Year, and President of the American Council For Technology and Industry Advisory Council.

"Much as Frank McDonough is Brian's mentor in *Spring Training for the Major Leagues of Government*, he was my mentor when I worked to increase the number of our federal clients building on our existing base of State and Local Government clients.

His wisdom born of experience was often delivered with anecdotes and examples known by only a few Senior Government Executives. He not only understands how government agencies work, but he knows how to transfer that information in an understandable, and often entertaining, manner.

Brian could not find a better mentor."

—PHILIP MCGUIGAN,
A Retired Partner of McGuire Woods LLP, was the principal author of Information Technology Outsourcing, A Handbook for Government, Second Edition published by the International City/County Management Association. He is currently a Director of Fundacion Amigos de Boquete, a Panamanian Not-for-Profit Foundation providing services to residents and to over 1,100 children in 12 schools in the Boquete District of the Republic of Panama.

Spring Training for the
Major Leagues of Government
by Frank McDonough

© Copyright 2016 Frank McDonough

ISBN 978-1-63393-174-9

Published by

◤köehlerbooks™

210 60th Street
Virginia Beach, VA 23451
212-574-7939
www.koehlerbooks.com

SPRING TRAINING
FOR THE
MAJOR LEAGUES
OF
GOVERNMENT

FRANK McDONOUGH

VIRGINIA BEACH
CAPE CHARLES

TABLE OF CONTENTS

FIFTY YEARS IN GOVERNMENT

I worked a long time in different jobs and in different organizations in support of the federal government. It all began one sunny day after I packed my belongings into my five-year-old blue Cadillac Seville, left the Patuxent River Naval Air Test Center in southern Maryland, where I served as a Navy Lieutenant JG in a flight squadron, and drove the 65 miles to Washington, D.C. I would live and work in the area for five decades, never anticipating the good jobs and experiences before me.

Crossing the 14th Street Bridge into Virginia for the first time, I spotted the Pentagon on the right side of the highway. Up on the hill, in the already old World War II building stood the Bureau of Naval Personnel. BuPers was where I started my new job in the Navy's Officer Assignment Division, launching my Washington, D.C. career.

Before it was over, I would work in three Navy organizations, three civilian agencies and IBM's Federal Systems Division in this order:

Bureau of Naval Weapons
Naval Research Laboratory

IBM Corporation
Department of Health, Education and Welfare
Naval Oceanographic Office
Office of the Secretary, Treasury Department
General Service Administration

During these five decades, there were many cultural changes in society and historic events, including Elvis Presley, the Beatles, and the Vietnam War, Neil Armstrong's steps on the moon, Woodstock, lava lamps, Watergate, the Gulf War, the Iraq war and the Afghanistan war. I worked in the administrations of nine presidents—from Jack Kennedy to George W. Bush— almost one quarter of all of the nation's presidents since the country's founding.

BuPers introduced me to computers because the Navy was a leader in 1962 in the use of the technology in personnel management, and I remained in computers and information technology for more than 50 years.

Since those days in BuPers, a technology boom led to ATM machines, the Internet, small computers, cell phones, the Blackberry, iPod, iPad, iPhone, other smart phones and more. These and other changes affected the government in three ways:

- Its role in society
- How the government conducts its wars
- How it does business with the public and the private sector

After I left active duty in the Navy, I worked as a civilian in the government, starting as a GS-9 and rising to GS-15, the highest level in the General Schedule of jobs for civilian employees before moving into the senior executive service. GS-15s run the operational programs of the government. Achieving grade 15 is evidence of a good career even if you go no further. Above the grade 15s are the five levels of senior executive positions. These are often in policy and senior management jobs. Happily, I made it into the ranks of Senior Executives, where I served in the second level for 24 years before ending my government career and beginning a consulting, teaching and writing career.

As happens in all jobs, I had good days and bad. I lost a good job in a political takeover of one agency. In another job, when I received more publicity than the agency head, he summoned me in from Lancaster, Pennsylvania to his office overlooking the Washington Monument and the Department of the Interior to fire me, but he relented at the last minute.

Along the way, I represented the United States in many international discussions with the G-8 Government Online Working Council, OECD, the World Bank, the International Council for Technology in Public Administration (ICA) and other World Forums.

I organized twenty conferences for senior officials to look ahead and develop plans for the future, and I have spoken at conferences on information technology management issues more than 300 times.

Periodicals have published my work 20 times in the past decade on subjects including future government, electronic government, and the knowledge society, policy issues facing governments in the digital age, and managing hundred million dollar systems. Between 2010 and 2016, I taught these subjects to seven master's degree classes in Mexico City for the University of Texas.

Mentoring became an important career development theme in recent years, and some asked me to serve in that role. Others suggested that I write about my experiences, unusual because as a senior official, I worked in six diverse agencies with much different cultures, served as a senior executive for more than two decades, worked for 10 different political appointees, and also because of my international, writing and teaching experiences.

I took their advice, and so the conversation begins.

"When he enters the fight, all he has is his enthusiasm, the moves, and strikes that he learned during his training. As the fight progresses, he discovers that enthusiasm and training are not enough to win; what counts is experience." [1]

INTRODUCTION:

THE ASSORTED VIEWS OF GOVERNMENT

If asked what you think of the federal government in Washington, D.C., your answer would depend on where you live in the country, your religion, your education, your politics, your knowledge of history and civics, your economic status, your age and health, and your perspective on life. Whatever your background, you pack strong personal opinions about Washington.

If you are a Republican, you probably feel that the government's policies are socialistic and at odds with what the Founding Fathers intended. If you are a registered Democrat, you complain at neighborhood gatherings that greedy multinational corporations, their lobbyists and easily bought congressional officials control the government and are moving the nation in a dead-wrong direction.

A recent immigrant has one assessment of the government. A graduate student in a good public policy program has a very different picture. If you are unemployed, you likely fault it on the government's economic policies and its unwillingness to regulate Wall Street and banks too big to fail.

If your child has a disorder like autism or your parent has Alzheimer's, you may complain that the government's research dollars at the National Institutes of Health and the government's endless grants to individuals, universities and corporations are misdirected, and that there should be fewer dollars allocated to AIDS research and more to the medical problem your family faces.

If you are anti-immigrant, you rail against the government when you walk the local shopping mall in Maryland hearing not a single word of English spoken by the shoppers or the sales clerks.

If you are a rancher in Montana or a tourist guide in Alaska, you may believe that government is a land grabber.

If you lost a son or your father in a mining accident in West Virginia, you feel that the government is responsible because it did not regulate the mine's owners and their unsafe practices.

Cabinet secretaries, agency administrators and academics write books offering high-level insights about government, but they are rarely aware of what goes on deeper within the agency. Like the Lord and Lady of an English manor house, they are unacquainted with much that goes on at the lower levels.

Former corporate executives sometimes try to compare the government to their experiences in the private sector. While the infighting, personality conflicts and tensions are similar, the corporate executive has much more control over the staff and resources than does the senior government executive; and the corporate executive has a simpler life with one principal objective: elevate the price of the company's common stock.

The government is a punching bag diverting the public from the complexity of life in America, while providing material for the editorial page commentators in *The New York Times, The Wall Street Journal, The Washington Post*, CNN and FOX News as they train the populace about government, while offering unsought advice to those in power.

Tom Rolston, a friend and formerly an IBM executive, summed it up when he said the public at large has no real insight into what goes on inside government agencies. This includes newly appointed officials, including Brian.

Who is Brian?

Brian, a fictitious character, is a composite of people I encountered during my decades in government service. He attended university, worked for a startup computer company and later started a small company in the suburbs of Washington, D.C selling software services to the federal government under Small Business Administration set-aside programs.

For 12 years, he donated modest amounts of money to each political party, attended professional meetings and danced at black tie charity events. He paid his dues.

Because of his contributions to the party in power, his name recognition and his experience running a small technology business, the White House offered him a senior job in the government to manage an important priority.

Like many before him and countless others yet to come, Brian has scores of questions about working in the federal government. His questions are the same as political appointees, senior executive service officials and GS-15s have, or should have, as they consider how to move up, into and perform in senior positions.

Therefore, he finds a mentor. In 44 chapters, Brian asks questions about performing in a high-level job; and his mentor responds with examples, statistics, anecdotes and advice.

Through Brian's journey, this book provides insights about working in, surviving and thriving in the federal government.

THE MANY RESPONSIBILITIES OF GOVERNMENT

The federal government and the presidency have accumulated extraordinary power since World War II, leading to a complexity that few understand, including many within it, and me to some extent, creating a fear that the government is too big and too intrusive.

Yet the federal government is one constant in our lives, easy to criticize, yet easy to praise during events such as the financial collapse in 2008-2013 or after natural disasters. In 2005, Hurricane Katrina in New Orleans caused property damage estimated at $108 billion, was the costliest natural disaster and one of the five deadliest hurricanes in US history. The death toll reached 1,830 people.

Hurricane Sandy in New Jersey in 2012 was the second-costliest U.S. hurricane. Damage exceeded $68 billion, and the storm killed 286 people.

In disasters such as these, only the federal government has the resources to help local governments recover. To help New Orleans and the Gulf Coast recover after the devastation of

Katrina, the federal government provided $142 billion in funds and other support.

To assist New Jersey, the President signed a bill providing $50.5 billion to help the state recover from the disaster. Federal Emergency Management Agency (FEMA) provided public assistance grants for some 5,146 projects related to Hurricane Sandy. In addition, the government provided the money for emergency projects, including debris removal and emergency protective measures, and for permanent repairs to roads, bridges, water control facilities, utilities and buildings.[2]

Within 48 hours of Sandy's landfall, FEMA had 1,200 people in the field, going door to door in affected neighborhoods. At the same time, FEMA personnel stored one million shelf-ready meals (including kosher meals) and a million liters of water at a predesignated supply base, ready for distribution by the National Guard and voluntary agencies. These were just the beginning of what became a two-year program for the federal agency.

Also, consider the size of the federal workforce as it responds to its many responsibilities:

- 1.9 million civil service employees
- 10.5 million Federal contractors and grantees
- 1.4 million military personnel
- 786,000 U.S. Postal Service employees [3]

The number of government programs and their influence are staggering. There are thousands of programs, no one knows the exact number, but here are a few examples.

There are 1,800 federal subsidy programs providing benefits to 41 percent (123 million people) in American society.

One hundred thousand schools across the nation have enrolled in the federal subsidized national school lunch program (only 540 schools have not enrolled).

The US military has personnel stationed at about 662 foreign sites in 38 countries around the world.

The General Services Administration manages 8,300 owned or leased buildings, and manages a 210,000-vehicle motor pool. In addition, GSA negotiates contracts with 1,500 companies providing goods and services available to all agencies.

The government's air traffic controllers control 87,000

flights in the skies over the U.S. on an average day, and at any given moment, there are roughly 5,000 planes in the skies. Moreover, there are no accidents due to their work.

In this book, we examine the management challenges below the President, his appointments in the White House, and agency heads. Down a couple of levels in the hierarchy is where most regulations, policies and new programs originate. Here, we can observe the government and its personnel, its structures, its culture and more as it does its daily work managing the thousands of programs enabled in American society.

The Purpose of Spring Training for the Major Leagues of Government

This book fills a space between two levels of publications. At the top level, political appointees, especially those heading cabinet level departments such as the Department of Defense, U.S. State Department, and the U.S. Treasury, write about their experiences in government. In addition, academics provide top-level insights based on research into government operations and policy.

At the lower end of the hierarchy are project management publications targeted to entry-level or mid-level managers for programs ranging from $25 million to about $100 million in life cycle costs. Some of these managers will one day become the high-level officials that this book addresses.

Between top level agency heads and mid-level project managers are those government officials working one or two levels below agency heads. They carry titles like Deputy Commissioner, Assistant Deputy Commissioner or other invented titles for officials positioned below the agency head.

This book answers questions that Brian raises. The insights, anecdotes and advice to Brian and by extension to real life officials have value for current and future generations of government executives and to others interested in government operations.

Advice to Brian delivers insights and advice for current and future government managers, especially those in the ever-changing pool of political appointees (8,000 was Obama's goal during his two terms), plus 8,000 Senior Executive Service officials and thousands more at the top level of General Schedule jobs (GS 15s), in addition to industry officials considering federal positions or selling to the government.

The goal of Spring Training is to accelerate the learning process of high-level officials:

- Improve their chances for success
- Help them avoid pitfalls that threaten reputation and performance
- Enable them to move smoothly through the ranks of senior government jobs
- Position them for advancement to even higher-level jobs in government or in the private sector

Spring Training for the Major Leagues of Government has insights for graduate students of public administration and the curious who seek information about how the government works one or two steps below the agency head.

For industry officials working on or seeking contracts with government, the book reveals a mindset of government managers that will stimulate ideas about how to develop a professional and working relationship with senior government officials.

In academia, professors could consider the book for final semester graduate students who intend to work in or market to the government.

Lastly, citizens seeking a greater understanding about the internal workings of government can use the book to learn how federal workers make decisions and manage the thousands of programs that serve the nation's 315 million people.

Let the questions and answers begin.

Brian Seeks a Mentor

Frank,

Thank you for your note of congratulations on my job offer to work as the senior program manager on the forthcoming two-billion-dollar national health care system, which will affect the lives of every person in the U.S. I cannot believe it! I never expected such a high-level offer from the White House. Nevertheless, while I have had success running my small company managing contracts for the government, I do not know much about what it is like to work inside its walls.

Would you be willing to serve as my mentor during my early months in the government? I would appreciate any advice you can provide to help me get off to a good start.

The United States federal government is the largest, most powerful, best funded, most expensive organization in the world. Our military and the intelligence apparatus are larger and more costly than similar organizations in all other countries combined.

Another way to view the power and size of the government is to look at the size of a presidential entourage when the president travels. For centuries, heads of countries travelled to other countries. It was and is important to make a good showing in the destination capital to demonstrate power and possibly respect for the host monarch. In medieval days, this involved packing up the important daily belongings of the king, queen and the entire court. These would be loaded onto wagons with wooden wheels pulled by as many as six horses, and along with servants, the royal guard, soldiers of the king's army, and the courtiers and perhaps led by two chained cheetahs, six elephants, dancers, and troubadours, the royal caravan would slowly and uncomfortably move along to their destination. The king rode on his warhorse, and the queen would ride either in a carriage or on her own horse.

Today, Air Force One and two additional identical Boeing jumbo jets serving as decoys replace the warhorse. When George Bush travelled to London in 2003, he brought 700 people with him, which *The Guardian* described as "worthy of a travelling medieval monarch." [4]

When President Obama visited London for a G20 meeting in April 2009, *The London Evening Standard* and *The Guardian* newspapers reported that the president arrived with an entourage of 500, including 200 Secret Service agents, a team of six doctors, the White House chef and kitchen staff, four speechwriters and 12 teleprompters, as well as the President's own food and water. In addition, he had 35 vehicles, including the Cadillac, known as the Beast with ceramic and titanium armor, tear gas cannon, night vision devices, and its own oxygen and resistance to chemical and radiation attack.

The military also demonstrates power beyond its bases in 38 countries. When the president travelled to India in November 2010, Fox News reporting on comments in the India Press noted "A foreign force this size probably hasn't been in India since the era of British colonization." In addition to the number of presidential staff personnel, protectors and vehicles noted by the British press, the visit to India suggested that the U.S. military sent along 40 aircraft and 34 warships to patrol the coast during the president's brief visit. *The Wall Street Journal* reported that the Secret Service ordered the host country to remove coconuts from trees at a memorial site the president would visit to ensure that nothing would drop on an important head.

These numbers are similar to those reported by the *New Zealand Herald News* on George W. Bush's visit to Australia in 2007. Sources indicated that the Bush entourage included 150 national security advisors, 250 Secret Service agents, 200 representatives from other federal government agencies, 50 White House political aides, 15 sniffer dog teams, the president's personal chef, and a team of 4 cooks. In addition, among the vehicles arriving in Sydney were three jumbo jets and another two giant cargo-carrying aircraft so large that they can carry other aircraft including helicopters and enough automobiles to ensure two identical convoys, one of which is a decoy. The estimated cost of the security for the president during the four-night trip in Africa was $60 million to $100 million. The cost was a bit of an embarrassment because two months earlier the White House cancelled public tours to save $74,000 a week in overtime costs for the Secret Service. [5]

Such an array of resources protects the president, but it also demonstrates to the leaders and the population in other countries the impressive resources of the United States. [6] [7] [8] Total these resources, and you will find that the personnel and resources that accompany our presidents are unmatched in history by kings, queens and benevolent and brutal rulers.

When you work in government, recognize that you are a part, however small, of this impressive juggernaut.

PART ONE

1
SIX CATEGORIES OF PERSONNEL WORK IN THE FEDERAL GOVERNMENT

There are four main groups of employees in the federal government with "fences" between them and little camaraderie. In addition, a fifth category, contractors, supports the government as an invisible workforce with almost five times the number of government employees and a sixth category, Congressional Staffers supports elected officials in Congress.

Elected officials:
Congress is the most powerful group in government because it appropriates money for government programs and because it writes the laws that govern society. There are 100 members of the U.S. Senate and 435 members of the House of Representatives. In addition, there are the president and the vice president, the only two elected officials in the Executive Branch.

Political appointees:
There are about 7,800 political positions appointed by the White House. Almost half of them are part-time jobs on boards

and commissions, according to John Kamensky, a senior fellow with the IBM Center for the Business of Government.

The full-time political appointees include:

- 1,200 appointments that require Senate confirmation
- 1,400 Schedule C officials-people appointed directly by the president without competition
- 800 non-career senior executives
- 800 members of the White House staff, including 100 assistants, deputy assistants and special assistants who control the president's incoming and outgoing correspondence and meetings
- Two "body men" who follow the president's every step, carrying his jacket and medicines and placing his phone calls

Some presidential appointments languish in the clearance process more than a year, causing some nominees to withdraw their application. No wonder then, when applicants run the gauntlet and actually get the jobs, they may feel a bit superior and members of a select club. Congress changed this process in 2011, attempting to streamline the confirmation process.

Recent new presidents have appointed more political supporters than their predecessors. George W. Bush, for example, named 12 percent more political appointees and 33 percent more Schedule Cs (a sub-category of political appointees) than Bill Clinton.

SENIOR CAREER OFFICIALS

There are 8,000 career officials in the Senior Executive Service, and they are at the top of the career ladder in the civil service system. Many SES officials have worked in the government for 20 years or more, and most can quite capably initiate and manage complex programs. However, there are a few dodos in this category as in any group of people.

Senior career officials make many of the judgment calls and tradeoffs that determine the success or failure of an agency's programs. They are also the key communications channel between political appointees and the lower levels of the career service and contractors.

THE CORE OF THE CAREER SERVICE

Working under the Senior Executives are about 1.6 million career civil servants, not counting Postal Service employees and the uniformed military. All occupy positions in General Schedule slots, ranging from GS 1 to GS 15. The GS 15s, excluding scientists, manage the day-to-day machinery of government, with those at lower ratings assisting. The number of government employees has not changed since 1950, but their skill sets have, as you would expect after 60 years in a period when information and telecommunications technologies have emerged with a blast.

Career employees assisted by contractor personnel (in certain jobs) serve as food and drug inspectors, passport handlers, tax processors, aviation controllers managing airline traffic, accountants, policy analysts, procurement specialists, and workers in hundreds of other specialties, including the care of wounded veterans, and ensuring that the elderly, poor and disabled at the lower end of society receive Medicare and Social Security support.

Two out of three government employees work in just four departments: the Department of Defense, Department of Homeland Security, Department of Veterans Affairs and the Department of Justice, including the FBI. Note that the majority of Americans rarely have any contact with these organizations.

The media often claim that rules protect the government employee to the point that it is impossible to fire anyone, creating the possibility that incompetents could populate the workforce. To the contrary, in fiscal 2013, the government terminated or removed 9,559 employees for discipline or performance problems. The Veterans Administration, one of the largest agencies, fired 2,247, the most of any agency. [9]

The government employee is well educated with 20 percent possessing a master's degree or above, compared to 13 percent in the private sector. Fifty-one percent of government employees have at least one college degree, compared with 35 percent in the private sector.

Nobel Prize selection committees have awarded prizes to fifty current or former federal government employees for contributions including eradication of polio, mapping the human genome and the harnessing of atomic energy.[10]

William Howard Taft, our 27th president, said it best in 1916 and his insights apply today.[11]

"Presidents may go to the seashore or to the mountains. Cabinet officers may go about the country explaining how fortunate the country is in having such an administration, but the machinery at Washington continues to operate under an army of faithful non-commissioned officers, and the great mass of governmental business is uninterrupted."

THE INVISIBLE WORKFORCE

In 2008, there were an estimated 7.6 million contractors serving the federal government. Seven years later, there were about 10 million. They do a lot of good work; in fact, the government could not meet its responsibilities without contractor support. However, as I will discuss in more detail later in this book, there are problems associated with contractors, including:

- A lack of accountability for poor performance
- Diminishing competition for government contracts as the big companies with deep pockets absorb the smaller ones
- The ability of the mega-contractors to overpower the government's priorities when their interests are threatened

Contractors outnumber the other five categories of personnel serving the government by a factor of almost five hundred percent; and they have greater resources available to them in terms of lawyers, lobbyists and money to influence elections. With access to high-level officials in Congress and the White House, they are content to be quiet and work discretely toward their goals, somewhat like the unseen hand that successful franchise owners play in National Football League team operations.

Congressional Staffers

There are about 20,000 staff personnel on Capitol Hill who spend most of their time writing speeches, doing research, and overseeing programs important to their senator or representative; and they develop new programs for their boss to propose as law.

With this brief introduction of the six categories of personnel that drive the American political system, here is how these powerful forces work with each other.

Who Has the Power?

Congress has the most power because its members control the amount of money given to the president and his agencies. Congress also creates new laws to control the White House and its agencies and to govern all aspects of American society.

However, the White House, with only two elected officials, thinks it is in control. It can stymie the intent of Congress by "misinterpreting" laws, and it can redirect funds appropriated by Congress, although Congress can respond to such actions, sometimes harshly.

The presidency is partly a job for someone willing to serve as a punching bag for whatever bothers Congress and any of the almost 315 million people in the U.S., while the power players in Congress and in the corporate world determine directions for the country and distribute the public's wealth. In exchange, they allow the president to declare war, say "no" sometimes to the power players, ride in Air Force One and Marine One, issue executive orders, and have access to the briefcase with the nuclear launch codes.

Congress, corporate executives and independent billionaires limit what the president can do domestically. For example, President Obama spoke many times about the need to rebuild the nation's infrastructure, and he proposed an $800 billion program to save Wall Street from the 2008 calamity in our financial markets. Four years later, in 2013, we learned that only 3 percent of the $800 billion went to rebuild infrastructure.[12] One reason is that the president does not have the authority to approve the rebuilding of those decrepit bridges and roads.

Congress, influenced by lobbyists, micromanages each decision. Thus restricted, the president's ceremonial role assumes greater importance providing daily silage for the media, keeping the public distracted with TV speeches, town hall meetings, disaster area visits, receiving foreign dignitaries, and travel to foreign capitals.

In the deep five-year recession that began before 2008— caused by Wall Street and the major financial corporations—the public looked to the president to create jobs, get the economy moving again and handle all the transitory problems that affect each person in the country. Yet the system, with its constitutional checks and balances between the presidency, Congress and the Supreme Court, does not allow one of the three institutions to dictate directions for the government. Again, President William Howard Taft provides important insights.

"The President cannot make clouds to rain and cannot make the corn to grow; he cannot make business good, although when these things occur, political parties do claim some credit for the good things that have happened in this way." [13]

The White House, although limited in its power to dictate direction for the country, is augmented by 7,800 political appointees, resembling an informal "elite guard" able to play several roles:

- Control the career workforce
- Implement programs to deliver what Congress legislates
- Influence public opinion on behalf of the White House
- Joust with Congress, especially with its many influential staff personnel
- And, especially if one is Republican in belief, support the transfer of government jobs to contractors

This elite guard comes to the center of government like British soccer fans after a morning of heavy drinking, careening in an unfamiliar city, marauding through the streets toward the stadium where the battle for a few goals will occur, amid much noise, loud voices and many fights with each other and the other side.

When a new president is elected, the career employees wait apprehensively inside the walls of government, anticipating the worst, spreading fearful rumors to each other about who and what is to come, while preparing to defend the institution from the "no-knowledge pack" they fear is about to descend upon them.

So it goes year after year, president after president, election after election. However, unlike the organized combat of professional sports, there are no victors at the end of the season. There is no Super Bowl Sunday. The players in government play their game endlessly without pause and are destined to do so into eternity. There are tiny, temporary advances, a three-yard gain and a cloud of dust, a successful Hail Mary pass to bring cheering supporters to their feet. Then the other political party takes over, gains a little advantage and eventually loses it.

There are referees as well in the game. Interest groups and the national media, especially *The Washington Post*, *The New York Times* and *The Wall Street Journal*, will call attention to rules infractions. In addition, when allowed, the public at the polls can vote for a new coach and general manager, hoping for true change.

ADVICE TO BRIAN

No group is all-powerful, and while there is serious competition within government, there are no victors. The game goes on without pause, as it has for more than two hundred years, and will carry on as long as we have a nation. Only the game itself is forever, not the players.

Taking the long view will help you to withstand day-to-day frustrations.

2

COMPARING GOVERNMENT AND PRIVATE SECTOR JOBS

Frank,

As you know, I have a good bit of experience running my former company while working on government contracts. Isn't the government similar to the private sector? Will my private sector experience help me to be successful in the government?

Private sector experience will enable you to bring fresh ideas to your government position. However, it will not help you as much as you may think. The government is different from the private sector in many important ways; it is a different species.

Government is like the kudzu vine. Once established, it grows rapidly, overtaking everything in reach, and its reach is ever expanding. The kudzu, which grows south of lower Pennsylvania, is becoming a common nuisance in the suburbs of Washington, D.C. The good news is that kudzu is limited by winter temperatures similar to the periodic restraints elections place on the government, effectively slowing it down for a season.

Conversely, thousands of companies, mostly corporations and nonprofit organizations sometimes called non-government organizations (NGOs), comprise the private sector. They want the unlimited reach of the government but cannot have it. They have shorter lives. They are like stand-alone trees with defined lives. Small companies are like Mimosa trees, which produce delicate pink flowers in the summer, living only about 25 years. Large multinational companies are like dogwood, willow and cottonwood trees that have roughly the same lifespan of humans, living until a larger competitor finds them in the later, weaker stages of life and absorbs or kills them.

The government is the parent as far as the private sector is concerned, and, as with children and parents, those dependent on government do not always love the government. In its role at the head of the table, the government creates an environment in which the private sector can survive, hopefully thrive, and create wealth to enable most citizens to continue to live better today than did most kings in medieval days.

The government can print and distribute money with nothing behind it as it did responding to the collapse of the Wall Street and banking systems from 2007 to 2016. The government can benefit favored companies by providing specific tax benefits and earmarks, by awarding contracts or by transferring government jobs to the private sector.

In addition, the government creates laws allowing companies to continue doing business the way the corporate world likes to do business. Infrequently, it creates laws requiring companies to do business while addressing the needs of the nation.

At the same time, there are additional and major differences between the government and the private sector.

Uniqueness of the Government Environment

Politics and the number of players influencing decisions in government are always surprises to newcomers.

Several cultures exist within the government, each with its own idea of what is the right direction in any given case.

Governments eagerly embrace every new "silver bullet" management process, leading to a lot of wasted time when officials should be spending their time on actual work.

There are endless laws, policies, processes and guidelines to follow that detract from doing "real" work.

Many political appointees lack experience to manage complex programs, which leads to strange and costly decisions.

The systems the government needs ordinarily do not exist because of their uniqueness, requiring development from scratch, with higher risk and cost.

The government budget process begins two years in advance, and, once set, it is difficult to change priorities or obtain additional funds, even though the needs and circumstances change.

Establishing new positions and hiring to fill them can take 18 months in the government personnel system.

Disciplining poor performance or firing an employee requires extensive documentation, taking a year or more.

When managing large-scale procurements, the government normally must advertise them and seek competitive bids, requiring a negotiation process that can take a year at a minimum, and the government may never make an award due to endless protests by companies anxious for the business.

Working in any large organization is a challenge. Some managers are successful despite the difficulties. Others are overwhelmed and discouraged and fail.

The first step is to recognize the realities, as we have begun to do in this chapter. In later chapters, I will suggest approaches to overcome the difficulties and pitfalls.

3
CHOOSING AN AGENCY CREATED BY LAW

Frank, it is becoming a little clearer now. I can see the various players and realize that the government is going to be a new challenge beyond my experience in the private sector.

I have a question from a friend of mine who has two job offers. One of them is a career appointment in a line agency, and it sounds like an exciting project. The other is a presidential appointment in an organization just created by a presidential executive order.

How can he decide between the two? What factors should he consider?

While both of these jobs are in the government, a career appointment and a political appointment are very different opportunities. Fortunately, answering one question will help him choose.

Did Congress or the president establish the agency or the program he will manage? In my own career, I worked in an agency created by a presidential order and in several created by Congress. I much prefer the latter.

When I worked for IBM managing several contracts at the National Institutes of Health, officials from the Department of Health, Education and Welfare offered me a job. They told me the White House was creating a new agency, the Health Services and Mental Health Administration. It would have more than 100,000 employees and would combine twelve major agencies, including the National Institute for Mental Health, the Center for Disease Control in Atlanta, the Indian Health Service, the Food and Drug Administration, the Public Health Service and others, into one organization.

My job would be to build and manage a major new computer center in the recently constructed headquarters building in Rockville, MD. In addition, I would have policy oversight over all of the computer hardware and information systems in the 12 agencies. In addition, the organization would have a division to develop systems for the administrator of the new agency.

For a month, I considered whether to remain with IBM or take the government job. One day, I thought I should go. The next day, I thought I should stay. It was not an easy decision, because working for IBM was satisfying and particularly prestigious at the time.

Finally, I accepted the government's offer because I had a mental picture of myself in such a major management job. I had four good years there, and with my three division chiefs—Jack Dolan, Ken Blythe, and Stan Evans—we did a good job. I might have spent the next 30 years there, but President Ford replaced President Nixon and abolished the organization, effectively restoring the twelve agencies to their former level in the hierarchy reporting to the Secretary of the Department of Health, Education and Welfare.

It turned out that President Nixon had created the agency by his own decree, a presidential executive order. Normally Congress creates agencies by enacting a law. If Congress created it, a president cannot unilaterally abolish it. However, if one president issues an executive order creating a new policy or an agency, the next president can abolish both. President Reagan, for example, issued an executive order blocking aid to organizations that provided counseling for abortions. President Clinton reversed the policy, but George W. Bush reinstated it, and, after taking office, President Obama rejected it. Had Mitt Romney won the presidency, we can anticipate that he would have reinstated the Reagan executive order.

For me, the abolishment of the agency by President Ford transferred my organization to the Food and Drug Administration. Before the transfer, I was a senior leader. After the handover, my new bosses in FDA offered me a menial job. I was not in their club, and it was evident I would not receive an invitation. Soon, their handpicked successor asked me to vacate my office. Fortunately, I was in the process of accepting a job across town with the Naval Oceanographic Office. I left FDA on a high note with a touching send-off by my staff.

Several years later, I joined the General Services Administration, an agency cemented in law. After World War II, a joint congressional/White House task force known as the Hoover Commission developed recommendations to streamline the Federal government.

The Commission recommended that the government create a central agency to manage government buildings and procurements by disbanding four small agencies and consolidating them into a single large organization. The product was General Services Administration (GSA), created by the Federal Property and Administrative Services Act that President Harry S. Truman signed into law on July 1, 1949.

Within GSA, I managed a program that itself was responsible for implementing two laws. The GSA and my program survived many challenges for years, although not forever, as we will discuss later.

ADVICE TO BRIAN

When you work in an agency created by law or, even better, when you manage a program created by law, your organization will survive when a new crowd takes over in the White House.

If you have a choice, and especially if it is late in a president's term in office, I recommend declining a job created by a president's Executive Order, and taking the job in the agency created by Congress, assuming you want to work in the government more than a few years.

In addition, there is another aspect to consider. If your friend accepts a job in a long-established agency with a mature culture and a rigorous checklist way of getting things done, it will be difficult to institute anything bordering on novel and innovative change.

On the other hand, a newer agency, such as the Department of Homeland Security created in the first decade of the 21st century, will resemble the Wild West, an environment without administronium, an environment in which innovation is possible, often valued.

A new organization can be stimulating and exciting because there will be less bureaucracy, fewer established demigods and more opportunities for personal growth.

Accepting a job in a fledgling organization is a matter of where you are in your career. Later, if you need to move on, it is easier to find another job when one is in a junior position—up through grade GS 13. Later, when you are at the top levels of the grade pyramid, new jobs are harder to obtain.

As a senior official, opt for an established agency given the choice, unless you are eligible for retirement and able to take a flier.

4
MEETING WITH FRIENDS OF YOUR BOSS

Frank,
My boss asked me if I would be willing to meet the representative of a company that wants to work for our agency. This person is apparently an old business associate of my boss. My boss said it would be just a "courtesy" meeting, but I am not feeling completely comfortable with request. What should I do?

One common situation in a government job occurs when your boss asks you to meet with a friend from pre-government days. Often, the friend just happens to be a contractor trying to sell to the government.

When your boss asks you to meet with his private sector friend "just to help him out," does he want him to get some inside information about your procurement, or is he just being nice?

Be careful, because this can present an ethical problem, especially if your boss is planning to award a small consulting contract, possibly to his friend. On the other hand, your boss may simply want you to meet with his old friend as a courtesy, with no intention of awarding the friend a contract. You cannot be sure what the game plan is or whether there is a game plan at all. Either way, you are in a jam.

Your boss has put you on a tightrope, probably without realizing it. You have to step carefully, because you can trip into one of two unfortunate outcomes:

You could alienate your boss. This is less dire than prison, but it can still damage your government career.

You can go to prison. Yes, it is true, although rare. While procurement rules do allow awarding some small contracts without competition, they do not allow awards based on friendship. If you are a party to a violation of the rules or even appear to be, you could be in legal trouble.

Here is how to deal with this puzzle. You must respond to your boss' request but do it in a way without risking censure and without offending your boss.

The first thing to do is to schedule a meeting with the friend and invite a contracting officer to sit in the meeting with you. Do it as soon as possible to set a positive tone. Give your boss's friend the same information you would give to any contractor, nothing more. Suggest other officials the contractor might want to call on and make it clear why you are making the suggestion. Tell your boss the meeting went well, assuming it did. If the friend asks for a second meeting, pass him along to one of your division chiefs familiar with this kind of situation. With a little effort and some smooth human relations, you will never need to meet again and expose yourself to trouble.

For major contracts, the stakes are higher. For example, 270 vendors once attended an *industry day* to learn about the GSA's planned procurement of $400 million of computer support services.

In procurements of this size, the pressure can be intense for vendors. A win can make a company healthy for several years. It is especially important for struggling companies. If a company's stock price is low and their revenue stream is weak, winning a major procurement can put cash in their coffers, save a CEO's job and restore Wall Street's confidence.

If your boss asks you to meet with an official of a company bidding or planning to bid on your agency's procurement, beware! In your boss's first request, you could not be sure a small contract award to a friend was the goal. However, in his second request you know that his friend's goal is to win a major contract, which changes the ball game and raises the personal risk.

Little is secret in major procurements. A company's competitors and all of your colleagues and subordinates in the agency are watching. Any meetings should include all prospective bidders. Otherwise, there will be protests after award. Even worse, if you accept lunches or other gifts from bidding vendors, jail is a possibility. Courtside seats at a Washington Wizards basketball game are not worth time in a cell.

The government procurement system can protect you. The general procedure is for the government to quit all contact with bidding companies at some point in the process, except for the procurement officials directly involved in awarding the contract. The cutoff time can vary. Sometimes the government will shut down further conversations and contacts after the procurement office issues the Request for Quotes (RFQ), but it can close the door at any point in the long contracting process.

The RFQ process will show which companies are interested in the procurement, and it can reveal the range of prices the government can expect when it issues the final Request for Proposals (RFP) to industry. After the government receives responses to the RFQs, it can then request formal bidding. By then, all contact between government and industry will have ceased, protecting unwary government officials, including you, Brian, from compromising situations.

ADVICE TO BRIAN

Exercise caution when your new boss asks you to meet with a friend and you know the friend works for a company seeking business with the government. This predicament will test your skills but follow my advice and you can navigate through the dangerous waters. When you meet, bring a procurement officer with you to keep you off dangerous ground. If one is not available, bring another person to serve later as a witness if needed; and above all, accept no gifts of any kind.

When procurement dollars are the target, uncertainty about motives coupled with hidden undercurrents should breed watchful wariness, for you know not what will rise from the deep.

5

MEETING WITH VENDORS

Okay, I understand that I should be selective about meetings to allow time to do the job the White House hired me to do. Before proceeding, let us return to the discussion we had about meeting with friends of my boss. You mentioned prison. I had no idea that was a possibility simply because of an error in judgment or transgressing a little known regulation. Can you tell me more about this? What do I need to know to be sure that I remain within the ethical lines?

Relationships with vendors can be valuable, as long as you navigate the ethical concerns correctly. Your insights need to be available to all vendors, not just a favored few. You are on thin ice if you meet with senior officials from one company and not others just before your agency is set to release a procurement solicitation for a few hundred million dollars. Meeting with officials representing only one company creates the perception that you are manipulating the procurement process.

If you do agree to a small meeting with one company, be sure to offer similar opportunities to other companies interested in bidding on your requirements. Also, do not meet with company officials by yourself. Bring along a member of the general counsel's office, the ethics office or the procurement policy office to silently monitor the conversation, stop you if the discussion is taking a perilous path and serve as a witness for you later if necessary.

Small meetings are dangerous, and off-the-record sessions are risky as well. A company representative may offer you such a meeting to allow you to tell it like it really is to a select group representing many companies, each promising not to repeat your insights to others. I did a few of these over the years and found the give-and-take feedback to be productive.

However, it backfired once. I spoke off the record to representatives of 40 companies at a small dinner in downtown D.C. After dinner, my host closed the door to the private dining room, and everyone it seemed, including the women, lit up a cigar. I talked candidly about a number of government-wide management and policy issues, not procurement issues, which we were focusing on in GSA, and there was a good Q&A period during which I received good insights. Later, at home, my wife told me I reeked of stale cigar smoke. I hung my suit out on the screened porch for a week and took two showers every day to try to remove the smell. Worse, one of the attendees at the supposedly off-the-record meeting called the IRS the following morning and said to the chief information officer, "Do you know what Frank McDonough said about your program last night?"

What I had said was the delays and cost overruns in its information systems modernization program indicated to us in GSA that we should place the program in a *time out* status, allowing time to re-evaluate the program's strategy, a direction we had been discussing with IRS officials.

IRS leadership was very upset, which led to a meeting between the GSA administrator and the commissioner of IRS along with her deputy, her CIO and me to discuss the transgression. As we entered her conference room, the three IRS officials reminded me of a painting of a solemn Venetian Doge and two deputies. Lacking only the silk robes and caps of office, the IRS officials planned to sentence me to walk the Bridge of Sighs to a lasting purgatory. Fortunately, GSA Administrator Roger Johnson also believed a *time out* was the way to go, so the meeting was not entirely soothing to IRS.

That is the risk of the off-the-record meeting. Although everyone attending agrees to keep the discussion private, an aggressive marketing manager seeking an entry to a government official may not honor the promise, as I learned.

Some government officials refuse to speak with vendors, whether in the office or in public forums. This is wrong and shortsighted. The vendor community deserves to hear your insights and plans. At the same time, you will get new information at each meeting.

Advice to Brian

Follow five simple guidelines, and you will have productive relationships with the companies selling to the government.

If you agree to small meetings with a single vendor, be sure to offer the same opportunity to other vendors.

Decline invitations to speak at off-the-record sessions. As valuable as they might be, it is human nature for vendors seeking an edge to reveal their "scoop."

Consult with the ethics and procurement officials, and legal resources in your agency to guide you and keep you out of trouble.

Above all, treat all companies the same.

Recognize that when you leave the job, your "friends" in industry will reach out to your successor and less and less to you over time.

6
GET TO KNOW YOUR ETHICS OFFICER

Frank
Your experience is troubling. It sounds like it is easy for an innocent to stumble into trouble with vendor preference. How big of a problem is this in the federal government?

Congress has stepped up the criminalization of behaviors in recent years. The Heritage Foundation reports that there are more than 4,400 criminal offenses in the federal code, many of them lacking a requirement that prosecutors prove traditional kinds of criminal intent. In an interview with *The New York Times*, Ed Meese, Attorney General in the Reagan Administration and later White House advisor to the president, said, "It's a violation of federal law to give a false weather report; people get put in jail for importing lobsters."[14]

In his book, *Three Felonies a Day: How the Feds Target the Innocent,* Harvey A. Silverglate argues that criminal laws are so vague that prosecutors can indict anyone they target because fuzzy legislation invites creative interpretation of the law. We saw examples of this in the cases against Hall of Famer Roger Clemons and Alaska Sen. Ted Stevens.

Criminalization of behavior without regard for intent creates a dangerous situation for federal officials, especially for those who work in or around the procurement system; in addition, the many law enforcement and investigative agencies are interpreting laws, regulations and policies inventively to help them to "get their man." Without advice, the average government official or the average American citizen will be unaware that he or she is violating federal law and is vulnerable to sudden, arbitrary prosecution.

Get into trouble, and you are on your own, my friend, as John Dean, advisor to President Nixon, learned during the Watergate trials and as Martha Johnson, Administrator of General Services Administration. learned in 2011 when her agency managers spent too much money on a conference. When the story broke in the media the following year, the Obama White House in an election year encouraged her to leave office immediately. Was this axe job unfair? Consider this.

Martha Johnson did not know much, if anything, about the "lavish" expenditures on this one conference, one of many conferences organized by GSA employees each year. When she learned of it, she initiated an investigation. Appearing before a congressional panel two weeks after she vacated her office, Oklahoma Rep. James Lankford pointed out the following.

"You resigned, though your office is the office that actually started this [investigation]. We would not have known about this unless your office had started the investigation. As the leader at the top, you resigned. And the people that were directly there making the decisions, signing onto warrants, going through these fraudulent contracts, they're still there."

Johnson, the press reported, breathed in and rubbed her brow above her glasses. "Yes," she said, "I believe they are still there."

Two years later, Kathleen Sebelius, Secretary of the Department of Health and Human Services, resigned after the calamitous rollout of healthcare.gov. However, 2014 was not an election year, allowing the White House to be more generous in this case, permitting Sibelius to remain on the job for an indefinite period while staff sought and cleared a replacement.[15]

Similarly, the Obama White House dumped Steve Miller, the Acting Administrator of IRS, in 2013 without showing any support for the IRS and without any attempt to tell the American people the difficulties faced by the IRS folks when investigating the mountain of politically oriented applications for tax-exempt status.

Here is an August 16, 2013 notice from the conservative Senior Executives Association, strongly recommending that Senior Executives purchase Professional Liability Insurance.

As you are undoubtedly aware, there has been an incredible amount of attention and scrutiny upon federal agencies and programs – and Senior Executives. Complaints and allegations of wrongdoing have simply become the cost of doing business for many federal managers and executives. Whether true or false, and whether exacerbated by media sensation, negative public impact or political agendas, the cost to defend your decisions, actions or inactions could be cost prohibitive if you don't have professional liability coverage in place - even if you are ultimately vindicated.

Federal Employees Defense Services (FEDS) professional liability coverage is available for $290 annually – only $145 after agency reimbursement. All executives and managers are eligible for reimbursement, and payroll deduction is available for all employees. Take advantage of reimbursement and enroll BEFORE you need the policy.

The FEDS policy also includes coverage at no additional cost for employment practices liability claims such as allegations of harassment, discrimination, retaliation, whistleblower reprisal and wrongful termination. In contrast, most Umbrella policies exclude employment-related acts, errors and omissions. The SEA recommends FEDS for every Senior Executive.

For more information, access this site, https:// seniorexecs.org/legal-assistance

Executive branch employees hold their positions as a public trust, and the American people have a right to expect government employees to place loyalty to the Constitution, laws, regulations and ethical principles above private gain. The rules can be complicated, but there are three core concepts:

Do not use public office for private gain.

Act impartially, and do not give preferential treatment to any single private organization or individual.

Avoid any action creating the appearance that you are violating the law or ethical standards. Creating the perception of a violation can be as damaging to your reputation among your peers as an actual violation.

Be aware, however, that information you provide to the ethics officer can become an official record and used against you. Do you remember David Safavian, the chief of staff in the GSA? He went to the GSA Ethics Officer seeking advice about a golfing trip he planned to take with a lobbyist, a former colleague in the private sector. The ethics officer approved the trip, and Safavian paid $3,000 from his own personal funds.

But he did not mention that the lobbyist—Jack Abramoff— had made a general inquiry to him about the availability of the government-owned historic Old Post Office Pavilion located four blocks from the White House. Abramoff thought he could put the building to better use as a hotel because it is one of the top tourist destinations in Washington and is conveniently located close to other attractions popular with tourists. Interestingly, the government later turned the property over to Donald Trump's real estate company to convert it to a hotel and mixed uses.

Safavian received no money from the lobbyist. He gave no favors to the lobbyist. Nor did the lobbyist benefit in any way from any action by Safavian. Yet two juries convicted him. In his defense, he said he had not thought that Abramoff's general inquiry was germane to the legality of the trip, especially since he paid his expenses out of his own pocket.

The prosecutors and the FBI often get their man not because of the crime itself but because people under investigation lie to the agents. Lying is what gets most officials in trouble. Do not shade the truth even if it will incriminate your political boss. Note well, there are several investigative organizations, not just FBI agents, that can question your activities and charge you with lying. One such organization is your agency's inspector general.

In another example, federal prosecutors worked for five years to prosecute former congressman and former two-term Illinois governor Rod Blagojevich, based on 23 corruption charges and one count of lying to the FBI. Before a retrial, a twelve-member jury took 14 days to convict Blagojevich of only one charge, lying to the FBI.[16]

Procurement is a complex process, and one can stumble into trouble because of inexperience, ignoring good advice from well-informed career officials or simply doing a favor for an old friend.

Darleen Druyun illustrates another case where messing with the procurement laws led to a jail cell. As a senior Air Force procurement officer, she served nine months in federal prison for favoring Boeing in contract talks in exchange for a job for herself, her daughter and son-in-law. Former Boeing Chief Financial Officer Michael Sears received a four-month prison sentence for illegally negotiating a job at Boeing for Ms. Druyun while she was still overseeing Air Force contracts in the Pentagon.

The risks are real. However, if you use good judgment and always consult with your agency's ethics office anytime you are in doubt, you should be fine. However, you and only you know all the facts, and if you reveal some and withhold others, the ethics office cannot help you.

The best thing is do not get involved in the first place. Do not socialize with potential contractor personnel while you are in government. It is okay if you attend an event as one in a large group of other government employees. However, if you are the only government official in a small group and you have the ability to make things happen for others in the group, steer clear. Even if you do not do any favors for anyone, the appearance of such a possibility will reflect badly on you.

ADVICE TO BRIAN

Every agency has an ethics officer. Get to know yours. If he is first rate, you will avoid a lot of trouble by following the officer's advice. My many dealings with the GSA Ethics Office helped me avoid trouble despite the complexity of government rules.

Everyone possessing some power, and this includes most government employees, needs a sounding board. Find one on your staff, someone unafraid to call it like it is even if it displeases you, and be sure to schedule semi-annual meetings with the ethics officer. You may not like what you hear in these meetings, but be patient because you are learning about complex regulations that are not always intuitive.

Hope this reassures you! Although there are many pitfalls, you can avoid them by seeking and following advice from old hands and the ethics officer.

One who insists "No, you can't do that" can be your most important ally.

7
STUMBLING INTO TROUBLE

Frank,
It seems there are many ways to get into trouble.
Are there any other pitfalls I should avoid?

There are plenty of ways for an unwary civil servant to get into trouble. Fortunately, most of them are easy to avoid, if you understand the rules and use good sense.

You will probably be required to testify before congressional committees, especially when lawmakers are considering legislation affecting programs like yours or when they are investigating failure. You must be cautious giving testimony to congressional officials.

I recall sitting on the side of the cavernous House Government Operations Hearing room in the Rayburn building on Capitol Hill with two congressional staff investigators. Except for the three of us, the room was empty. While I answered their questions under oath in the nonconfrontational setting, with the warming afternoon sunlight streaming in and with eight lanes of traffic rhythmically, hypnotically passing on the expressway outside, I found it easy to slip into a false sense of security.

Something in the congressional hearing process encourages you to tell more than you know. Perhaps you want the members of Congress and their staff to see you as very knowledgeable. Maybe you want to help more than you really can. If you are not careful, you will go to the edge of your knowledge and beyond, into the land of conjecture. I observed this tendency in myself early in my work with the Hill so I would guard against it. Even so, in the warm sunlight, after a few hours, the danger presents itself repeatedly. After an hour or so, it becomes easy to forget the cardinal rule to be very precise while under oath.

Here is why it is so important: If the congressional investigators record your answers and then ask you the same question three months later in a public hearing, your answer should be the same. However, if in the previous session you let yourself go beyond what you really knew, your current answer might be different. You may not even remember the original question. If there is a difference in your response, Congress could accuse you with lying—the charge which leads to most convictions.

Fortunately, congressional representatives never threw three-month-old questions at me, but you can see how easy it is to slip into trouble.

You might want to bring a lawyer with you if congressional staffers summon you to the Hill for a discussion while they investigate some aspect of your program. If you do, though, you can turn a personal, cordial meeting into something adversarial. Go alone, however, and you must trust the congressional staffers. After a few years, I elected to trust. Can you trust? Should you? In the end, it is all about people and relationships. The personal stakes are high considering that censure or jail are possibilities, though jail is unlikely in most cases.

There are plenty of other roads to trouble. People on your staff can file grievances charging racism, sexual harassment, coziness with certain vendors or waste of government resources such as buying business class seats for long-distance travel on airlines. Occasionally, an employee will file a grievance attempting payback, possibly for a poor performance appraisal that you delivered, or the employee may file a grievance simply because he dislikes you. Then again, the employee may have a valid complaint.

You can survive one grievance or even a few as long as they

do not all come at the same time. However, if several employees file grievances in a short period, upper management may begin to pay attention, and you are in for trouble.

As a high-level official, your actions are visible, and many people will be observing you. As you make decisions, some may have a negative effect on the observers. They may go after you if you give them ammunition they can use against you.

Do not obsess about this; just be realistic. Being aware that people are scrutinizing your activities will help you to do the right thing at all times

At one time, thousands of dollars passed through our office because one of our programs was an expensive senior management development program. At the time, I had been in the government 25 years, had lots of experience and thought I knew all the answers about avoiding trouble. Nevertheless, I always went to Virginia Bannister, my administrative officer and friend, when I needed advice. She had even more experience than I did managing government money. Often she would tell me forcefully that I could not do something I had thought was okay, and I would always follow her advice. Between us, we worked carefully and successfully for the thirteen years that we ran the program.

In a 2010 case, the administrator of GSA and her commissioners needed a Virginia Bannister when their staff personnel were planning a management development conference they would hold in Las Vegas. Many criticized the exercises for team building, which included assembling bicycles, training exercises commonly used by leading corporations. Other aspects of the team-building program provided titillating reading for Congress and the media, raising cries that the conference was over the top and a bad use of taxpayer money. Those in control ignored the advice to tone down the conference. Failure to heed the advice and rein in the spending cost the administrator, a respected commissioner and others their jobs.

Each senior official needs an experienced advisor well aware of how the system works and not afraid to say firmly when it needs to be said, "You cannot do that." Wise officials will listen and follow the advice.

In addition, there is a newer contemporary way to stumble

into trouble called *political correctness*. Comments about religion, Jews, gays and lesbians, and guns are among the topics that will track you for life. Also, speak about intelligence agencies or the law enforcement apparatus, and they may place you on their watch lists. Criticize the IRS, the Social Security Administration or Homeland Security, and they may put you on a watch list. In modern life, it is best to live under the radar and not to speak or write about these organizations or topics until close to death—if you must do so at all.

Is government a nasty environment to work? Well, it certainly can be disagreeable, but if you follow a few simple rules, you will survive and enjoy the experience.

Advice to Brian

Be wary in all interactions. Important people in industry will want to become part of your inner circle socially, on the golf course and as advisors. Beware! They come to you because of your position and the resources you manage. They may like you, but the fondness is temporary. Be wary of the forms of flattery that accompany power and fame. They are for the position, not you.

In addition:

Assume that people are observing you at all times and have several outlets to publicize any of your activities they view as offensive.

Recognize that some actions, appropriate in your own business before joining government, may be entirely inappropriate in government.

Always be aware of the public perceptions you create as you work day to day. I often think of Allie Latimer, general counsel and later special assistant for ethics and civil rights at GSA. She always emphasized that the government should work at a higher standard than private sector businesses.

Never fall victim to your ego or go beyond what you really know when talking to investigators.

Find and listen to your "Virginia Bannister," who is unafraid to tell you "you cannot do that."

Follow these five rules to avoid the traps lying in wait for unsuspecting managers, and you will find that government work is a richer, more satisfying experience than you ever imagined.

8
Don't be the Fall Guy

Frank,
When I ran my company, I read the trade papers
and The Washington Post *and saw the media pillorying*
government managers for one deed or another. If things
go poorly in my new agency, not just in my program,
what should I anticipate?

In the days after Hurricane Katrina in New Orleans, when President George W. Bush spoke at the Mobile, Alabama Regional Airport, he said to Federal Emergency Management Agency Director Michael "Brownie" Brown, "You're doing a heck of a job." Yet the credibility of the government suffered because the devastation and the poor government response had been visible to a shocked world for days on all television channels.

Soon after the president's praise, the White House, responding to heavy criticism from Congress and the media, sacked Brown. This was a rare example of holding a political appointee accountable.

Brown was not alone in the poor response to Katrina. Brown had informed the president about the possibilities of a major storm, and the president deserves some blame. But Bush rightfully counted on other players, including Michael Chertoff at the Department of Homeland Security, Kathleen B. Blanco, Governor of Louisiana, Ray Nagin, Mayor of New Orleans, as well as Brown at FEMA. Nevertheless, the American public will remember Michael Brown as the villain in the Hurricane Katrina fiasco in which 1,400 died and thousands were permanently dislocated.

There always has to be a fall guy. The public and the media require one. In Katrina, it was Brown. While it is rare for anyone in the White House or elsewhere in the government to pick out a fall guy to satisfy the media and the public, a fall guy always appears. John Dean was the target during Watergate according to Bob Woodward in "The Last of the President's Men." George Tenet at the CIA took the hit for producing the poor intelligence that led to the Iraq War, even though he may have been one of the few people aware of the facts. Seemingly, none of his peers in Defense or superiors in the White House listened.

In Katrina, a major problem was the longstanding lack of trust and willingness to cooperate between the several federal agencies participating in the recovery. In addition, federal, state and local government personnel often dislike each other, making cooperation difficult, although they will collaborate in mega-disasters such as 9/11.

During the peak of Hurricane Katrina, when Mayor Nagin pleaded for help for New Orleans for three days, he was really saying, "Please, you federal and state government people, please work together, and help my people, my city and me."

However, the trust and coordination were not to come, as they rarely do within and between US government agencies. When they do, they are only temporary.

There can be a danger to you in cases before the facts are known and if there is room for doubt on who did what to whom and when. Then, it can be possible to pin the blame on an innocent bystander, which might be you if you were even marginally associated with an event under scrutiny.

Bill Bransford, general counsel for the Senior Executive Association, advises career officials: "Remember that a program review going badly can reflect poorly on you. A political appointee under scrutiny may seek a scapegoat in the form of a vulnerable [career] Senior Executive."

There is a time when it is every man for himself. Read Bransford's article on this subject and note his emphasis on being prepared, being careful and always telling the truth even if it reflects poorly on your boss, the political appointee.[17]

There are exceptions, of course. Some officials, despite the consequences, will not try to pin the blame on a subordinate. The Secretary of the Department of Energy, for example, appeared before Congress in 2011 when the Solyndra Company collapsed after getting a $535 million loan guarantee from his organization and said, "The final decisions on Solyndra were mine." [18]

ADVICE TO BRIAN

When the laser eyes of Congress, the national media and the public focus on the alleged poor performance of an expensive program, and as a career official, if you are associated with the program in any way, you will be more vulnerable than your boss, especially a political appointee unwilling, naturally, to be tarred easily by an unfolding debacle. If you are the principal cause of the problem, take your medicine; otherwise, be on your toes, because you could unfairly end up as the fall guy.

This is a time for spin, a time to emphasize the good points of the program. Take the initiative. Develop a position paper addressing five points that you and your managers can use to respond to the criticism:

- The circumstances that led up to the crisis
- The misunderstandings that exist about the recent circumstances
- The outcomes that might occur based on the current situation
- The notable achievements to date of the program
- The actions your agency is taking to correct future problems

In addition, draft a press release to provide concise speaking points for your bosses and the agency's public affairs office. Your political managers will be able to use this information in public, and they will know you have the information as well, reducing the likelihood you will become the fall guy.

9
CHALLENGE WIDELY HELD BELIEFS

Frank,

It seems that the government people I meet these early days know so much and speak with such conviction. I know that I need to choose my advisors carefully, but for all of the information I receive, how should I respond? I am thinking particularly about information and advice I receive from "old hands" that have been around for decades. Can I pretty much depend on what they tell me?

It can be useful to challenge generally held beliefs. Here are some examples of common beliefs, all false:

Thomas Crapper invented the toilet

Thomas Edison invented the light bulb

Henry Ford invented the automobile

Guglielmo Marconi invented the radio

Al Gore invented the Internet

Apple's products are immune to viruses

In government, there are many commonly held beliefs that program managers should question and dig deeper. For example:

It is cheaper to outsource technology work than to do it with government employees.

Department of Defense managers handle hundred-million-dollar programs better than managers in civilian agencies do.

A project management training course is the key to success in eliminating large cost overruns in many expensive programs.

Management processes from the Office of Management and Budget and the Chief Information Officers Council are making startling improvements in the management of hundred-million-dollar technology programs.

Technology used in Iraq can solve the immigration problem in the U.S.

One widely held belief, alive for 40 years, claims that technology is moving so fast and government policies are so rigid that agencies are falling behind and working with out-of-date tools.

Agencies and industry complained that the government's computers were obsolete, preventing innovation because of the procurement rules; and they blamed the Brooks Act and GSA's implementation of the Act for the problem.

One of the most vocal critics of the Brooks Act and GSA's regulations was a Department of Energy official. Responding to the critics, Martha Dorris on my staff and I studied the location of the obsolete computers. We identified hundreds of 20-year-old, small special purpose scientific computers at the Energy Department that substantially increased the average age of the fewer, but large-scale modern computers across the government.

Martha and I discussed our findings with the DOE official. At first, he did not accept the data. However, analyst that he was, he returned to his office where he did his own analysis. He found that we were right: many of the small scientific computers in his agency were often 20 years old; and he created a program to upgrade them. His action reduced the average age of all computers in the entire federal government by several years.

After that, opponents of the Brooks Act quieted down about the obsolescence issue. Challenging this generally held belief about the cause of obsolescence in the government unveiled the true cause and took a lot of heat off the Brooks Act and my program, enabling the government to move forward based on facts, not conjecture.

The lesson here is that doing your homework often reveals that conventional wisdom is dead wrong. Unfortunately, there are so many issues and so much fiction flying around that one seldom has time to challenge all of the possibilities.

Nonetheless, it will enhance your reputation as a thoughtful manager and you will do a better job if you acquire more knowledge about important issues than anyone else on your staff, in industry or on the Hill. Obviously, you will need to be selective. To assist you, identify a first-rate analyst, someone brash and willing to call anyone and go anywhere to obtain information, like an annuity sales representative calling your home from an 800 number on Sunday afternoon.

Advice to Brian

The old saying that things are not always what they seem to be suggests that there will be times when you should challenge widely held beliefs and engage in some creative research to unveil the truth

10
WORKING WITH YOUR DEPUTY

Frank,

Thanks for that. I am already hearing widely held beliefs that I suspect are invalid, at least partly so.

Now that I have accepted the job offered by the White House, I have another concern. It sounds like my new job is a lot of work, close to 24/7, especially if I am also spending time analyzing widely held beliefs. Can I expect any help?

I am glad to be able to report you will have help. You should have at least one deputy, and there are three ways to use one:

Give your deputy those items you do not want to do. Some say this is giving the deputy the dirty work.

Use your deputy as a "shadow" to follow you all day in order to be aware of everything you know. Then your deputy can provide continuity when you are not available. In most cases, this is a waste of talent and experience, but you will see examples of this approach while you are in government.

Follow the example of a good marriage. The complications of modern life require two people to get it all done, so divide the work with your deputy.

In our marriage, we consider all assets as our assets, but we each have certain responsibilities. As we do these, we seek insights from each other about the best way to perform important tasks. I manage the outside of the house, the landscaping, the cars, and some investments. Mary Alice manages the inside of the house, including decorating, food, our travel arrangements, social engagements and her investments. We have an annual budget, separate checking accounts and credit cards. Each month we review all charges to see where the money goes, which disciplines spending. At the end of the year at tax time, we sum up the spending for the year to see what it takes to run our lives. Many times, we say that it takes two people to get it all done in contemporary society. So too at work; divide it with your deputy.

ADVICE TO BRIAN

Follow this good-marriage model and make your deputy responsible for a chunk of the substantive work, not the routine or unpleasant tasks that you dislike. This will allow your deputy to develop his own identity, and it frees you up for the tasks most important to the success of the program. If there is harmony and trust, two people can accomplish what one person alone cannot achieve.

11

SPEAKING AT CONFERENCES AND TO THE MEDIA

Frank,

I just spoke to the manager that I will be working for, and she confirmed that I will have an experienced deputy working with me. So that is good.

She also mentioned that I am expected to give speeches and interviews with the media as the program progresses. I am a little nervous about this because I never spoke in public in my private sector jobs, only in-house, and never for a crowd bigger than a dozen or so company insiders.

Can you give me some guidance?

Speaking in public and to the media goes with the territory. You must do it, and you will get more comfortable as time goes by. However, there are a number of considerations.

Wherever you go, whenever you speak, you create a record that will follow you the rest of your life. This can be helpful, or it can haunt you as you move on in your career, especially if you might run for political office in the future.

Many government officials make speeches, and you will seldom hear complete frankness from them. One notable exception was David Walker, the former comptroller general of the GAO, Congress's watchdog agency. President Clinton appointed him, but because the position has a fifteen-year term, his service carried over into the George W. Bush presidency

He was always very frank in his public speeches. He predicted a tsunami looming in the form of the massive public debt created by George W. Bush and his appointees. Walker spoke publicly 150 times a year. Because of his 15-year appointment, he could speak frankly, as few others can, without fearing loss of his position.

Walker could say things like "The US government does not have a strategic plan and never has," or "Today we have government without representation." He could say these things and still have a desk to go to the next day. You will have many opportunities to give speeches, but you will not have a guaranteed fifteen-year appointment, so you will need to be more circumspect when you are at the podium in a public forum.

All conference organizers chase after the new faces in town. They are happy for you to show up and speak, even early in your job when you have produced no results and are still planning. You will have so many requests to give speeches you could easily spend more time behind lecterns than in your office. Once, I reviewed my calendar for the previous year and found that I was out of the office at meetings and conferences 20 percent of my working time. I cut it to 10 percent the following year and thereafter.

As one example of the new face chase, President Obama appointed Vivek Kundra to be the chief information officer for the federal government on March 5, 2009. Seven days later, too early to know much about the new job, he spoke as the conference keynoter at the FOSE conference, one of the biggest annual technology conferences in Washington.

While Henry Ford said you could not build a reputation on what you are going to do, things are somewhat different in the big systems world of the federal community. Here you can collect a lot of attention before you do anything substantial or anything at all.

I advise you to give some speeches, but mostly at conferences held in Washington, close to your office. Flying from Washington to Hawaii or San Francisco to speak to 30 people for an hour is not worth your time in most cases.

As the costs come down, we will all use systems such as the Musion Eyeliner on Stage Tele-Presence technology because it eliminates long-distance travel. CISCO, one of the licensees of Musion's technology, has demonstrated live performances with CISCO's chair, John Chambers, in Bangalore, India when they "beam in" two of his executives located in California, allowing the three of them to stand together on stage in front of a live audience in India.

The beauty of the Musion Eyeliner technology is that the beamed-in persons appear to be on stage in front of the live audience; and the communication facilities are so good that there is no pause between the speakers in California and Bangalore or in the movement between the video frames. In addition, the beamed-in figures see the audience as if they were there in person, adding to the reality.

In 2014, there were 158 rooms worldwide equipped with Eyeliner technology. Until this technology becomes ubiquitous, choose the speaking opportunities that will allow government and industry officials to get to know you and your goals. Discussing your program in front of the right people can convince them of the value of the program and motivate them to become supporters. In addition, the contacts may help you find a good private sector job when it is your time to leave the government.

When conference managers invite you to speak, ask how many people will attend the conference. Because they tend to overstate the anticipated audience to entice government officials to speak, you should reduce their estimate by 50%.

Then ask what day and what time they will schedule your speech. The earlier you speak the better. For example, if it is a three-day conference, the morning of the first day is the prime time to speak, because all of the people attending the affair will be present and attentive. Later, the audience will thin out, and by late afternoon of the second day, some attendees will be out sightseeing, doing office work or just taking a power nap. Moreover, by the third morning, many attendees are already on their way to the airport

Find out when you will speak and decide if there will be enough people in the audience for it to be worthwhile. In addition, the conference organizers might try to change your scheduled time after you agree to speak. As the date for the conference draws near, some speakers drop out, and the organizers rework the schedule. If they move you from a good position to a bad one, you can drop out as well.

The other question you should ask is whether you will speak in a plenary role as a featured speaker or as a member of a panel. Audiences like panels. Conference organizers like them as well because they can add more names to the agenda to attract additional attendees. More important, seven panels over three days with six participants on each panel will ensure at least 42 people will attend the conference.

I would not participate on a 55-minute panel with more than three speakers. In addition, if the organizers do not schedule the panel in prime time, I would question whether it makes sense to participate.

If you decline an invitation because you calculate you will be speaking to a room of empty chairs, the conference organizer will probably push back, claiming it is not the number of people you speak to, but the number of the right people. This is correct, but the truly right people are not likely to remain and participate after the early sessions.

MEDIA INTERVIEWS

The trade publications *Government Executive, Federal Computer Week* and *Government Computer News* together reach 200,000 people in the federal community. They can help to publicize your program. Reporters representing these and other industry trade papers are normally trustworthy, and if they want to interview you, it is usually wise to agree. These reporters are likely to understand how the government works, and they will present you and your program in a generally favorable light. However, if *The New York Times, The Washington Post* or a television network calls, you need to be cautious. Normally, they are investigating something. They smell a story. You should sniff danger.

Interviews with national media reporters are an opportunity for disaster or a chance to deliver your message to a wide audience. When they call, ask what questions they have. Then, make an excuse to get off the phone, providing time to develop your response. Do not to enter into an extemporaneous discussion with a national media reporter until you have had time to develop your message.

Four Tips for Working with the Media

Tell stories. Reporters, as with all people, find stories interesting, sometimes captivating, as opposed to textbook language discussions.

Before the meeting, develop short, snappy sound bites that get your message across and provide the reporter with a suggested headline for his article.

Keep your answers short and crisp. Aim for a smile and a relaxed demeanor. Early in my career, I had a habit of droning on too long, answering one question to the point that I became lost in a muddle. With experience, when I sensed that even I was getting tired of a subject, I would stop and ask, "Is this too much? Do you want to move on to another question?" Always, the answer was "yes."

Watch out for leading questions. Arch Lustberg, a former American University drama professor and a New York City theater producer, taught almost all of our 1,300 Trail Boss graduates how to work with the media and Congress. He ran a lively class and would challenge a randomly selected class member to respond to a loaded question such as, tell me how will you respond to the reporter who asks, "Why does your agency allow companies to rape the forests of the United States?"

Arch taught us never to repeat the reporter's question, as many corporate and government executives will do as they fall into the trap and respond, "Our Company does not rape the forests of the United States." That reply will end up on the evening news, or it can become the headline in the newspaper or magazine. Instead, Arch counseled, respond with a smile and discuss what your agency or company is doing to make America greener.

Advice to Brian

Do not be a hermit. Speak to the media, especially the trade press, and participate in conferences. You will gain from these experiences, and you can use them as opportunities to sell your program. Just be sure to prepare well before you speak on the record. In addition, be selective and, if the offer to speak is from an unfamiliar source, clear it with your ethics office.

Finally, keep yourself special and space out your acceptances because audiences tire of too much of a good thing; and keep George Burns's advice always in mind: "Have a good beginning and a good ending, and have the two as close together as possible."

12

LEARNING FROM SENIOR OFFICIALS IN OTHER COUNTRIES

Frank,

Thanks for your advice. I just signed up for a Toastmasters speaking class to develop some techniques, so hopefully when the time comes to stand before an audience, I'll have some skills and be able to control my nerves.

I had dinner with a friend last night who suggested that I could learn some lessons from experienced government officials in other countries. Is this true? Are the governments of other countries similar enough to ours that there could be examples for me to follow?

What do you think about my friend's idea?

Your friend is right. One time in Cyprus on a chartered bus driving along the sea to a conference dinner, I talked with Wu Choy Peng, the CIO in Singapore who led her nation state to many awards in electronic government. She told me her government outsources everything to build a technology industry that can create national wealth. She said it took her eight years to learn to manage the intricacies of all of the outsourced programs.

Because they depend so much on contractors, the government of Singapore evaluates vendor performance monthly, levies penalties for poor performance and awards bonus points for good performance. This allows the government and its contractors to actively manage their programs and institute corrective action before problems run out of control.

The lesson I took from our conversation and now pass on to you is to deal with contractor problems immediately. If you think something is going wrong on a project, investigate it. The contractor might tell you that everything is fine, but do not take his word for it. You may end up stuck with an underperforming contractor while you pay too much for substandard work

Obviously, our U.S. government does not rely on contractors as completely as Singapore, but we use them extensively and we need to manage them effectively. Singapore's experience with outsourcing is just one example of how the experience of another country's government can provide useful insights for your job.

ADVICE TO BRIAN

It is important to reach out beyond Washington, D.C. for good ideas that work in other nations. From time to time, review the following sites for ideas to use in your job.

European Union (has a committee on every IT subject imaginable and is a pioneer in cross government management) [19]

International Council for Technology in Government Administration: (49-year old IT policy organization with 26 member nations) [20]

The OECD has 30 member countries with 250 publications each year on all subjects, including IT. [21]

You will find wisdom in many places and knowledgeable officials willing to share.

13
WORKING IN THE HEADQUARTERS BUILDING BUILDS RELATIONSHIPS

Frank,
My new bosses allow some managers to telecommute or to work from other locations rather than in the headquarters building where office politics might reign. For me, this has an attraction. Do you think working offsite is a good idea?

Working from home or offsite would be a mistake.

Think about it. If you are carrying on a romance with a sweetie and she lives in the same apartment building as you, the relationship is more likely to blossom than if she lives across town, a one-hour drive when traffic is light.

When you work in the main headquarters, you are available for invitations to ad hoc, impromptu meetings from your boss and peers. However, if you are located across town, they will not invite you to such meetings. You might not even know they took place.

When you work in headquarters, you will soak up information passed around informally in the parking lot, in the elevators and in the hallways, and you will develop relationships as you run into people. You will be able to arrange spontaneous luncheons with peers and bosses, all of whom have information to help you position your program. You will have the opportunity to meet people across the agency in impromptu ways, and you will better understand the organization and its moods. These are reasons why some companies such as Yahoo and Google discourage telecommuting, which, by the way, is a poor choice for ambitious midlevel managers hoping for promotions in an organization.

If you work in headquarters, you can drop into your boss' office after hours for a short chat, a bit of advice and the opportunity to plant a few ideas about your program that he might discuss in meetings with the head of the agency.

At the same time, your staff needs to have access to you easily and frequently. If assigned an office at headquarters away from your team, you will have to manage your time between the two sites. Be sure to hold your weekly staff meetings in the headquarters building to allow your managers to relate to the larger agency.

Current technology allows many options to work from remote locations, and they can make it seem almost as good as being there together. For planned meetings, linking in remotely works fine. For everything else, there is no substitute for working in the same building as your managers and peers.

Advice to Brian

If space is not available for you and your staff in the headquarters building, request a single small office for just you, your secretary and space for a conference table to accommodate meetings of eight people.

Use this office three afternoons a week so people will expect to see you there on those days, as sure as the sun rises to meet us every day.

14

ACCEPTING THE INFLUENCE OF GOVERNMENT UNIONS

Frank,
What about the federal employee unions? Do
they cause trouble for managers? I have had limited
experience with unions in my private sector positions,
but I know they can complicate a manager's job.

President Kennedy allowed unions to include federal employees in their actions, even those employees who are not dues-paying union members. This has had mixed results. On the positive side, employees have the union as a protector when they feel management is unjust. In addition, the National Treasury Employees Union, for one, has effectively lobbied for timely benefits and pay increases for the career service.

Unions can speak out publicly on issues when career officials, fearing retribution, cannot. For example, after the November 2008 presidential election, some political appointees refused to leave government, although leaving is the tradition after an election. With the aid of President Bush, some appointees were able to take career positions, a process called *burrowing-in*. Unions however spoke out loudly against the practice and attracted the attention of the press, including *The Washington Post* and *The New York Times*. Other major media outlets spotlighted the practice, and they were especially critical.

There is, of course, nothing new in this cynical practice. Dozens of political loyalists burrowed in during the final months of the Clinton administration. The score of Bush burrowers brought with them the worst pro-business, anti-regulatory biases that made this administration such a disaster.[22]

After the election but before Obama took office in 2008, the Bush administration's efforts to place some of his loyal supporters in career civil service jobs became an issue as it does with every outgoing president. Burrowing in occurs when political appointees tunnel their way down in the organization and try to hide away in the career ranks.

Normally, political appointees leave the government when a new president takes over; however, many do not want to leave for several reasons.

They will never get a better job.

They make more money in their government position than ever before.

They want to continue the outgoing president's game plan as long as possible.

They have grown to love their work and see themselves as indispensable to the future of their program.

They simply want to stay in the Washington, D.C. area until their children finish school and go off to college.

After Obama's election, *The Washington Post* called attention to the outgoing Bush administration's attempts to keep some political appointees in government by transferring them to career-level jobs.

Robert Irvin, senior vice president for conservation programs at Defenders of Wildlife, an advocacy group, criticized burrowing in at the Department of Interior. "It's pretty obvious they're trying to leave in place some of their loyal foot soldiers in their efforts to reduce environmental protection." [23]

Career people observing these actions can enlist others to draw attention to burrowing-in actions. Unions and advocacy groups are on the alert for such actions. In addition, the Office of Personnel Management has a process, which slows down, but rarely prevents placement of political appointees in career civil service jobs.

In general, the number of such actions is small. The Clinton administration, for example, placed 47 appointees in career jobs in its last 12 months in office. Yet, the emotional response to burrowing-in actions can be red hot.

On the negative side, when employees oppose a management action, they file grievances with the union. Grievances are sometimes justified, but they often lead to a seemingly endless process that frustrates managers attempting appropriate action against poor performers.

ADVICE TO BRIAN

As with other powerful organizations, there is good and bad associated with unions. The best way to deal with unions, as with all government players, is to develop a reputation for honesty, fairness and consistency with employees from your first day in office, and always be available to sit down and talk with union officials. If you are arbitrary, nasty or isolated from employees or unions, you are in for a rough time in government.

Whatever your politics, accept that unions have power in government. Spend some time to get along and move along.

15
OBSERVING THE MODERN DAY "SPOILS SYSTEM"

Frank,

I want to hire two former colleagues from companies that I worked with in the private sector. If I bring them into the government in political appointee positions, I can hire them quickly. However, as you say, I likely will lose them after the next presidential election. Alternatively, I could create two new career positions and bring them on board as career civil service employees. This would take a lot longer, perhaps a year according to some old hands. I am aware of the tensions that either action will cause with my new staff so I want to do it right and with sensitivity; but I do not want to wait forever to bring their talents into my organization. Someone said in a serious way that I am reviving the dreaded spoils system. Can you give me some background?

Here is some perspective from the late conservative radio commentator Paul Harvey. "In times like these, it is helpful to recall that there have always been times like these."

Brian, a bit of history will serve you well in the months ahead. The modern civil service is closely associated with the decline of feudalism and the growth of national autocratic states. In Prussia, as early as the mid-17th century, Frederick William, elector of Brandenburg, created an efficient civil administration staffed by civil servants chosen on a competitive basis. In France, similar reforms occurred because of the Revolution that began in 1789. They were the basis for the Napoleonic reforms that led to the first civil service program in any country.

Development of a professional civil service followed several decades later in Great Britain and even later in the United States, where victorious political parties delayed reform because they enjoyed the political benefits of distributing the spoils.

In a spoils system, the government awards its jobs to loyal members of the party in power. "To the victor belong the spoils." The earliest presidents, including Thomas Jefferson, awarded jobs to party loyalists. During the next 100 years, the corruption and inefficiency bred by the system reached staggering proportions in the administration of Ulysses S. Grant from 1869–1877. The public reaction helped bring attention to the need for civil service reform, but it took the assassination of a sitting president for true reform to occur.

The Pendleton Civil Service Reform Act of 1883 established the Civil Service Commission and professionalized the government workforce. This was the response to the murder of President James Garfield by Charles Guiteau, apparently a rejected office seeker under the spoils system. Succeeding the assassinated president, Chester Arthur supported establishing the civil service system.

The Pendleton Act made it unlawful to fill various federal offices with political supporters. Today, officials in the federal government ignore the law from time to time. Sandra Borden, formerly with the United States Coast Guard, observed President Reagan's political supporters appointed noncompetitively, even to the lower GS 12 level jobs, nine levels below the agency head.

The spoils system is even more common in state and local governments.

In modern civil service systems, the government usually

selects job seekers by examination and promotes them based on merit ratings. In democratic nations, governments design recruitment and advancement procedures to protect the civil service from political patronage.[24]

The federal civil service copied earlier practices in France and Great Britain, but the US system today is different because it is loaded with political appointees at the top. In Great Britain, there are 200 political appointees in the entire government. In the U.S., the Agriculture Department alone has 227 political appointee positions, and there are some 7,800 in the government as a whole, including 4,000 in the 28 core agencies in the government.

The main goal of the civil service personnel system is to prevent patronage, and the system has done a decent job of it for more than a hundred years. In recent decades however, would-be government reformers have been challenging the system, and it now appears to be on its last legs. Half of the civil service workforce is already under alternative personnel systems, and the trend appears to be accelerating.

Democrats and Republicans have worked systematically for years to weaken the career civil service system to employ more of their own supporters and impose greater control over career government employees. Jimmy Carter began the dismantling. Democrats and Republicans have followed Carter's leadership.

University professors of public administration emphasize that leadership by career officials is in the public interest. Unfortunately, modern age presidents do not share this belief.

The Senior Executive Association identifies seven techniques used by recent presidents and their appointees to place more of their supporters in jobs and exercise greater control over senior career executives.

Each new president routinely increases the number of political appointee positions in the government.

Those in power place more and more political appointees deeper in each agency, often replacing career officials.

Recent administrations convert an increasing number of career-reserved Senior Executive Service positions to SES general positions, allowing the White House to fill them with political appointees.

Political appointees eliminate career SES positions by reorganizing and consolidating organizations and then filling the new position with a political supporter. As one example, in 2006, the General Services Administration converted four of its highest-level career jobs to political status.

Political appointees ignore laws and policies and allow their colleagues to burrow down into the career ranks where they will remain for years, instead of leaving government when the president and their party leave power.

Once in office, political appointees increase the number of organizational layers in government, effectively isolating career officials further from the top political leadership.

Political appointees continually increase oversight and clearance procedures over speeches, correspondence, policy, the hiring of mid-level personnel, performance appraisals and bonuses, public appearances, and virtually all actions in an agency, thereby stripping senior career officials of their traditional authority.

These actions, originating in the White House, are seldom in the best interest of the public. They simply reward campaign supporters and place zealots, or incompetents in some cases, in government jobs.[25]

The civil service system has evolved through the decades and is not perfect, but it does provide a measure of protection to the government workforce from political ideologues, those with the rigid agenda and strong emotions that darkly hint "don't tell me, I know what is right, just do as I say or else, sometimes known as the Tea Party type of person."

The George W. Bush administration tried to eliminate the federal personnel system and replace it with one more to their liking. This created significant tension between his political appointees and the career establishment, as demonstrated during a panel session hosted by *The Washington Post* and organized by the Council for Excellence in Government. Pat McGinnis, president of the council, presided at the session held on November 2, 2005.

Two high-level political appointees attended. One was Clay Johnson, deputy director of the Office of Management and Budget and later an aide to President Bush in the White House.

The other was David Walker, comptroller general of the GAO, a congressional organization chartered to conduct investigations into executive branch performance. They were there to argue in favor of the personnel changes desired by President Bush.

The unions stood in their way. John Gage, president of the American Federation of Government Employees, and Colleen Kelly, president of the National Treasury Employees Union, attended to speak in opposition.

Interestingly, no federal employees or managers with experience working inside the federal personnel system were on the panel. Instead, surrogates represented them.

President Bush proposed scrapping the career service in favor of an unstructured system that Johnson and Walker promised would solve problems— problems they repeatedly spoke of but never defined. Gage and Kelly attacked the Bush administration idea, claiming it would bring even more unqualified presidential appointees into federal jobs. They warned that patronage and cronyism would resurface, as in the bad old days before the Pendleton Act.

Clay Johnson, with an easy southern drawl, spoke as if the Bush administration invented the federal personnel program, ignoring more than 100 years of history and experience in Washington. He offered many vague assurances, as people do when they really do not understand the issues. "We will do it with them rather than to them," he said, speaking of the federal workforce.

The panel discussion continued with growing acrimony between the two sides. The more the administration representatives talked about their proposed changes, the less the union leaders seemed to like them. John Gage described it as "attempts to strip employees of their rights," while Colleen Kelley said employees understand and trust the current system, and there is no need to change it completely.

Gage also discounted Clay Johnson's claim that reforming the 120-year old system could happen relatively quickly or that federal personnel could become familiar with it during 10 hours of training.

By the end of the contentious discussion, it was clear the administration and the employee advocates had radically different ideas of what the system's problems were and whether there were any at all.

McGinnis said in closing the inconclusive session: "With the body language among the panelists, there is not a great deal of trust here today."

ADVICE TO BRIAN

This story introduces different viewpoints about the relentless push to weaken the civil service system by allowing political appointees to diminish the historical balancing role of career employees and to place more presidential supporters in career jobs.

Political appointees generally savor the long-term trashing of the Civil Service personnel system and its protections from the spoils system. Career employees fear the results on themselves and on the government as a whole. However, they can do little to counter the endless attacks.

It is like a case of public administration anemia where successive White House administrations slowly replace seasoned judgment with a diluted mixture lacking in experience, reason, the lessons of history and respect for the government as a whole.

Muzzled career employees can only seek surrogates to carry the message to the public. Unions, the media, sympathetic non-government organizations and academics are all sources that can carry forward fresh examples of spoils system activity.

Regarding your question about hiring two former colleagues from industry, I would bring them on board as GS 15 Schedule C political appointees, then try to convert them to career positions before the next presidential election, recognizing that this is burrowing in which many dislike. Nevertheless, if they have proved themselves to your other employees as valuable to the team, and if they are likeable and personable, you can probably prevail.

16
Managing Personnel, Often an Oxymoron

Frank,

Thank you for your insights and recommendations about how to bring two colleagues on board. I also have a general question about working within the federal personnel system to reshape my staff over time as needed for the technology and management challenges that lie ahead. I have heard that the personnel system is complex, time consuming and as frustrating as seeking help from a commercial company's call center.

As a junior manager at IBM, I found there was a written policy for everything, same as when I was in the Navy. Deviations from the manual required a trip to IBM's corporate headquarters in Armonk, New York, to seek approval. However, I had real authority in hiring, promoting, developing, paying, evaluating and disciplining my staff.

As a government manager, by contrast, I had real authority to make decisions that IBM's division presidents could not make.

I could initiate hundred-million-dollar systems initiatives, but like other government managers, I had no real authority over some personnel issues. Human relations policies developed by successive White House administrations have systematically stripped real personnel management authority from managers.

Before I proceed, let me mention that it is not impossible to fire a poorly performing federal employee. In fact, in 2009, government managers terminated 11,275 employees (.007 percent) for poor performance or misconduct, and an unknown number left voluntarily after receiving poor performance appraisals.[26]

However, the rules are complex. President Reagan's administration, for example, ended mandatory retirement, allowing federal employees to work as long as they want to any age, even when they are no longer able to perform their job.

Reagan's rule affected my organization. We had an employee who should have retired 10 years earlier. Anyone with the sad experience of placing an elderly parent into a nursing home or an assisted living home knew this employee needed assistance and special care. An assisted living facility or even a nursing home could provide the help and support he needed.

This man could not walk out of an elevator if it settled an inch below the floor level. He could not lift his foot over the one-inch riser at the door to the men's room. He had done no work in years. In an interview with our personnel officer, he admitted he did no work anymore and said he did not intend to do any work again.

My staff worried about him because he would fall from time to time. At times, his toupee would sit askew on his head. Sometimes his condominium neighbors called us in the agency to express concern because they had not seen him for a few days.

He also suffered delusions. After President Clinton's election, this employee told his colleagues he would become the commissioner of our 2,000-person organization with control over $27 billion in information technology assets.

When I asked his manager when he planned to take action, he told me that he had given this sick man an outstanding performance rating the previous year, negating the possibility of any short-term action. I asked why he had given such a high rating to someone who publicly admitted to doing no work. The rating manager said it was out of respect for his age.

At this point, we began to address the performance rating issue. The personnel system does not allow a manager to reduce an employee from an outstanding rating to an unsatisfactory rating in one step. The process needs to unfold over several years with many meetings between the manager and the employee. In addition, the human resources officials need to be involved each step of the way, because missteps can lead to lawsuits. The union will be involved regardless of whether the employee is a union member.

We did not want to fire this 76-year-old employee with 51 years of service for non-performance; but we had no other choice since he refused to retire and because he was drawing a paycheck without doing a lick of work.

For sixteen months, a more senior manager on my staff, Dale Christensen, reluctantly worked his way through the complex process to fire the man. Finally, he reached the end of the process, when we could issue two required letters to the employee. The first letter is an *early alert* advising the employee that firing action is next. It allows fifteen days for his response. The second letter would fire him.

In the later stages, we met twice with my boss, the commissioner, to brief him on the case and to ensure he would do his part when the time came.

His part at the end was to stand aside, let the process work and not become emotionally involved. Our commissioner assured us he was aware of the situation and would support us when the time came.

When we issued the first letter, the employee immediately went upstairs to the administrator's suite to complain to the top official in the agency. The chief of staff intercepted our man in the reception area. With some medical knowledge and elderly parents, she suspected that advanced Parkinson's disease was one of his health problems.

Things seemed to be proceeding logically until my boss called one of his confidants and me to his office and said the administrator wanted the firing done in a "more humane" way. He asked that the firing letter be rewritten and softened; and he said he wanted us to arrange a work–at–home assignment for the elderly employee for a period of three to six months.

I reminded my boss about the complexity of firing an employee and that his last-minute humanitarianism would muck up the process. We had taken almost a year and a half to work through the personnel process to get to this point. The legal and personnel offices had reviewed every word in the two letters because the process is so legalistic. It would not be appropriate to rewrite the letter.

How, I asked, could we dream up a work-at-home assignment while we were firing the individual for non-performance? Giving a paid work assignment while firing an employee would send a confusing message, suggesting that we felt he was fully capable of doing his job. This was not the case.

Fortunately, my boss would accept a little pushback from time to time, and this time he did, suggesting that I go upstairs and try to change the mind of the chief of staff. I did, and she saw me right away. I gave her more information, but she liked the idea of giving the man an assignment at home after the termination. I reminded her about the long and complicated process in place to protect employees from arbitrary management actions. It had taken us 18 months to work through the process to where we could reluctantly fire this person. Finally, she fully recognized the situation.

The information I provided was new to her, but I had not convinced her to allow a clean firing without a work-at-home assignment. However, we did agree that he reminded us of our own elderly, failing parents in years gone by when they needed special care and attention.

The next day, the commissioner called to tell me he still wanted an after-firing, work-at-home assignment. I argued once more against this course of action because it would wreck the case. "You and everyone agree that taking him off the government's payroll is the right thing to do," I said. "It has taken us 18 months to bring this obvious case to this point. I do not understand the gratuitous concern at this late date."

"I am not asking your approval," he said. "I am going to do it."

Later in the day, I met with Dale, the manager working all this time to allow the long overdue action, and with the two personnel specialists guiding us during the past 18 months. The three were as incensed as I was about the gratuitous behavior by our boss, coming late in a case where everyone agreed we should not retain the man in a government job.

All senior executives are well aware of the futility of trying to deal with non-performing employees or those seemingly guilty of misconduct. G. Gerry Shaw, former general counsel for the Senior Executives Association, provided additional examples of the government's problem.

In one case, an employee discharged a firearm in the office. She was a driver for employees working in remote wilderness areas, and her job was to pick them up and return them to home base. Periodically, she did not pick them up. These individuals, abandoned in the deep woods without food, water or protection from the weather, often hiked out of the forest on their own. When the agency tried to force the employee to perform her work, she filed a sex discrimination complaint. The agency's public health physician further complicated the situation by saying the woman had a mental problem and could not maintain touch with reality unless she remained on the job.

In another agency, reported Shaw, a female manager had a habit of making disparaging remarks to Hispanic male subordinates. When employees complained, she requested a reassignment. Later, she filed an Equal Employment Opportunity Commission (EEOC) complaint, alleging that sex discrimination was the basis for her reassignment—even though she asked for the reassignment.

In another case I was involved in, a junior GSA lawyer assigned to an employee grievance case agreed with me that the complaint was not valid. However, since the division, now in my organization, had lost a grievance case years earlier when it was part of another agency, the lawyer hypothesized the judge would look at us unfavorably because of the earlier, unrelated case.

After I was involved in a few of these EEOC-type complaints and the hearing system associated with them, my deputy, Fred Sims, told me that the hearing examiners had quotas encouraging them to avoid decisions and to emphasize the "agreement process," which allows the hearing examiners to require the government to defend itself. This process is so onerous that government officials give up the fight and agree to a settlement in favor of the claimant.

In this environment, my organization never won a case, no matter how frivolous the formal grievance.

Getting back to our non-performing employee problem, I suggested that the director of Human Resources meet with our commissioner and the administrator's chief of staff to determine if all parties were familiar with the case, clear on their goals and fully aware of the risks of late-in-the-day decisions like idea for the work-at-home assignment. They met, and three days later, the commissioner agreed to drop the idea.

We were now ready to move forward. The next step was to talk to the employee about the agency's reluctant decision to fire him and to offer to accompany him to investigate assisted living homes in the Washington area.

The next day I went into the men's room near my office. This facility was the size of three coat closets and unchanged since 1915. As I stepped in, I smelled urine. The employee in question was the only other person in the room. I asked if I could hold the door for him. He did not answer while moving out with a slow shuffling gait.

I asked Dale Christensen about this, and he confirmed it: Our man often wet his pants. Even in the men's room, he went either on the floor or in his pants, another disheartening confirmation of his failing health.

Three days later, Christensen came to my office and said our man had agreed to retire voluntarily from the government and would do so in seven weeks.

In the government, nothing is for sure until six months after it happens, but the signs were positive. We were pleased for the individual and for our other employees who would see that management could pursue a deliberate course of action in a caring, human way, despite the thorny thicket of regulations that often confound action involving people issues.

In government, it is not over until it's over. Since the employee was delaying his retirement for seven weeks, anything could happen in the period. Under this arrangement, we stopped the termination process to allow his voluntary retirement. If he changed his mind and decided not to retire, it would take a lengthy period to rebuild momentum.

Nonetheless, for the first time in 18 months, proper action seemed to be at hand. Now, we could begin to plan to honor a man who had served his country for 51 years.

The chief of staff told me she would get a special "congratulations-on-your-retirement" letter from the President, and, a meritorious service plaque from the GSA administrator. Christensen began to plan a reception in the administrator's historic suite of offices, and he and a few on his staff offered to clean our pending retiree's apartment.

A few days after his decision, the employee walked with a lighter step, assisted by a newly acquired pine-colored cane.

ADVICE TO BRIAN

There are two lessons here. The commissioner eventually backed away from his work-at-home assignment idea, demonstrating the wisdom of the ancients: *Knowing how to yield is strength (Lao Tse)*. This is a key to success in a high-level government job.

At the same time, removing poor performers is hard work. The system is simple on paper: Develop a performance improvement plan according to the personnel system, monitor it carefully, and assign frequent performance ratings. If an employee consistently performs poorly, despite counseling and warnings, you have built the record you need to fire the employee—in theory.

However, in practice, the *simple* process is very time consuming, taking well over a year even in straightforward cases, and anyone can derail it any time, even on the last day before termination.

Faced with a poor performer, you need to decide whether it is worth your time or the time of one of your senior managers to pursue the termination process. You will likely make your decision based on a few factors, including the limited number of positions you have in your organization, and whether the individual is causing morale problems.

In your time in the government, you will find 10 percent of your staff will be able to help you move the organization to new heights. The vast majority, 80 percent, will go along and assist, doing their jobs capably. The other 10 percent will make it difficult. My advice is to spend your time with the 90 percent who perform well.

The most important task in your early days on the job is to identify those top few exceptional performers that can assist you to move the organization forward. These special performers may report directly to you, or they may be two or three levels below you. If so, the challenge is to get them involved with you without wrecking the existing chain of command, which would create confusion, and damage morale, normally high when a new boss arrives.

In government, you will need to work within the federal personnel system to hire qualified performers to help you manage your program. This can be difficult. The process can seem endless because there is always another issue, regulation, law or process to overcome.

Brian, find someone on your staff or hire someone who knows the personnel process and the people in the Human Resources office. It should be someone the personnel people like or at least respect. Your person needs to be easy going, yet persistent. A heavy hand type-A personality is not who you want in this assignment.

Your selection should be the only person in your program allowed to deal with your agency's HR Department. Do not expect the HR folks to give your personnel actions special priority, but they will be more responsive if they know and can work with the one person you appoint to interact with them.

You need to support your designated contact person. Nurture your connections to the agency leadership so you can, if needed, call on the top bosses to help you move a personnel action. You, of course, would never go over the heads of the HR department. However, the idea that you could, and might, may help speed up some personnel actions from time to time.

As you can see, federal personnel management is considerably more complicated than you may expect. The examples in this chapter point out vividly that you will need help from several sources in your personnel management transactions.

You cannot fly on one wing.

17
RECOVERING WHEN "THEY" GO AFTER YOU

Frank,
I have heard about new bosses demoting lots of senior-level career officials when a new administration comes to Washington. Is there anything I can do to protect my status? What recourse do I have if I am unjustly reassigned or demoted?

Learning how the system works enables you to protect yourself if people try to force you out of your job, as happens to all senior career officials once or twice in their career. Adverse action against you is just part of life in the government.

Sometimes the action is quite personal. Alan Dorris, a senior career official, described working in the Bureau of Public Debt when the Nixon White House appointed political appointees as deputies to work for senior career officials. Often called *minders,* their job, Dorris felt, was to keep an eye on the career officials and make sure they were loyal to the president and adhered to the party line.

Career officials needed a Republican friend to survive in the bureau in those days. Fortunately, Dorris had one. His friend called him one day and said, "They are going to push you out. They are going to give you a deputy, and in a few weeks they will ask you to step aside."

His friend advised him to take the issue to the personnel department. Dorris resisted, but the friend counseled, "Personnel is a conduit straight into the commissioner's office, and the new commissioner doesn't want to rock the boat too early in his tenure."

Dorris did not go to the personnel office, but two weeks later, the personnel officer called him. "You're going to get a deputy, and we'd like you to stand aside for six months and see how it works out." Dorris refused and promised to protest any effort to push him out with any method available.

As predicted, the personnel officer called the commissioner and said something like, "We've got a problem here with Alan Dorris, and he's going to raise hell about our idea of asking him to stand aside."

The commissioner then called Dorris and reassured him that the Bureau did not intend to push him aside. Three months later, the agency's management promoted the political deputy to GS-15 and moved him to another office across the street. Dorris survived, partly because his friend had given him an early warning and partly because he understood the personnel system well enough to recognize he had some defensive options. Dorris believes he survived because he pushed back.

After Nixon's downfall, many of his political appointees bailed out all across the government.

Political parties have learned how to force experienced senior career officials to quit or transfer so they can replace them with party loyalists. Alan Dorris is the rare one who resisted and survived to tell his story.

In another example of a personal attack, consider the case of Brendan Sullivan, well-known lawyer of famous people such as Oliver North of the Iran-Contra scandal during the Reagan administration, and Sen. Ted Stevens (R-Alaska) during the George W. Bush administration.

When Sullivan served as a supply officer in San Francisco during the Vietnam War, the Army assigned him to defend an enlisted man who had escaped from the Presidio, an Army post. Accepting the job, he thought that the Army went by the book, giving accused their rights—but he found this was not the case. He pressed in ways that defense lawyers rarely do in military courts, and the Army pushed back, employing what he said was intimidation. Unsuccessful, the Army reassigned Sullivan to the Vietnam war zone with one week's notice—normally 90 days' notice were given—just six months before he was due to be discharged.

Walter Cronkite took up the case on his evening broadcast, although he presented Sullivan as a radical. *The New York Times* published a story about the case. In addition, Sen. Charles Goodell (R-New York) and Sen. Alan Cranston (D-California) issued a joint statement that "assignment to a war zone must not be used as retaliation against those who voice unpopular views or champion unpopular causes." After receiving much negative publicity, the Army backed down and cancelled Sullivan's orders to Vietnam.[27]

In another example of government going on the attack against someone viewed as holding opposing views, Gina Gray, who served in the Iraq war zone, worked as a public relations officer at Arlington National cemetery, the nation's most hallowed burial ground. Her boss fired her after an argument because she challenged his decision to forbid the press to access a funeral suite, although the family had invited the press to cover the funeral.

She then worked for two years to expose the mismanagement at the cemetery. While the Department of the Army provided false status information to Congress, and while the Inspector General was slow to investigate, her persistence led to media attention revealing dysfunction at the cemetery. Gray estimated that there was a minimum of 15,000 burial errors at the cemetery. She had asked why her superiors gave her job to the daughter of the commanding general of the Military District of Washington, who was responsible for several facilities including the cemetery. In addition, she asked what became of the millions of taxpayer dollars supposedly spent on electronic grave records at the Arlington National Cemetery that do not exist.[28]

Throughout 2011 and 2012, new revelations continued to

surface about mismanagement of the bodies of service personnel at Arlington National Cemetery.

"Going after someone" happens at the highest level of government. President Nixon allegedly ordered aides to recruit Secret Service agents to dig up the dirt on Ted Kennedy. It is unclear whether the Secret Service cooperated with the president. Nixon, however, pressed for more wiretaps and a combing of tax records, not only on Kennedy but also on other leading Democrats. "I could only hope that we are, frankly, doing a little persecuting," he said.[29]

Senior executives must support political appointees in their policy directions. This responsibility also includes the duty to tell the political appointee when a proposal is a bad or illegal idea. This is when the trouble can begin, because some political appointees do not appreciate bad news or what they regard as resistance.

Bill Bransford, former executive counsel for the Senior Executives Association, points out that senior executives are often in a tight spot when they stand up to political appointees. Alternatively, they can keep their heads down and avoid conflict. More are doing the latter, according to Bransford, as they see fellow executives suffer from unexplained and irrational personnel decisions.[30]

On the other hand, sometimes when they go after you, it is not personal. They simply want to give your job to someone else. To do this, they can give you a poor performance rating based on factors that are not in your job description, as happened to a senior executive in the GSA who was a pioneer in E-government initiatives in the federal government. In such a case, you have the option to fight it out through the Merit System Protection Board or possibly in the federal courts. However, even if you win, the process will damage your psyche, and if you remain in your job, many doors, formerly open, will close, making it impossible to do your job.

There is another circumstance, one where nobody is wrong. Trust and chemistry are important between people working together on important issues. In addition, one needs to be in harmony with others in the group, whether they are political or career officials. If trust and chemistry are lacking, you may find yourself outside the inner circle, looking in while occupying a non-job. Some call this "serving time."

Advice to Brian

During your government service, you may find yourself demoted to a special-assistant job assigned to a dingy office without access to the people running the agency. The press no longer calls for your comments. Invitations to deliver speeches become rare. You are an outcast. You are serving time.

Suppose a new political appointee comes to town and wants to move you, a senior career executive, out of your job so the new assistant secretary can have his own team or maybe you have a disagreement with your boss. In this circumstance, as a senior executive, you should understand that your boss could do whatever he wants. Sure, he has to give you 15 days' notice and discuss the matter with you, but he can do whatever he wants. The matter is a bit more complicated if he wants to move you outside the commuting area, say from Washington to Fairbanks, Alaska; then 60-days' notice is required. Your best strategy is to try to have a say into where and when he will move you. Check out vacant senior executive positions in the agency, identify jobs you would like and campaign for one of them.

If you work in government for many years, it is likely someone will come after you, especially after a new president takes office. Unless your case draws media attention, you have a couple of choices if the new political appointee sends you to purgatory. You can keep your chin up and be above it all, or you can complain about your predicament to anyone willing to listen. Few people are likely to care, and some are actually happy to see you suffer because of your past deeds affecting them.

I have seen senior officials choose each road. Some take the high road, performing in their reduced role without complaint, possibly returning to a prominent position when the agency leadership changes, as it always does eventually. There is no guarantee, though.

However, those taking the low road, complaining endlessly, usually become bitter and fade into oblivion. If you feel you cannot bear your exile, it is better to leave the agency or even the government entirely before allowing your character and reputation to become permanently impaired.

In many ways, it is not if they go after you, but when. The question is how well you respond when it happens to you.

18
APPRECIATING NON-GOVERNMENT ORGANIZATIONS (NGO's)

Frank,

The Alan Dorris story and your advice about taking the high road are very insightful. I hope I never have to consider which road to take. Your earlier comments about working within the federal personnel system indicate that it is very complicated, and, of course, I experienced a bit of that when I applied for my job. However, I had no idea about all the nuances. I need to spend some more time learning about it.

By the way, what can you tell me about non-governmental organizations? I think my job is going to require me to stay in touch with some, but I do not know which ones or exactly what I am supposed to do. I know you can't help me with the specific details—I'll get filled in on that when I start—but what are the general things about NGOs that I need to know early on?

You will encounter many organizations operating in the gap between the government and the public. Some are influential, relentless in their pursuit of legislation or policy favorable to their constituencies. The International Red Cross, Red Crescent and Amnesty International are examples of the 29,000 or so international NGOs and the estimated 2 million domestic NGOs in the US. In technology and E-government, you will most likely deal with the Council for Excellence in Government, the Senior Executives Association, the Technology Association of America and others seeking to influence federal information technology policy.

As you can see, some of these are primarily relief organizations, and others are lobbying or trade groups. They all fall under the broad definition of NGOs. Des Vincent, a colleague in the International Council for Technology in Government Administration, defines NGOs as organizations with three defining characteristics:

- NGOs benefit to a significant degree from volunteer work
- They are self-governing and independent of the state
- They are uninvolved in the distribution of profits to shareholders

NGOs perform a wide variety of public services funded or partly funded by the taxpayers, including hospice care for terminally ill patients, childcare services in disadvantaged areas, and advice and guidance for young people. At a different level, some NGOs play an important role by campaigning for change. Examples include campaigning for the first laws to protect children from abuse and helping to create international humanitarian laws.

While they do good work, they can draw justifiable criticism. The media often criticizes some NGOs for poor service and improper use of funds, such as paying for first class seats on aircraft, luxury suites in hotels and lavish dinners in five-star restaurants. Their salaries can be outlandish as well, often exceeding that of the President of the United States and senior congressional officials by a factor of five or more. Worse, some NGOs collect donations but distribute only a token percentage to the supposed beneficiaries.

Except for periods of crises, change in the federal government will come not from within the government itself; rather, it will originate from pressure by state and local governments, industry, the NGOs and the voters.

ADVICE TO BRIAN

Identify any NGOs sharing the same interests as you. They can become allies and help in several ways.

They can carry a message to the Congress and to the public, while the White House or your agency policy officials have you muzzled.

NGOs organize discussion groups and conferences. These give you an opportunity to publicize your message and build support for your program.

Through NGOs, you can meet people sharing similar government related interests.

Many NGOs perform valuable, though sometimes one-sided, research on selected issues. Should their interests coincide with yours, their research can be beneficial.

Although you may choose to work closely with certain NGOs, always seek opposing views and preserve your independence.

19

RATIONALIZING HOW THE PRESIDENT AND THE PUBLIC MAY VIEW YOU

Frank,

As we discussed, I am going to be doing very important work, important to each citizen in the country. When I travel outside of Washington, should I tell people that I meet along the way that I am a senior official in the federal government?

Working a few levels under the president is an eye-opening, rewarding experience, but outside of Washington your reception can be as dispiriting as if the maître d' seats you just outside the restroom for your 25th anniversary celebration.

Dr. Samuel Broder, an American oncologist and medical researcher, was a co-developer of some of the first effective drugs for the treatment of AIDS; and he was director of the National Cancer Institute from 1989 to 1995, overseeing the development of new therapies. He received several awards for his work, including the Arthur S. Flemming Award, a presidential award given to outstanding government employees. Others receiving the award include astronaut Neil Armstrong, the first man on the moon, and Paul Volker, the former chair of the Federal Reserve.

Dr. Broder said it best as he resigned from public service in 1995, observing that a major factor in his decision to leave government was his frustration with the fashionable view of government as an impediment to progress.

"When I first came here 22 years ago, government service was still something people generally admired," he said. "It was a very positive career choice. And, I think it might be good to take a few steps back and remember that although we do have to make government more efficient and face fiscal realities, there are certain core functions of the government that are extremely important, including scientific research for the alleviation of suffering."[31]

This statement is as timely today as it was in 1995. Making the government a scapegoat has a long history, but it began in earnest in the modern era with Ronald Reagan. In running for office against incumbent Jimmy Carter, Reagan campaigned against the government itself. In his first inaugural address, he said "Government is not the solution to our problem; government is the problem."

President Clinton continued the practice of bashing government to pave the way for his reforms. In his State of the Union message in January 1998, he publicly expressed outrage at the IRS and did so again on radio a week later. He and Vice President Al Gore frequently portrayed the government in need of change in order to support their program, the National Partnership for Reinventing Government (NPR). The aim for the initiative, Gore stated, was to create a government that "works better, costs less and gets results Americans care about," creating a picture for the average citizen that the government does not work well, costs too much, and gets results unimportant to Americans.

NPR was a good program. In order to sell it to Congress and to the public, however, Clinton and Gore demeaned the government, inflicting further damage on the reputation of the government and its employees.

Since Reagan, the history of bashing the government continues with each new president and presidential candidate, and more recently, with each congressional candidate. Barack Obama continued the practice with his pointed use of the demeaning term *bureaucrat* when he pronounced in 2010 that government bureaucrats would not run his new health care program. Later, when his contractors brought mountains of bad publicity to his signature health program, he may have reconsidered whether he should have employed more bureaucrats.

Moreover, it is not always pleasant to tell other people about your employment. One time on a golf course in Georgia, the starter assigned me to play with three strangers. We had a good time for three hours. Then, on the 16th tee, while we waited for the fairway ahead to clear, one golfer asked me in a Southern accent, "What do ya'll do for a living?"

"I work in computers for the federal government," I said. Immediately, I could tell that my answer provoked tension, and the sociability ended. They were very hostile to President Clinton's programs, especially in health, and they told me so.

Another time, I was waiting in line for a tour through the Canadian Parliament building in Ottawa. Two older couples from Phoenix were in the line ahead of me, and we had a nice chat as the line inched moved forward. One gray hair asked what I did for a living. When I replied that I worked in Washington for the federal government, the conversation ended; they lost interest in talking with me. Luckily, the tour soon began.

Two days after the 1994 election, turning Congress over to the Republicans, I hooked up with three retired "good old boys" from North Carolina for a round of golf. When I said I was from Washington, they reacted strongly. One said the election, passing control of Congress to the Republicans, was a message of disapproval for President Clinton and added, "Wait two years until we send him another message," referring to the 1996 elections when Clinton would have to run for re-election. There was no offer to join them for a beer on the 19th hole after we finished the round.

Most Americans have few interactions with the federal government. An exception is the IRS, and for all of its efforts to be a good citizen, the IRS does much to create ill will between the government and the public. In the 2009 tax-filing season,

Americans made 75.7 million phone calls to the IRS's toll-free help line seeking advice; however, IRS did not answer 22.4 million calls for three reasons:

- The taxpayers hung up after a long wait
- They were disconnected by IRS
- They received a busy signal

The following year, the agency's goal was to answer only 7 out of 10 calls from taxpayers seeking assistance. In addition, when an IRS representative does answer a taxpayer's call, the fortunate taxpayer waited an average of 11 minutes and 38 seconds before being connected.

In 2013, about 40 percent of callers never reached an IRS representative. Those who did get through had held on an average of 18 minutes.[32] The situation was worse in 2014.

Further, the public can be alienated because of an intense dislike for the President's goals in war, health care reform or the environment. In addition, many citizens become cynical about their government because of the personal lives and conduct of members of Congress and their endless earmarks for their pet projects and financial supporters.

The endless spin used by the government to influence the thinking of the public reduces trust in the government, especially when the subject is yet another war to preserve unstated American interests.

Occasionally, lower level employees bring discredit to the government's reputation. One example is the 2012 case of the prostitutes and Secret Service agents carousing in Cartagena, Columbia two nights before the president's arrival for an international conference.

Another is the 2010 Western Region's $823,000 employee team conference for GSA employees, a story that broke in the news in 2012. Unfortunately for GSA, 2012 was a presidential election year, and the GSA conference became a political football for the Republicans to bring discredit to President Obama and those "villains" in Washington. One congressional representative even called for the abolishment of GSA but quieted after industry representatives said that the congressional representative, new to government, was unaware of all of the services and policies

GSA provides to all agencies inside the government.

While examples of career employees such as these are rare, they bring negative attention to the government, negativity that endures for years.

As you travel outside Washington, do not be surprised when members of the public are cold to you. They view the government as a heartless monolith or worse; they view you as the government.[33] When presidents knock the government and demean government employees, people across the country, often unconsciously, lower their opinion of those laboring in the government.

ADVICE TO BRIAN

Government employees suffer public disapproval because people associate them with a president's unpopular policies or personality. In addition, if the public dislikes Congress in general, as do most Americans, and if they had an unsatisfactory transaction with an agency, the public will dislike the government workforce and you by extension. Successive presidents feed the fire when they publicly bash the government for their political gain.

There is one other factor. Schools do not teach civics to young citizens. Most young Americans reaching adulthood have little knowledge of the history of the United States and the government's role in society. Moreover, living outside Washington far removed and isolated from the national government, with few interactions except taxes, Medicare, Medicaid and Social Security, the public accepts generalities about the government and its employees.

The old-time guidance not to lend money else you create an enemy applies to the debates between Democrats and Republicans to reduce the federal debt. Republican stronghold states such as Alaska, Alabama, Kentucky, Louisiana, Mississippi, New Mexico, North and South Dakota are generally hostile to the government and argue for a smaller government. These same states historically rail against the federal government while they tap the public till, and take more from the federal government than they contribute, happily accepting transfer payments from Democratic-controlled states such as California, Connecticut, Delaware, Illinois, Minnesota, New York and New Jersey. The latter states pay the most to the federal government and get the least in return.[34]

Alaska especially is a state where the public may give you a frosty reception because you are a government employee. Alaska's politicians, such as former governor Sarah Palin, and the public routinely charge Washington with intrusiveness and other crimes, although the state receives more money from the federal government than any other state on a person-to-person basis. Alaska survives on drilling, mining and federal pork. According to a state legislator, the federal government returns $5.76 to Alaska for every tax dollar the state sends to Washington, far more per capita than any other state.

Unfortunately, as a gigantosaurus, the federal government is easy to criticize when a person lacks knowledge, is a political, or media climber, or uninformed. Although government work is interesting, stimulating and important to every person living in the nation, some in America lack esteem for federal jobholders. Accept it, you cannot change perceptions built up over a lifetime.

20

USING POLITICAL SPIN AND MANIPULATION

The most dangerous of all falsehoods
is a slightly distorted truth.

G. C. Lichtenberg (1742–1799)

Frank,
When I read Fact Checker in the Washington Post
archives, assessing the validity of the statements by
public figures, it seems that I should treat much of what
the presidential candidates say in public with great
skepticism, just as I would treat offers for a free lunch,
or guarantees by a used car sales clerk. Is it the practice
to play loose and easy with the truth in the government?
I understand they call it "spin." Can I use spin, and if so,
when, and in what circumstances?

Everyone practices spin, especially countries, political parties
and companies. Known a century ago as "winning the hearts and
minds of Americans" and today known as propaganda, spin is

used to mold public thinking. Spin in the U.S. dates back at least to 1917 when President Wilson created the Committee on Public Information to shape America's attitudes toward the war.[35]

With its staff of 75,000, it created and published propaganda to glorify the war and the American contribution to destroy the evil Germans. All varieties of media delivered the message, including articles, cartoons and advertisements in newspapers, journals and movies. CPI inserted its products to shape public opinion in public school lessons, university textbooks and Sunday sermons, in films and lectures in movie theatres, Indian reservations, and anywhere the public gathered. It printed its messages on posters displayed in public places and storefronts and on pamphlets distributed by the millions. CPI was active abroad as well.[36] In addition, it had a role in censorship to ensure that opposing views did not surface for the public to consider.

In hindsight, American propaganda in World War I was the beginning of spin, and it controlled American beliefs in wartime, surprising in an American democracy.[37]

All organizations in contemporary society have a highly developed ability to spin the facts to put the best face on an issue. Government employees routinely read articles in the newspapers about projects they are involved in and are surprised by how different the reported story is from what they know. The difference can be spin.

In public relations, spin can signify a heavily biased portrayal of an event or situation in one's own favor, suggesting disingenuous, deceptive and/or manipulative tactics.

Government and corporation officials talking to reporters will attempt to put the best possible face on an event or an issue. Good reporters can see through this in some cases—but not all reporters are good.

With experience in the world of political spin, you learn not take anyone's words at face value. If a source close to the White House deems it so, war can be peace, freedom can be slavery, and ignorance can be wisdom.

The Department of Defense is a leader in the practice of spin. After September 1, 2010, military personnel killed in Iraq had Operation New Dawn, not the Iraq War, engraved on their headstones. Similarly, those who died in Afghanistan have Operation Enduring Freedom carved on their memorials. Some families and veteran's groups said that ". . . those slogans are little more than propaganda tactics for politicians and the Pentagon to sanitize the wars and drum up public support."

"It's not a new dawn," said Oscar Aviles, whose son, a Marine Corps lance corporal, died in Iraq in 2003. "It's just a lot of pain and anguish." [38]

The Defense Department, alarmed by the world global outcry over its use of drones to kill, took the word *kill* out of the names list and spun more innocent names with little meaning, names somewhat like the passwords used to protect desktop computers— seven letters, two numbers and a few special characters.

As with American companies, the Pentagon works to spin the news provided to the American people. Spinning from Afghanistan and Iraq uses the *embed* process; but the consequences are more serious than spinning the features of a soft drink, a new model automobile or an updated smart phone. Pentagon spin from a war zone occurs from two actions. First, the military limits the number of reporters embedded with combat troops in war zones. In Iraq, the number of embedded reporters was on average twelve.

In addition, the Pentagon controls access to reporters more likely to give favorable coverage. Under the agreement that reporters sign, they acknowledge the military can terminate them without appeal, ensuring that reporters with embed status are unlikely to produce unfavorable coverage, although some have done so and were terminated. [39]

The Department of Interior's Minerals Management Service, a troubled agency since its formation in 1982 and tarred by its central role in the BP Gulf of Mexico oil spill in 2010, used spin to divert attention from its troubled past. It simply changed the name of the agency to something even more obscure, the Bureau of Ocean Energy Management, Regulation and Enforcement.

To extend the diversion, it employed another Washington tactic for an agency in trouble by initiating a study that would last until the pressure was off.

Government is not the only practitioner of spin. The fructose industry, facing research findings that pancreatic tumor cells use fructose to divide and proliferate, lobbied the government to allow it to change the name from fructose to corn syrup to deflect criticism of the product.[40][41]

Organizers of political rallies on the Washington Mall often exaggerate attendance at their events to convince others that many share their beliefs and America should listen to their message. Glenn Beck, right-wing television commentator, held a rally on August 28, 2011. He, along with Sarah Palin of the Tea Party, was there to "restore honor" to America.

Congresswoman Michele Bachman estimated the crowd at over 1.6 million because she said we were there to see it. Using a scientific approach by flying a camera-rigged balloon after receiving clearance to do so from four federal agencies, the company Digital Design & Imaging Services of Falls Church, VA, reported that the real attendance was 87,000.[42][43]

One great example of spin occurred when the government changed the name of the Department of War, a name that had existed in various forms since 1789, to the more passive name: the Department of Defense. Considering DOD's activities since 1946 in Korea, Vietnam, Grenada, Iraq, and Afghanistan, well away from our shores, should the government restore the department to its original name to reflect its true mission?

Washington Post White House correspondent Ann Devroy reported that most people in Bill Clinton's Washington found the question of spin verses lying largely irrelevant. The city operates under what she described as a "tacit understanding"— even though we say you should not lie, the definition of lies and the definition of truth are all somewhat malleable.[44]

Spin can take the form of action, not just words. The US inflation rate as reported by the US Inflation Calendar of the Labor Department was 1.7 percent in June 2012. However, pricing action by companies suggests that inflation is much higher. In the same month, I bought my favorite thin, low calorie cookies and noticed that the contents were reduced 20 percent in weight from my purchase the previous month, but the package and the price were the same as last month. At first, I thought the paper bag weighed as much as the cookies.

My shaving cream came in a smaller can and the total weight was 20 percent less than the product I purchased just two months earlier, but the price was the same. How many consumers would notice these subtle changes in content?

Companies are silently adjusting to inflation by reducing content and charging the same amount, rather than raising prices for their products. These are examples of relatively harmless spin, a game played by government and industry to mask the true level of inflation.

A cruel use of spin occurs when politically conservative and private sector interests persistently pronounce that Social Security will not be available when today's young people are in need of the lifeline that Social Security provides to retirees. The objective is to create fear that the system is collapsing, which would allow privatizing the system, an outcome that major financial institutions would relish should they gain control of the hundreds of billions of dollars flowing into the Social Security system.

Despite the campaign to create alarm, the reality is that the system is not going broke. In 2011, Social Security ended the year with a $2.7 trillion surplus. The funds from worker's payroll taxes will cover all retirees' payments until 2021—even if the government makes no changes to the program. After 2021, SSA can cash its Treasury Bonds and provide full benefits until 2037. After 2037, income from payroll taxes would cover 75 percent of retiree's payments for decades. Of course, in the interim Congress could make other marginal changes, and the numbers become even more positive. [45] [46]

Former Secretary Clinton is typical of the majority of appointed or elected officials and those who would be. In 2015, she hired public relations experts to redefine her public image for the next presidential election. As one result, polls revealed that the public feels she is too programmed. [47] The potential drawback of these makeovers was described by Republican strategist Fred Davis, who told the Post that if Clinton's marketing "seems like a craven attempt to try to put fresh paint on an old house, then it will backfire." [48]

In addition, companies dependent on government contracts finely tune spin. Boeing, Lockheed Martin, Northrop Grumman and many other well-heeled companies attempt to influence government decisions in three ways:

- Taking full-page ads in *The Washington Post* and in other media sources
- Using their extensive network of lawyers, lobbyists and elected officials
- Working through industry associations to influence government decisions

In 2011, with the successful use of Predator and other unmanned aircraft in Afghanistan, it was becoming clear that the age of unmanned aircraft, thinking robots and laser warfare was approaching. The hundreds of air squadrons and fleets of aircraft carriers may soon to go the way of the Army's Bradley Fighting tank— into the chapter of history books titled *Obsolete*. Yet the spin doctors hired by weapons manufacturers and some hired by local governments work with Congress to continue manufacturing soon-to-be obsolete systems and to keep the jobs in a congressional district.

In a mega aircraft buy, on February 29, 2008, the Pentagon announced a $40 billion award to the Northrop Grumman and European Aeronautic Defense and Space (EADS), Airbus's parent company. The contract would provide 179 refueling and long-range transportation carriers for the Air Force. Over time, the requirement could rise to another 321 tankers and a total value of $500 billion in 2008 dollars.

Boeing had dominated this market, so this loss was serious. Moreover, there would be no more United States Air Force refueling tanker procurements for several decades. Therefore, this situation was more than serious. It called for all-out war to turn the Air Force decision around.

After the award to Northrop Grumman, the spin started immediately. Sen. Patty Murray (D-Wash.), whose state is home to Boeing's largest plant, said, "We are outraged that this decision taps European Airbus and its foreign workers to provide a tanker to our American military. This is a blow to the American aerospace industry, American workers, and America's men and women in uniform." [49]

Norm Dicks (D-Wash.), "the congressman from Boeing," a senior member of the state's Congressional delegation, and a member of the House Defense Appropriations Subcommittee, said the contract award shocked him, and he predicted an uprising on the Hill. "There are a lot of members who won't accept this," he said.[50]

Boeing and its supporters described Boeing as an all-American manufacturer, while portraying Northrop Grumman as a foreign intruder taking American jobs. This was a false picture.

For example, the Department of Transportation issued a report on the same day as the Pentagon award announcement, citing that American passengers fly on jet aircraft made with parts manufactured overseas, parts that the Federal Aviation Administration rarely inspects. Boeing was one example because it bought parts from China, Italy, Japan, Brazil and many others for both its current 777 aircraft, a plane it considered bidding to the Air Force, and the advanced Dreamliner 787.[51]

In building its passenger plane for the future—the 787 Dreamliner—Boeing manufactures only the vertical tail fin. It farms out 70 percent of the work to nearly 50 partners and top-tier suppliers at 135 sites spanning four continents.

Boeing flies around the world in four specially modified 747 planes called the Dreamlifters, collecting parts and delivering them to Seattle. Demonstrating its excellence in design, engineering, manufacturing, logistics and procurement, Boeing can assemble the pre-fabricated parts and build a new 787 Dreamliner plane in 3-7 days.

The following table identifies the source of major components of Boeing's newest aircraft.[52]

Boeing's 787 is a Global Affair	
Wing tips	S. Korea
Wing	Japan
Forward fuselage	Japan
Wheel well	Japan
Doors	France
Horizontal stabilizer	Italy
Center fuselage	Italy
Engines	United Kingdom
Landing gears	United Kingdom
Cargo doors	Sweden
Fairing	Canada
Trailing edge	Australia
Leading edge	Oklahoma
Engine nacelles	California
Tail fins	Washington
Forward fuselage	Kansas
Aft fuselage	South Carolina
Vertical fin	Washington (Boeing)

In February 2011, under pressure the Defense Department changed course and awarded the contract to Boeing, the "All-American Company."

In another typical use of spin by both government and industry, General Motors in April 2010 launched a major public relations campaign, cheering itself for "repaying" the government $6.7 billion previously loaned to the company by the Treasury Department. President Obama and Treasury Secretary Timothy Geithner both praised GM for the repayment action.

GM, in its publicity campaign, said the repayment was evidence that the company had turned the corner. "GM is able to repay the taxpayers in full, with interest, ahead of schedule because more customers are buying vehicles like the Chevrolet Malibu and Buick Lacrosse," said Edward E. Whitacre Jr., the GM chief executive.

Sen. Grassley (R-Iowa) in a congressional hearing listened carefully to the Inspector General of the Treasury Department and learned that the government had given GM two pots of money to rescue the bankrupt company, and that GM had simply paid off one federal loan with money from the other pot of federal money. Grassley called it the government enabled "Troubled Asset Relief Program (TARP) money shuffle."

After Grassley revealed the true source of the money, GM and Treasury denied the findings and tried to put more spin on the case, with Treasury saying the cash was "the property of GM," although the money came from a taxpayer-financed escrow account held for GM at the Treasury Department.[53]

Spin becomes a habit. When they leave government, cabinet heads and agency administrators write or outsource the task of writing about their government experiences, and they provide important insights. Sometimes, these top-level officials rewrite history, creating a self-serving, revisionist account of their work in government, not always based on reality.

Jena McGregor appraised Dick Cheney's, Donald Rumsfeld's and Michael Brown's memoirs from the George W. Bush administration.

"With rare exceptions, the political memoir genre has become little more than an opportunity for leaders to burnish their own image and settle old scores. With hefty advances from publishers and a politically divided reading public that tends to buy books that reaffirm their beliefs rather than challenges them, we should expect little else."[54]

ADVICE TO BRIAN

As a program manager, take a balanced view of spin, it can only do so much. If your program is missing target dates, spin is only a short-term technique to buy some time.

If your three-year program is late, now requiring four additional years to complete, anticipate a critical review by Congress's investigator, the GAO. It is inadvisable to assert that GAO really does not understand your program or to claim that their analyst missed the big picture. GAO probably knows more about your program than you do. Besides, they may hit you with additional, more lethal ammunition if you go public in your attack.

When you are on the receiving end of a GAO report, my advice is to agree with the findings, while pointing out that you and your team saw some of these problems coming months earlier, resulting in prompt corrective action.

In this case, spin is a good possibility. GAO may have pointed to setbacks in a few major goals in your program. However, you can shift the debate to sub-goals, pointing out, for example, of the 200 sub-goals used to measure contractor performance, 130 are on target, the contractor is correcting 25, and your team is renegotiating 45 with the contractor.

Changing the discussion from major goals to sub-goals is an honest tactic enabling you to muddle the picture and divert attention from the criticism. In this example, your positive conclusions based on sub-goals and GAO's negative conclusions based on major goals are both correct.

When you introduce a new level of complexity, you may persuade people, short on analytical time, to agree with you that the status of your project is not entirely as GAO claims. You live to fight another day, given the time you bought using spin. However, GAO is correct; your program is in trouble. While you have bought time to try to fix it, overseers are now closely watching. A second critical report by the GAO or one by your agency's Inspector General could be fatal to you and your program.

Be sensible. Do not let the spin pot boil over. Do not spin to the point where you begin to believe your own stories and drift into untruths. You are not a magician in a dark Victorian laboratory with blinking lights, steaming beakers and some old discarded body parts, creating magic. Be conservative with spin. Most importantly, study the GAO report and fix the problems in your program.

PART TWO:

Twenty-Five Insights Needed after Beginning Your New Job

CHANGES AFTER WORLD WAR II LED US TO TODAY WITH ITS BENEFITS AND PROBLEMS.

Frank,

I have been reluctant to mention this but now I must. When I told my friends that I was joining the government in a high-level position, they congratulated me; but I could tell they had concerns. Later, they told me they felt I would be entering a staid, tired organization that lives in the past and never changes. They said they feared I would become zombie-like from the stress trying to institute change in an environment where few want it.

Governments change grudgingly, but they do change, especially when the culture changes. Here are some statistics describing life in the US. Can you guess the year in America when life was as follows?

- The average life expectancy was 47 years
- Only 14 percent of homes had a bathtub
- Only 8 percent of homes had a telephone
- There were only 8,000 cars in the US, and 144 miles of paved roads
- The maximum speed limit in most cities was 10 mph
- Alabama, Iowa, Mississippi, and Tennessee each had more people than California
- More than 95 percent of all births took place at home
- Ninety percent of doctors had no college education
- Only 6 percent of Americans graduated from high school
- Marijuana, heroin and morphine were all available over the counter at the local corner drugstore

The year was 1906, not so long ago. Think about how our nation and government have transformed in the years since. We have seen new government regulations in sectors such as prescription and social drugs and medical certification. We have seen new government programs in education, Social Security, Medicare, Medicaid and medical insurance, the national highway system, basic and applied research, massive investments in the military, in new intelligence organizations, and in space exploration, to mention a few areas that led to major change.

At the same time, the government rarely changes because of internal pressures. Rather, it changes in response to major events such as the Great Depression of the 1930s, two world wars and six other wars since 1945, riots in American cities in the 1960s, and as a result of the Muslim terrorist attacks in 2001. Furthermore, there are trends in religious beliefs, scientific and technical advances such as computers, Internet and social networking, along with global economic competitiveness, improved health delivery and demographic changes due to Asian and Hispanic immigration, all of which are altering the government's policies and programs and the country's culture and social structure.

In 1946, after World War II ended, the federal government needed to streamline, reorganize and consolidate on a large scale. Presidents and members of Congress had created many government organizations to address the two world wars framing the Great Depression. As World War II ended, government needed to adjust to a peacetime economy.

Reorganizing a national government is a risky undertaking. The special interests are more concerned about the narrow needs of their constituencies than they are about the nation. They work relentlessly to shape changes to preserve their interests, increase their profits and build wide-moat monopolies, and they are generally very successful.

In addition, both political parties must agree with any major changes to the national government. Yet, this is a challenge because Democrats and Republicans have sharply different ideas of the role of the government and who should get what piece of the national pie.

Recognizing the issues dividing the parties, President Harry Truman, following the Lodge-Brown Act of 1947, assembled the Commission on Organization of the Executive Branch of the Government, later known as the Hoover Commission. The Commission's job was to recommend administrative and organization changes in the government. [55]

Truman, a Democrat, appointed former President Herbert Hoover, a Republican, to chair the new commission. Six Republicans, including Hoover, and six Democrats served on the commission. Included were well-known political figures of the era—Secretary of State Dean Acheson, Secretary of Defense James V. Forrestal and Joseph P. Kennedy, father of future President John F. Kennedy.

After meeting for two years, the Commission forwarded its findings along with 273 recommendations to Congress in a series of nineteen separate reports. Six years later, a follow-up study reported that the government had fully implemented 116 of the recommendations and had partly implemented another 80. [56 57 58]

As he accepted the report, President Truman said, "Good management and good organization require far more than the transfer and consolidation of bureaus." Truman went on to say, "The commission's reports reflect this point of view. We all recognize there are no easy shortcuts. The solution does not lie in any one action of the Congress or any one order of the president."[59]

Its work complete, the Commission dissolved in June 1949.

The first Hoover Commission and, to a lesser extent, the second Hoover Commission created the government we have today. Later, when the government created new agencies such as the Department of Energy, the Environmental Protection Agency, the Department of Homeland Security and NASA, the staffing policy was a basic number of government employees augmented by armies of contractors. Homeland Security, for example, has 180,000 career employees and some 200,000 contract employees, causing two senators to question whether DHS was in charge of its policies and programs or whether it had ceded core decisions to contractors.[60]

Today, our government struggles to work within an industrial age structure inadequate for the age of globalization, technology and terrorism. The government looks and acts tired and as worn out as an uncared-for 25-year-old automobile, rusted, faded, cracked and leaky, because the government's numerous vertical stovepipe agencies are unable to meet today's challenges requiring cross-agency solutions.

We expect too much of today's poorly organized government, unreasonably hoping that it can handle today's issues. Leadership needs to take a "whole of government" view. We need a Government without Boundaries, in which agencies collaborate and cooperate with each other, a need so evident in Hurricane Katrina, in the underwear bomber case in 2010, and in cases involving the 16 intelligence organizations; and, by the way, do we need sixteen?

President Obama in his State of the Union speech to the nation on January 25, 2011 drew a laugh when he commented that the Department of the Interior regulates salmon in fresh water and the Department of Commerce regulates salmon in salt water, and it, "... gets even more complicated once they are smoked," he said.

While the government has made some progress by using collaboration software such as Microsoft's SharePoint, substantial change is unlikely to occur for six reasons.

The ever-increasing numbers of marginally qualified White House political appointees are often unable to visualize the big picture.

Contracts negotiated with the private sector often prohibit the government from consolidating and reorganizing its programs without financial penalty during the life of the contract.

To protect the number of its committee chairs, Congress bars even modest administration attempts to eliminate redundant and duplicative government programs and agencies. During the Great Depression, Congress granted consolidation authority to the White House. However, Congress rescinded the authority in 1984 when Ronald Reagan was president.

When Congress created the Department of Homeland Security, herding 28 agencies into the new Department, its members were unwilling to relinquish any authority and insisted that they retain authority over "their" agencies before they would allow the White House to proceed with the reorganization. Consequently, the Department gets its marching orders from more than 108 committees and subcommittees, fragmenting the government's efforts to integrate and respond to the threats of terrorism and other national emergencies.

In another example of congressional oversight, Congress has given authority to some 51 federal agencies monitoring the flow of money to terrorist organizations.[61]

Powerful special interests, including thousands of non-governmental organizations (NGOs) and the media, work every day to influence the affairs of government.

Interest groups distribute large sums of money to influence the direction of government and often fight change to keep things as they are.

Successive presidents of both parties disenfranchise the career workforce, disrespecting their knowledge of the big picture and their knowledge of what government could become.

The CEO of Burlington Northern Railroad, speaking of the need to rebuild the nation's infrastructure of roads, rails and bridges, said that there are 107 federal programs dealing with infrastructure, making it impossible to solve the infrastructure problem in a coordinated, dollar-efficient manner.[62]

Before closing on this subject, here is one additional case. The Department of Agriculture and the Food and Drug Administration share responsibility for egg safety, depending on whether an egg is inside the chicken or has been laid and whether the egg is whole or has been cracked open.

After earlier outbreaks of the salmonella virus from eggs, the Centers for Disease Control entered the picture, adding a third federal agency and additional decision-making complexity to egg management. Congress, to maintain the number of its powerful committee chair positions, retains these divisions of responsibility over eggs despite the health risks they pose to the public and the difficulties they present to the agencies attempting to solve national health problems.

The salmonella outbreak in 2010 in 17 states caused nausea, vomiting and fever in many people and death in people with weakened immune systems. Government agencies need to collaborate and consolidate across their boundaries to address today's problems. Unfortunately, the government remains fragmented, while the salmonella case is one example of the consolidation that has occurred across industry.

The Wright County Egg company, with its five "farms" in Iowa, produces hundreds of millions of eggs that the company redistributes to 18 distributers in the nation under such pleasant names as Farm Fresh, James Farms, Pacific Coast, Lucerne, Sunshine, Hillandale and Dutch Farms. If you think your fresh eggs are coming to you from one of these firms with a farm fresh name, think again. They all come from the Wright County Farm in Iowa, one massive example of consolidation of many in the US.

Advice to Brian

Brian, with this brief history, you can see that the federal government faced up to organizational problems in the past, particularly after World War II, and it needs to do so again because of the rampant duplication and overlap between agencies. While reorganizations are often difficult, and some use them to create the illusion of progress, there are times to reorganize to reduce confusion, inefficiency and wasted money. For the federal government, the time is now.

As a senior level official, be prepared for reform and change. Stay flexible; keep an open mind. Those who resist change often become of the victims of it.

21

SIX CONDITIONS TO MONITOR WHEN REORGANIZATION IS IN THE AIR

Frank,
We have a new agency head, and the rumor
mill predicts that she wants to implement a major
reorganization. Will this be a time to hunker down or a
time of opportunity? I have some ideas she might want
to consider. How best can I present them?

When your higher-ups are contemplating a major reorganization, you need to maneuver carefully as a cat similar to Nick Wallenda who completed a high-wire walk over the Grand Canyon on a two inch cable in 2013.

Timing is everything. The terrorist attacks of 2001 in New York City and at the Pentagon in Arlington, Virginia were catalysts to combine 28 agencies into a new power base called the Department of Homeland Security. The attacks also dramatically increased the authority and influence of the intelligence and law enforcement agencies. Such catastrophic events are rare, but they can provide the needed sense of urgency for government officials to fast-track reorganization plans.

Logic does not matter when elected officials or political appointees decide on the need for change. You can challenge the plan, but timing is crucial. Challenge too early, and your comments will be forgotten when the discussions get serious. If you raise your concerns too late in the game after the group has come together on the direction for action, you will experience an uncomfortable moment of silence before the chair stares you down and moves the discussion to other issues. Bring your concerns forward too often, and invitations to future discussions will become infrequent.

A manufactured war or a necessary war provides opportunities to expand the Department of Defense, benefitting the weapons manufacturers. Similarly, the recession in 2007–2013 created the opportunity to "grow the economy" by rearranging or diminishing the powers of those civilian agencies regulating the private sector or providing services to the public.

Often it is difficult to identify the source behind a reorganization proposal and to determine whether it has the power to push the proposal forward. Watch for hints and feints suggesting that the president himself is behind any given scheme. Either he is or he is not. Too many rumors with no real evidence of presidential commitment will suggest he is not behind the proposal and the case is weak.

Congress has more power in these matters than the White House; but Congress must negotiate or the White House will drag its feet during implementation, or it will ignore the new law for as long as possible, possibly a very long time.

Power-broker discussions in public by agency or corporate officials are often exercises in spin to influence public opinion. Similarly, much information reported by the media never makes it into the final version of the new law. On the other hand, chairs of Congressional committees can slip new items into the legislation in the dead of night without the White House or many in Congress being aware of these actions, or their implications.

ADVICE TO BRIAN

If a truly major event occurs that might allow a major reorganization while you are in government service, expect a rebalancing of power, presenting an opportunity to increase your influence and that of your program. All of the infighting for power will take place at a level above you, so it is important to develop contacts in the quieter, earlier days during regular government operations so upper level managers will know the true merits of your organization when they reallocate resources and power.

You should always have an outline of an action plan in your pocket ready to propose when the government needs to take extraordinary and rapid action during a crisis.

Brian, if you see an opportunity for your program, you must not move too early when alternative balls are flying wildly in the air or too late when the power brokers have made their deals. Be ready with your ideas developed well in advance, perhaps years earlier before the opportunity arises.

Your role is threefold:

- Observe
- Provide supporting analyses
- Be alert for opportunities for your program

Let's move on to the 24 specific insights to help you once you are on the job

22

THE FIRST INSIGHT, ONCE YOU ARE ON THE JOB

Frank,
Even though change can be difficult in the complex
federal government, my job is to bring change to the
government. Can you give me some advice on how to
make it happen?

The government changes slowly when major policy issues such as Social Security benefits are in play. While technologies such as the Internet, e-mail, social networking and electronic delivery of citizen services have brought positive change to government administration, in other ways government has not changed much in 40 years.

Let me quote a few paragraphs and ask you to tell me when the author wrote them.

If rhetoric could solve the "massive crisis" in American health care . . . we could all hope that the immense social, professional and fiscal deficiencies of this problem were about to be attacked adequately. However, that is not the case, as it never has been.

Effective preventive care is largely nonexistent. The cost of being sick is increasing today at a rate double the cost of living.

There are unconscionable wastes in the duplication of hospital facilities and not enough facilities for patients who do not require the crushingly expensive services needed to treat the acutely ill.

The real question is whether doctors, hospitals, medical schools and prepayment health insurance groups will have the good sense to change a lot of the traditional practices and beliefs, which simply have no application in the light of the demands of today.

Brian, would you agree that the author wrote these words this year? Would it surprise you if I told you that an official wrote these words 20 years ago?

How about 30 years ago? Well, I would be too conservative. The editor of a leading newspaper published these insights almost 50 years ago on July 15, 1969. My point here is to encourage you to flavor your ambitions, especially those for change, with a strong dose of realism.[63]

When catastrophes occur, elected officials are quick to initiate changes they had wanted to make since they campaigned for the White House or Congress. [64]For example, the George W. Bush White House and the intelligence and law enforcement communities used the 9/11 terrorist attacks to obtain authorities and budgets they had only dreamed about for years. After the Boston Marathon pressure cooker bombings by Muslim students, the FBI suddenly expressed the need for additional authorities, including new access to Facebook accounts and those on other social media platforms.

In government, you will observe that each White House team wants to remake the nation using the power of government to suit its ideologies and the goals of the moneymen who helped them win elected office, and they are successful at the margin. However, you should also be aware that the government is like nature; it normally changes slowly over long periods. Moreover, it does not change because a president wants change, but it can change precipitously because of calamitous events never anticipated.

ADVICE TO BRIAN

Recognize that significant change occurs slowly in government unless there is a catastrophic event. Implement change in small increments, while waiting for a crisis in government creating the opportunity for true change. Then, you can unveil your entire program for the transformation you feel is necessary.

23

A Single Member of Congress Can Change the Government

Frank,
This is interesting, the history of change in the government. I have heard you talk before about the Brooks Act. It sounds like it was a big deal. What was it all about it? Did it bring change to the government? What can I learn from the Brooks Act era?

In addition to the change that results from crises, change can occur when one powerful individual like Congressman Jack Brooks has a personal vision and is able to focus his energy on it for many years.

The Brooks Act was born in the mid-1960s in the dark of night in a deal between Congressman Jack Brooks and President Lyndon Johnson, both of Texas. Brooks was close to many Texas power brokers, including Sam Rayburn, Speaker of the House for 17 years—a record—and President Johnson. When you see the famous picture of Lyndon Johnson on Air Force One, with Dallas Federal District Judge Sarah T. Hughes swearing him in as the nation's 36th president after President Kennedy's assassination, Jack Brooks is one of 14 crowded in the aircraft's cabin behind the new president.

Creating a computer industry in the US with many companies instead of one or a few was the initial purpose of the Brooks Act. Later, it focused on the numerous failed modernization efforts at the FAA, the IRS, the Patent and Trademark Office, the Social Security Administration, the National Oceanographic and Atmospheric Administration and other agencies.

Without the Brooks Act, IBM would have dominated all computer acquisitions in the government. In the early days of the industry, the federal government was by far the most active buyer of computers in the country, and IBM was the dominant supplier. If the government had made all of its purchases from IBM, as many agency officials preferred, there would have been very little opportunity for any competing providers to emerge.

IBM's competition included several Fortune 100 companies called the *dwarfs*. The group included Burroughs, Control Data, General Electric, Honeywell, National Cash Register and Univac.

IBM adjusted to the Brooks Act procurement rules and enjoyed continued success. Happily, other companies, given the opportunity, were able to emerge and grow.

Thirty years after the government enacted the Brooks Act, I attended a Christmas party with then current Unisys and former Univac employees at their annual gathering to remember the good old days. Bob Beardall, a long-time Unisys employee, looked out over the room filled with his friends and former colleagues and said, "They owe a lot to Jack Brooks."

"What do you mean?" I asked.

"These guys were given an opportunity to sell to the government. The Brooks Act forced agencies to look at all suppliers, and Univac won its share," Bob said. "As a result these guys bought houses, raised families and sent kids to college because of the opportunities delivered by the Brooks Act."

The legislation called the Brooks Act was not Brooks' only influence on federal procurement. In the mid-1980s, his staff member, Jim Lewin, convinced Brooks that the GAO ruled too frequently in favor of agencies in bid protests. As a result, the congressman introduced the Competition in Contracting Act authorizing GSA's administrative law judges to hear bid protests by vendors. This is when the real troubles began.

The language establishing the Board of Contract Appeals was drafted by Dave Cohan of Cohan and White, and by Leonard Suchanek at GSA. Later, Suchanek became the chair and chief judge of the board. For 12 years, the board had the power to cancel or modify contract awards by all agencies. It could also award financial payment to companies winning their protest.

The GSA bid protest program led to a growing cadre of specialized lawyers in Washington representing technology companies protesting the award decisions they lost. About 100 lawyers made a good living from the new work, and they were strong supporters of the GSA's Board of Contract Appeals.

Even in the 1980s, it often cost companies $1 million or more to develop bid proposals responding to government procurements. Some could cost more than $10 million. Today, the costs can reach $100 million. Companies that did not win awards usually protested to see if they could *get well* one way or another before the Board.

Eventually, losing companies began to protest virtually all award decisions, leading to long delays and expensive legal processes. If the contract was a re-compete of ongoing work, the company already performing the job was usually the first to protest. Until the protest was resolved, often after a year or more, the incumbent contractor would continue to perform and receive income. They had nothing to lose and everything to gain by protesting and delaying an award destined for another company.

In protesting, companies often claim that an agency's procurement specifications are unclear, making it difficult to prepare a good proposal. Alternatively, they may attack the evaluation plan, claiming it favors one of their competitors.

Sometimes, they charge that the winning company's bid is too low, considering the complexity of the job. Such claims can be true. *Lowballing* is common practice when bidding on government procurements. Some companies bid abnormally low prices, anticipating they will be able to suggest changes after award to break the contract, allowing them to charge higher prices to the government. Some companies play this game quite successfully.

When the GSA Board of Contract Appeals was active and even today when the GAO hears protest cases, agencies routinely add 6 to 12 months to their procurement cycle to accommodate the protests sure to come.

Sales managers, and what we now call capture managers, often lose their jobs if an expensive bid does not produce an award. Filing a protest hoping to reverse the award can be a capture manager's effort to buy time to win another contract award or find another job.

The Brooks Act was the primary rule for all federal computer acquisitions for 34 years.

When Jack Brooks lost his bid for re-election, 10 years after authoring the Competition in Contracting Act and more than 30 years after authoring the Brooks Act, lawmakers, policymakers in the Office of Management and Budget and influential members of industry moved in to scrap both bills and replace them with the Clinger-Cohen Act.

Of course, the story doesn't end here. Governments are like pendulums, swinging from one extreme to the other in the unending search for equilibrium.

Ten years after the end of the Brooks Act and well into the Clinger-Cohen era, contractors were aggressively increasing their bid protests. As of August 13, 2013, contractors had filed 2,786 protests in the previous 365 days with the Government Accountability Office, an increase of about 77 percent in five years. GAO sustained 17 percent of the protests, and agencies decided to amend their process in about 31 percent of the cases, allowing rebids.

With the 2013 report, GAO for the first time included the most common reasons for sustaining protests:[65] [66]

- Unequal treatment of offers
- Unreasonable price or cost evaluation
- Failure to follow the solicitation evaluation criteria
- Inadequate documentation about decisions

The government reimburses companies for their legal costs when they win a bid protest appeal. In addition, the government gives winning protesters the right to bid again on the procurement. The odds of winning an appeal is nearly

30 percent at a relatively modest cost of less than $100,000, modest since the payoff may be an agreement for millions or billions of dollars in contracts. These are powerful incentives encouraging vendors to protest government awards.[67]

Unfortunately, the delays associated with the congressionally authorized bid protest process can in extreme cases double or triple the time required to award a contract.

As we advised the government managers enrolled in our management development program—the Trail Boss program—and even today, agencies set aside additional time in their procurement plan to accommodate the inevitable protests. Kevin Carroll, former manager of the Army's contracting program, said that the increase in bid protests and the shortage of contracting officials to deal with the protests are doubling the time it takes to award the average contract.

In a single Army procurement, six companies filed protests after bidding unsuccessfully on a $20 billion program to revamp the Army's computer networks. Resolving their complaints delayed the program for a year. In this example, there would be no opportunity for the losing companies to win any Army networking work for nine years. Kim Nguyen of Pragmatics, reflecting the view of many companies, said the stakes were too high to accept defeat.[68]

Advice to Brian

The bid protest process, used by companies to influence government procurements, has a long and contentious history. It led in part to the demise of the Brooks Act era, but the protest problems persisted in the Clinger-Cohen era and will in the Issa-Connolly era.

If you are managing a major program run by contractors, you cannot avoid protests. Nevertheless, here are some actions you can take:

- Build an additional year into your schedule to allow for the inevitable bid protests.
- Do not make your procurement so large and so long that you will freeze several companies out of related opportunities for the foreseeable future.

- To try to ward off protests, employ all of the reviews, checks and balances developed by agencies over time. Do not go overboard, however, because a capture manager in a company may be desperate if he or she spent the bid preparation money and did not win an award. Expect a protest from an anxious person, assuming his corporate management agrees to take the action.

The second bullet needs re-emphasis. A large procurement awarding a small group of companies with exclusive access to an entire product area for years will guarantee a fight from desperate, losing bidders.

Remember this is all history. Yet the Brooks Act governed federal procurement for 34 years, and there are five lessons to remember about this discussion:

- If a president gets behind change and the Democrats and Republicans support it, change is possible.
- A law passed in the dark of night, such as the Brooks Bill, even if tacked onto another bill, will most certainly lead to change and can have a profound and unanticipated effect on many programs.
- Major change happens slowly most of the time, but when a crisis propels it, change can happen fast like a moving express train.
- There is a 60-year history of managing information technology in the federal government. It did not start with the latest chief information officer or E-government chief.
- Nothing is forever; even the long-lasting Brooks Act had a funeral.

24
TRACKING NEW LEGISLATION
IS PART OF YOUR JOB

Frank,

Your last letter about the rise, long history, and fall of the Brooks Act and the bid protest problems will be helpful in my new job. You mentioned the Clinger-Cohen Act that followed the Brooks Act, but it seems like it did not solve the government's problems. Looking ahead, what should I do about the possibility of new legislation that might affect my program?

New legislation can provide a fresh start and an opportunity for you and your program if you have good contacts on the Hill and if you can learn about draft legislation early enough to influence its contents.

Let's talk about the Clinger-Cohen Act that governs the acquisition and management of information technology in the government.[69]

The Clinger-Cohen Act resulted in large part from a series of meetings in the Old Executive Office building housed in the White House complex.

At least thirty officials attended each meeting, representing organizations from all over government. In a sense, these meetings were for show to cement the impression that there was wide support for the actions already decided upon by the inside power group. Bringing like-minded people together to write a report for decisions already made by insiders is a good way to deflect future criticism of the decision. This is a common procedure, although in this case there was no expectation of criticism. The group wanted to kill the GSA Board of Contract Appeals bid protest process and the process by which GSA delegated its procurement authority to agencies.

They did this by creating the Clinger-Cohen Act, abolishing the Brooks Act and decentralizing procurement authority, and by handing it over to agencies.

The Clinger-Cohen Act required each agency to establish a chief information officer position, although the Act did not require a single CIO for the entire government. The group shaping the Clinger-Cohen Act did not want a czar for technology, a government-wide CIO, because they feared a future White House would appoint a marginally qualified political appointee to the job possibly as payoff for support during the election campaign. They also believed the federal government was far too large and diverse for one person to oversee its countless technology programs.

As it turned out, a *de-facto* CIO in OMB evolved, but with uncertain power. Mark Forman held the job at first, and Karen Evans followed him. Later, when President Obama took office, he took the next step and established a national chief information officer position and a chief technology officer position, appointing two men who had helped in the presidential campaign, men who remained in their jobs only two years.

Often, agencies do not implement new legislation as Congress intended. This was true with Clinger-Cohen. While Brooks remained in Congress for decades, guarding the law he created and ensuring that agencies implemented his law as he intended, Representatives Clinger and Cohen are long gone from Congress. At this point, no legislator actively protects the Act.

The Act was well researched and written by Paul Brubaker and his staff in Congress. It covered all of the emerging issues of the time, and it continues to provide a policy umbrella for the community, but it was too prescriptive, preventing it from fully evolving with the times.

What have been the results of the Clinger-Cohen Act? Despite some success, full implementation has been limited. While there are CIOs in every agency, too often they are political appointees lacking knowledge of the government, the programs they manage and experience in the management of major systems.

Many current CIOs are not in the inner circle of the agency leadership. Many CIOs work on lower level infrastructure issues such as helping to keep communications networks and computer technology current. In addition, they spend considerable time trying to implement new OMB management and policy processes.

Clinger-Cohen required agencies to develop business cases before making technology investments. However, in practice, contractors crank them out for agencies following a cookie-cutter formula. These business case products meet Clinger-Cohen's requirements, but do little for the agency.

Another priority in Clinger-Cohen is performance-based acquisition (PBA), a technique for structuring all aspects of an acquisition around the purpose and outcome desired, as opposed to detailing the specific work that the contractor will perform. PBA has been around since 1990, is on everyone's radar screen, but has not won general acceptance.

In addition, the Act's emphasis on architecture standards and schemes has absorbed important time and resources in agencies, but these are very complicated and difficult to implement.

Nevertheless, the Act created a CIO infrastructure vertically in agencies and horizontally across the major departments to address the new technology issues in the increasingly interconnected and mobile government.

The sole measure of success in the federal IT community is whether the program delivers major systems on time and within budget, while meeting the goals set when the government made the decision to build the system. Everything else is secondary and meaningless in the shadow of this goal. Many hundreds of midsize and smaller systems meet this single measure, contributing to the successful operation of the federal government.

On the other hand, the many failed systems of recent years suggest that the Clinger-Cohen legislation has not improved the delivery of the larger government systems, although, in fairness, $100 million and multi-billion dollar systems are not easily developed. We will talk more about managing complex systems later in this book.

The pendulum swings. Sometimes legislation centralizes government management; sometimes it leans toward decentralization. There are advantages and disadvantages to each approach. There are opportunistic advocates and dissenters for both styles of management.

After years of decentralization under Clinger-Cohen, some now feel it is time to recentralize. In one example, the Obama Administration in 2009, facing huge and unprecedented budget deficits, complained that the Clinger-Cohen Act and the ensuing decentralization led to growth in the number of data centers from 400 to 1,200. This caused increased spending, duplication and impenetrable boundaries between agencies. The Obama administration promoted cloud computing as a way to reduce the number of centers drastically and save money. The Issa-Connolly legislation emphasized Data Center Consolidation and required that the Executive Branch should meet its goal to close 1,235 data centers by 2015.

ADVICE TO BRIAN

Bob Chartrand, formerly of the Congressional Research Service, once showed me a report identifying 200 pieces of information technology legislation initiated by Congress in just one year. You should identify any legislation your appropriation and oversight committees are drafting that could affect your program. If you have a working relationship with key staffers on those committees, they may tell you what is underway. Even better, they might ask you for suggestions to be included in the proposed legislation. Sometimes I was able to suggest literal language for a new bill. This is a long shot.

To be useful, you must learn about draft legislation early on. After the senator or representative has approved the language in the draft bill, it will be too late to provide your insights.

You may want to devote one person part-time to stay in touch with congressional staff personnel on your appropriation and oversight committees. Your agency will discourage this, pointing out that there is a Legislative Liaison Office in your agency to do it for you. However, the head of your agency takes priority, and his issues with Congress may leave little time for your program. Make the assignment quietly without attracting attention.

Staying on top of new legislation is another critical aspect of your job.

25

OBSERVING HOW
THE WHITE HOUSE GETS ITS WAY

Frank,
While the White House hired me and I want to
support the party line, I expect and hope for some
independence as I do my job. Will they micromanage
me? How does the White House exert pressure across
government, since there are only several hundred
people there and the government has two million
civilian employees plus another 2.6 million, including
reserves in uniform?

Although the White House selected you for your job, you
need to be aware of how it influences the activities of government
employees.

New presidents and their 800 senior staff members in the
White House, along with their 4,000 political appointees in the
28 core agencies, have a series of options to control agencies and
to implement their economic, ideological, political and social
goals.

It is not easy to implement a new president's agenda because members of Congress have their own ideas about what is good and proper for the country; moreover, there are 1.6 million career civil servants in place, some with their own ideas about the proper direction of government.

Theoretically, the president and his supporters can change directions by taking the following actions:

- Articulating the vision
- Placing the right people in key jobs to enforce the vision
- Communicating and motivating the workforce
- Using the media to sell their direction to the public and to influence Congress
- Installing performance measures to let all know that results are important
- Creating new programs and selling Congress on the need

However, the government is the great ship of state, and like driving the massive, older naval aircraft carriers, it takes time, skill and a good wind to change direction. Sometimes the government, like people, resists change; sometimes the new administration needs to replace people and reorganize to get the change they want.

Here are eight ways used by the George W. Bush White House and its army of government supporters to take control.[70]

At NASA, for example, the administration eliminated civil service staff by replacing long-term career managers with political appointees and by allowing the newcomers greater control over the career scientists and administrators.

Political appointees ignored, edited and, in some cases, changed the findings in the reports of their senior scientists and career administrators before allowing publication.

White House appointees introduced new management systems to grade federal agencies on results, appointing themselves in charge of defining success and failure. Then, they were able to use their findings to influence career officials.

By taking authority away from career servants with long experience in regulatory policy matters in the Environmental

Protection Agency, the Department of Labor, the Food and Drug Administration, and other departments and agencies, the White House actively influenced the content of specific regulations normally issued by expert scientists and experienced policy officials.

The White House proposed, especially in the DOD and Homeland Security, to replace the civil service personnel system with new, government-wide pay-for-performance rules, making it easier to promote, reward or fire employees, foregoing the traditional due process.

The George W. Bush Administration advanced the pay-for-performance concept with his competitive-sourcing program, forcing thousands of federal workers to compete against private sector contractors to retain their jobs.

After Bush, the White House continued to implement a series of actions and publicity campaigns to weaken traditional watchdogs such as Inspector Generals and the Office of Special Counsel in the Justice Department, limiting among other things protection for whistleblowers identifying waste, abuse and fraud in the government.

To make its actions less transparent to the voting public, the administration implemented new restrictions limiting the release of government information to the public, including a huge jump in the number of documents labeled *classified*, making some of its practices unavailable for scrutiny.

While these actions help the White House and its supporters to emphasize their goals, there can be unintended consequences, and these can be severe. [71]When the White House weakened the Office of Special Programs in the Justice Department, the long-term results were significant.

Carrie Johnson, a *Washington Post* reporter, identified more than 900 cases alleging that government contractors and pharmaceutical manufacturers defrauded taxpayers out of billions of dollars. These cases languished in a Department of Justice backlog built up over a decade. According to lawyers involved in the dispute, the Department could not keep pace with the surge in whistleblower charges during the George W. Bush administration because of staff shortages resulting from the Bush White House policies.

Even if whistleblowers file no new cases, said Patrick Burns of Taxpayers against Fraud, it might take the Department of Justice 10 years to clear out the current backlog. The government investigates only 100 cases a year, and whistleblowers file up to 400 cases each year. Maintaining a small staff ensures that judges will not hear whistleblower cases until years after the event occurred, if ever.

In mid-2008, the huge backlog attracted renewed interest in Congress and in nonprofit groups, because many of the cases involving waste in the Iraq and Afghanistan wars, rising health-care payouts and privatization of government functions offered tidy opportunities for profits without oversight.

When federal agencies have the resources to intervene in cases potentially involving fraud, the results can be significant; *The Washington Post* reporter wrote that companies returned $13 billion to the US Treasury in recent years due to whistleblower cases. Conversely, keeping an agency's staffing level too low to do its job results in lost revenue; more significantly, it allows fraud to continue.[72] In addition, it allows White House officials to limit the regulatory and investigative activities of agencies.

ADVICE TO BRIAN

When the White House uses its unique power and exercises the eight special tools it has to control and force change in the Executive Branch, there is little the career manager can do other than watch and learn. Only public attention from the media, Congress and non-government organizations can slow or stop the momentum.

26
PROTECTING YOUR BOSS

Frank,

As you know, in my small business, I was the boss. There was no one over me. Working for someone will be an experience for me. Suppose I get a boss that wants to blow up the government or something slightly less ambitious. I mention this because some new political appointees arrive in the government with a chip on their shoulder concerning the government itself. If I find myself working for such a boss, how should I respond, knowing that an action he contemplates is impossible?

Not everyone in a management position is good at developing government policy. You may find yourself involved in poorly thought-out policies conceived by your boss. Here is an example of a high-level official attempting unsuccessfully to issue policy to change direction in government.

The first time we met with the new head of our agency to brief him on our program, our issues with Congress and our government-wide responsibilities, he interrupted in the first minute to tell us that he wanted to give us his insights, rather than hear from us.

Career civil servants cherish opportunities to listen to the new boss and to understand his priorities. Over time, however, a boss, unwilling to listen, causes problems for himself and his organization.

In this case, the administrator of GSA told my boss, the commissioner and me that he wanted to impose a freeze on information technology purchases in the government. He knew that the federal investment in unclassified information technology at the time was $27 billion per year. This included salaries, contractor services, mainframes, super computers, personal computers, networks and software. Seventy percent of the total figure maintained the thousands of legacy systems—such as accounting, tax returns processing, air traffic control—helping to run the massive operations of the federal government, the largest organization in the world.

Because of his experience as chief executive of a computer hard drive manufacturer, his mantra was that the government should get better prices for personal computer technology. However, PC technology accounted for only $4 billion of the $27 billion; yet he proposed to apply a freeze to the total federal IT budget.

Responding to his order to initiate the freeze, I drafted the first version of a letter addressed to the heads of the 16 Cabinet agencies and to the heads of the approximately 100 other agencies in government. I reviewed the draft letter with my immediate boss, and he said to include in the letter a requirement for a complete inventory of each agency's information technology products and services—a good idea, I felt.

Later, in my office, my deputy Fred Sims and I discussed the effects of a complete freeze on the line agencies responsible for doing the work of the government. We then built several escape routes into the letter to allow exemptions to the freeze in cases involving health, public safety, national emergencies and other urgent requirements. In addition, we added the words: "The suspension [freeze] does not affect the delivery of services supporting current operations . . ." Finally, in the draft letter, we set a 90-day time limit on the freeze.

Here is the draft letter we wrote:

Based on President Clinton's initiative to reinvent and reduce the size of the Federal government, I am ordering an "IT FREEZE," which suspends Information Technology (IT) acquisitions for products and services until the following actions can be completed by each major agency.

Inventory your current IT products and services.

Develop a baseline list of ongoing and anticipated expenditures for IT products and services by year for three years.

Review the baseline from a cost, need and re-engineering standpoint to validate the approach to meeting program requirements.

Cancel orders and acquisitions for IT products and services no longer necessary.

Confirm orders and acquisitions for IT products and services that continue to be necessary.

Validate existing performance measures for the larger acquisitions or development of new measures.

It is requested that you provide me with the results of these reviews, dollars saved and actions taken in six months so the "IT Freeze" can be lifted.

The head of the department or agency may grant exceptions to this suspension based on health, public safety, national emergency requirement, and other urgent situations. The suspension does not affect the delivery of service supporting current operations, though these expenditures are included within the scope of the baseline review and are a potential source of savings.

If your departmental staff has questions about this initiative, Commissioner Joe M. Thompson or I may be contacted.

Sincerely,

We incorporated the escape routes for two reasons.

First, the business of government must proceed. The 54 million Americans then receiving Social Security benefits and supplemental payments, or any of dozens of other benefits and services, must receive them on schedule, else the credibility of the government itself would suffer.

The second reason was to protect our boss. When word of the freeze hit, we knew there would be cries for his head, louder than several previous cries he had already provoked.

Thirteen committees in Congress decide which initiatives to fund and not fund. The freeze would stop action on important initiatives powerful members of Congress had already approved. Normally, we would discuss this reality with the administrator, but we were rarely able to get him to listen. Therefore, we inserted provisions in the letter softening the freeze to protect him and to allow the critical business of the government to proceed during the freeze.

In late December, a few weeks before the Republicans took control of Congress, my immediate boss, the commissioner and I met in a hastily scheduled meeting with four members of our 18 member Interagency Advisory Committee.

Present were:

- Renny DiPentima, deputy commissioner for IT systems in the Social Security Administration (SSA)
- John Carabello, dean of the Information Resources Management College in the National Defense University
- Lloyd Moseman, deputy assistant secretary and senior IT policy official in the U.S. Air Force
- Tony Valletta, deputy assistant secretary for Command, Control, Communications and Intelligence in the DOD

The IT spending freeze was the topic. The reaction from these four experienced executives was worrying. DiPentima said it would cause a furor in Washington. Industry would charge the Hill howling to Congress, he said, because companies had invested millions of dollars in bids hoping to win federal contracts, contracts that the freeze would delay indefinitely or cancel. In addition, companies affected by the freeze would likely sue for damages.

DiPentima went on to say that his agency had a deal with Congress to reduce the Social Security Administration's workforce by 5,000 people. Without technology, there was no way the agency could keep its promise, he said.

Valletta said DOD had a good, cooperative relationship with our boss to date, but if he pushed ahead with the freeze, the cooperation would end. DOD, he said, had made commitments to Congress to achieve certain readiness goals, and they were dependent on IT to achieve those goals.

Moseman noted that President Clinton was trying to reduce the size of government, and all agencies were planning to meet the program and staff reductions by investing in information technology.

Carabello described other freezes in the preceding 20 years. They break down overnight, he said, because the government must operate, and exceptions to the freeze soon become the norm. The administrator and GSA would suffer greatly trying to introduce a freeze only to see it collapse fast, he counseled.

Our GSA administrator, whose tenure had been rocky already, had little political capital left in Washington, DiPentima said. Squandering what he had left on a losing proposition would be foolish, he warned, as the others nodded agreement.

Moseman proposed an alternative direction in which the administrator would ask cabinet and agency heads for voluntary action rather than imposing a mandatory government-wide freeze.

Later, an unidentified person leaked information about the forthcoming freeze to officials in OMB, abruptly ending the proposed freeze. Their analysts concluded the projected savings would be marginal, not worth the chaos.

Circuitously, the right decision evolved, and our boss retained his public reputation—although it suffered a little in our tight circle, including with my boss who reported to the administrator, the four select members of our Interagency Advisory Committee, and me.

Advice to Brian

Someday, your boss may want to support White House goals by proposing a dead wrong program unlikely to see the light of day. After you do your best to show him the pitfalls, without success, here are four steps to take.

- Stay cool. There is a long, winding road between an idea from an agency head and implementation across the government.
- Develop a plan with specific actions and dates to demonstrate a well-planned initiative to agencies.
- Draft a policy to implement his plan. Incorporate escape routes to protect your boss's reputation and the ability of agencies to do their job.
- Bring other respected people into the discussion to provide additional good advice to your boss; and, as an added benefit, they may pass information about the case to the right people, perhaps at the OMB or Congress.

Do not be discouraged by this case. You will observe bad decisions in any profession and from any manager. If you are persuasive, you can sometimes convince them to change their minds about a bad policy idea. If you cannot, then, while being careful and wise, you can often protect them, while mitigating the worst effects of the proposed policy.

Stay alert!

Case Study, a Bad Idea That Spun Out of Control

The GSA is the nation's largest property owner, the largest single customer for information technology, the nation's largest car rental company, and the nation's largest user of hotel rooms and commercial airline seats to mention only a few of its responsibilities.

GSA owns or manages 9,600 buildings and manages $27 billion in information technology and telecommunications expenditures. In addition, GSA manages a fleet of more than 215,000 vehicles, preserves 478 historic properties, manages the nation's stockpiles of strategic materials, and manages dozens of programs to assist the White House and all federal agencies to obtain needed resources.

With expenses of $1 billion per year, GSA returns $4 billion in savings each year; it allows agencies to acquire goods and services quickly and at a good price. If the government did not have a GSA, it would need to invent one. Yet GSA has been an easy target over the years. White House officials, for example, have reduced GSA's work force from a peak of 42,000 employees in 1980 to 12,600, a 70 percent reduction, in 32 years.

While GSA serves the entire government, it has no natural constituency such as veterans, farmers or senior citizen organizations to fight for it. While Congress generally supports the GSA, it will often use it as a whipping boy when members seek publicity. The latter tends to occur regularly, before congressional elections.

The rest of the time, Congress embraces GSA because it provides a central point for items such as new federal buildings and lavish courthouses in run-down sections in their cities. In addition, GSA's centralized programs make good sense, and most members in Congress appreciate them when politics are not in play.

Industry has a love-hate relationship with GSA. It provides a single procurement and billing system when a company is selling to the 28 core agencies and 100 other small agencies and government commissions. Yet companies resent GSA in its self-appointed role as each company's most favored customer while demanding the largest discounts each company offers.

Industry's advocacy organizations wage largely unsuccessful campaigns seeking relief from GSA's aggressive pricing programs. However, over the years they have wounded the agency by taking their crusade to Congress, to their own members, to others in industry, and to the new political appointees arriving with each new president. Each election provides GSA's critics an opportunity to complain anew about GSA's aggressive pricing practices. In time, many influential people have developed a decidedly negative, though uninformed, view of the agency.

There is a lot of detail in the following case study because it identifies interplay between the main players in a major reorganization attempt— the Congress, the president and vice president, a powerful OMB budget official, and several senior government officials.

On November 8, 1994, the American public voted out many Democratic members of Congress, giving Republicans control of the Congress for the first time in 40 years.

To outdo aggressive Republicans bent on reinventing the government, President Clinton had only a few weeks before the end-of-year holiday season, with Congress out of town, to demonstrate his commitment to change. In this short period, he needed to seek ideas, package them into a believable program, present them to the American public and the media, and place Republicans on the defensive.

Without any analysis, the then administrator of GSA proposed to reduce his agency's staff by 94 percent. Anxious to reduce the size of government as they promised in the presidential campaign, President Clinton and Vice President Gore jumped on the idea, as did David Hahn, a powerful OMB budget official. Before long, the idea took on a life of its own, and the GSA administrator soon lost control of the initiative.

The White House/OMB plan was to shrink GSA's employment from 17,415 employees in 1994 to about 7,000 employees by 1996 and 989 in 1997.

There were four options, although the government had no experience with the last three.

- Cancel GSA's business lines outright
- Transfer them to other agencies
- Privatize the business lines by transferring them to a private sector company
- Sell the business lines to employees to enable them to leave the government and operate the new company

Late in the day, on New Year's Eve, just hours before the evening festivities began in the nation, the GSA building was almost vacant. My boss, one of the four commissioners in GSA, convened his managers for an emergency meeting.

He reported that the administrator had telephoned from a ski lodge that morning and demanded a progress report for ideas from the commissioners to reduce the agency to 989 employees.

When his four commissioners told him they needed about 30 minutes to brief him on the steps they were evaluating to privatize the agency, the administrator insisted on a five-minute version. He wanted quick examples so he could tell the White House the programs he proposed to privatize and reduce the number of his government employees by 94 percent.

I wondered if he was in the breakfast buffet line in his hotel or on the ski lift, or was he sitting on the toilet as former President Lyndon Johnson reportedly did when holding short meetings with his staff or visitors.

Each of the commissioners had formed teams to plan the transfer of massive programs to contractors, including the management of 10,000 buildings, while protecting the government's interests. They were trying to figure out how to hand over 10,000 GSA employees to one or more private sector companies while providing some protection for these career employees. The administrator did not want to hear any detail.

My boss continued to report on the administrator's phone call. He told us that the room became as silent as a colonoscopy waiting room while the four commissioners listened in grim silence to the administrator complaining over the phone from the ski resort. "Those idiots at OMB want to take General Services Administration apart piece by piece," he told them. "I need to be able to show aggressive action. I need examples of functions we are going to move out of government."

He demanded five examples by 8:30 the next morning—New Year's Day.

Before we left for our separate New Year's Eve celebrations, GSA's deputy administrator joined the meeting and gave us her own insights. She told us not to bother with the idea of combining GSA with OMB and the Office of Personnel Management. The administrator, she said, had already proposed a similar idea to Vice President Al Gore and to OMB Director Leon Panetta, and they had shown no interest. The power and momentum was flowing, she said, from the Republicans now controlling Congress. She took issue with the OMB papers specifying 989 people as the end number for GSA, saying that we did not know what would be the final GSA number.

She said we should not worry too much about the arguments

for a smaller government. Republicans always believe that smaller is better, she said, but her view was that sound business decisions, based on a plan, should decide the direction, if any, for change. This was the first mention of the need for a plan during the rush to downsize GSA. Developing a plan would buy time to help shape the discussions, and she pledged to help build the sophisticated analysis needed to plan GSA's future.

Even if the president's plan was dead on arrival on the Hill, she went on to say, our planning exercises would be worthwhile. Every developed nation in the world was looking at outsourcing or privatization.

She emphasized that the government had no approved goal to reduce GSA's workforce for the next two years, so there was no reason to feel pressure to develop proposals in a rush. She said privatization is a tool, not the outcome, and that OMB officials did not seem to understand the meaning of privatization.

For days, the administrator had been unrelenting in his demands for suggestions of functions that GSA could hand off to industry. He had emphasized that we should forget about savings for the taxpayers. They were not important, he said, in view of the larger objective to reduce the size of government. Then, in a complete reversal, he signed a letter to Congress insisting on the need to move cautiously, emphasizing that we should not make changes in GSA unless real savings occurred.

I puzzled over this latest change in direction. Later, I learned that a Maryland congressman told the administrator's staff that the proposed reductions in GSA were interesting, but he did not endorse them. The government needs to do more study, said the congressman.

Two weeks later, the whole issue vanished. Feedback from Congress and analyses at OMB ended the downsizing discussions. Nevertheless, there is more to this story.

The heroes of this case, according to a former deputy administrator at GSA, were Julia Stasch, the administrator's deputy, Gerry Carmen, a former administrator of GSA, and Susan Brita, a former chief of staff at GSA and a senior staffer on a powerful committee in Congress. Years later, in the Obama administration in 2010, Brita would return to GSA as the deputy administrator, the number two official in the agency.

While Carmen and Brita were working behind the scenes in Congress to bring rationality to the issue, Stasch asked the administrator, "Are you going to let them do in the agency without any analysis?" This and the Maryland congressional representative's negative reaction led to an 18-month study, allowing time for the issue to fade into history.

The study concluded that it was a bad idea to reduce GSA to 989 people. The administrator then scheduled several meetings on the Hill during which he said, "I have had a change of heart. We can do better if we retain GSA at its current size although improvements can be made."

As I mentioned earlier, GSA had 42,000 employees when I joined the agency in 1980 and 17,415 in 1994 at the time of this case study. By 2012, long after this administrator had left GSA, OMB had reduced the agency to 12,635 employees. Successor White House and OMB staffs continued to hack away at General Services Administration's employment level, working toward the goal set 18 years earlier by another White House and another OMB.

Advice to Brian

This case study demonstrated elected officials and political appointees jointly attempting a major reorganization. However, the proposed mega-reorganization to reduce GSA from 17, 415 to 989 employees was too ambitious to digest, and since it lacked supporting data to justify the action, the proposal had no credibility and faded away without action.

Almost all presidential candidates campaign against government during the electioneering period, and they need to make a show of delivering when they take office. Occasionally, they do not follow through. The George W. Bush campaign, for example, argued for reducing the size of government and improving its management. Once in office however, his administration expanded the government's role and drove the budget surplus they inherited from the Clinton administration to a deep deficit, which they passed to the Democrats and Barack Obama in 2009.

So, if the incoming president and his supporters want to abolish your program or agency, do not lose heart. Campaign promises before an election are merely nice possibilities after winning office.

Two points:

1. As a senior official, you will learn that your real job is to protect your program and your organization from those that want to absorb it or kill it.
2. Career officials are not entirely helpless facing extreme ideas from political appointees. With long-term relationships on the Hill and at OMB, seasoned career officials can quietly encourage others to question the merits of threatening proposals.

ANOTHER CASE REQUIRING PROTECTION OF THE BOSS

Personnel actions must make sense. My boss at GSA once informed me that the Executive [Oversight] Board decided to recall three senior executives serving temporary assignments elsewhere in the government. Temporary assignment is the farmed-out solution for a senior manager on the outs with their current boss, often a new political appointee. Agency leaders can send their top executives elsewhere for any of several reasons:

- The executive is performing poorly
- They want to put their own person in the career executive's job
- There is a rocky working relationship between the career executive and a new political appointee

My boss told me he had taken one of the three individuals and was going to assign him to me to be in charge of our $27 billion delegations program, in which we did business with every agency and every major system manager in the government.

I knew the man, a good man, but he had mismanaged GSA's largest system ever attempted. One GSA administrator took a rare step in the government—he cancelled the program. There were discussions about bringing charges against the manager. In the end, the leadership settled for an Inspector General report to publish on the record, for all to see, an explanation of what went wrong.

I told my boss about the history and questioned his plan to

place this man in charge of our government-wide delegations program.

This information had no effect on my boss. He told me that higher-level managers had caused the problems with the canceled system and that I should be more forgiving. This is like a case with young children, he said. You will always be surprised by the one that does the best.

Inclined to fight the decision, I asked a staff member to research Inspector General Reports, GAO reports, congressional hearings, and newspaper and journal articles for materials. I did not want a mountain of information, just a few items to give my boss a better sense of the events that caused the major system failure. In one hour, my staff member turned up two IG reports and four trade newspaper articles. One review charged that information presented by the project manager was grossly inaccurate and questioned the value of continuing periodic management briefings with him.[73] [74] [75] [76]

An Inspector General report clearly laid the blame on the man my boss was forcing into my organization.

The report identified $200 million in waste due to poor program management and several other factors:

- Insisting on continuation of computer programming in the absence of a detailed design plan
- Diverting contractors to do jobs other than what the government hired them to do
- Dismissing criticism out of hand as unfounded
- Ignoring the advice of contractors to downsize
- Creating chaotic relationships with his contractors
- Providing unrealistic, inaccurate and always optimistic status reports to management
- Falsely reporting milestones and tasks to be on schedule
- Filing reports that did not identify serious problems
- Providing progress reports, which did not properly inform management about the true situation.

This information had no effect on my boss. Fortunately, there were other people digging into various files to refresh their memories.

Brad Bass, a reporter with the influential *Federal Computer Week,* set off an alarm inside GSA when he called our public affairs office requesting a copy of the Inspector General's report documenting the failed system. Bass also asked for confirmation of the rumor around town that the former manager of the failed system would oversee all of the government's major information systems.

Anne Marshall in our public affairs office sent an alarming message to my boss, others and me. She indicated that both Bass and Kevin Powers of *Government Computer News* were working on articles that would not be friendly. She said many sources outside of GSA—including some on the Hill—had already provided the reporters with historical information.

She advised us that this particular appointment could not have come at a worse time for GSA. The agency was already fighting hard just to stay alive because of proposed plans to reduce the agency by 94 percent to less than 1,000 employees. Marshall said both reporters had copies of the Inspector General's audit report documenting the failed program and were well aware of the part that my boss's chosen man had played in that program. In addition, she said that Powers had a copy of the GAO report documenting the failed system for Congress.

She told us there was nothing we could do to counteract the stories. With this information, my boss grasped the gravity of what he was about to do. He convened an impromptu group in his office to brainstorm the situation. I linked in from London on a conference call. The solution that developed was that my boss would call Bass and "clarify" that the man in question would serve as staff, not in a management role. He would be a special assistant, advising the commissioner as needs arose.

One assignment could be to consult on Business Process Re-engineering with the commissioner's division leaders and their clients. BPR is a methodology to rethink all of a business process with the goal of revising it to make dramatic improvements.[77].

This assignment made sense because the man had taught this subject during the previous five years while on temporary assignment at another agency. These ideas formed the basis of a new job and thus ended this controversial episode.

ADVICE TO BRIAN

You may want to shake up your new organization, transfer career officials to other posts and make room for some new faces.

Before doing so, seek advice from the agency's Human Resource people, your public relations staff and your own senior career executives. They will have information and a context that you will not have, somewhat like the caddie and professional golfer relationship in the last few holes of the Masters Championship in Augusta when chaos and emotions are high and it is hard to think. This is a time when caddie and golfer bond, and as in so many of my examples, in government you are the golfer, the one who needs to execute often under pressure, while the caddie has information that will help you to keep a clear head and execute winning shots.

In the previous chapter involving a proposed draconian reorganization of GSA, and in this case concerning the placement of an adrift executive, political bosses initially disregarded dissenting ideas, and it took several attempts by various players to win acceptance of their message.

In addition, Brian, remember that senior career executives must protect their political bosses from themselves, even at personal risk if they repeat their concerns more than a few times. In these two cases, Congress, the media and agency officials joined in to make the point that the proposed actions were foolhardy.

When they finally got the message, the political bosses reversed course, took quick action and averted a public relations disaster. Even political bosses can change their decisions.

27
REORGANIZING YOUR SHOP

Frank,
I've been considering all you've told me so far, and
it sounds like there might be times when the best thing
to do would be to reorganize to shake things up and
arouse some needed change. What do I need to know
in order to approach such a task in the best possible
manner?

Reorganization is a fine art, a favored solution used by new leaders of organizations, Congress and the White House because it is relatively easy to do, and it demonstrates action to the American public. Later, however, there can be unintended consequences.

Many government attempts to improve performance by reorganizing fail. An Englishman once told me that in Britain, when someone contributes a lot of money to a politician, we make him a Lord, but we do not put him in charge of anything important. In America, our political leaders too often reward their friends and contributors with appointments to important jobs.

In his first term, President Ronald Reagan appointed a dentist to lead the Department of Energy. Some in Reagan's White House thought DOE's major role was fuel management and cited such mundane tasks as having printed 4.8 billion gasoline-rationing coupons for a planned rationing program as among its key duties.

The dentist was gone from the federal government in a year; but DOE continued performing its main mission designing and manufacturing nuclear weapons for the DOD while managing the nation's most important research laboratories, including the Lawrence Livermore National Laboratory, which provides science and technology solutions to the most pressing national and global security problems. DOE survived.

Another way to bring change to an organization is to appoint an aggressive bully to head it, someone to take the heat. A bombastic leader can become a lightning rod for all the hostility engendered by reorganization, allowing others to pull the strings behind the curtain and reorganize.

After the September 11 terrorist attacks, Congress and the White House dramatically reorganized the government, creating the Department of Homeland Security by consolidating 28 agencies and some 128,000 people. In addition, they created the Office of the Director of National Intelligence (DNI) and the National Counterterrorism Center (NCTC), attempting to force the 16 agencies in the intelligence community to share information, a near impossibility before the attacks in New York City and the Pentagon.

Even then, the intelligence community eight years later in December 2009 failed to detect the underwear bomber aboard Northwest flight 253, although the individual was already in an American intelligence computer system and even though the bomber's father had alerted the American embassy in Nigeria about his radical son. This case, among others, suggests that the two reorganizations were not working as intended.

Ten years after Congress created the Department of Homeland Security following the terrorist attacks in New York City and at the Pentagon, current and former officials agreed that the relatively young department was still suffering from poor management and unclear focus.[78]

Reorganization is one way to change the direction of government, especially if in the process you are able to remove and replace senior managers opposed to your plans. Reorganizing allows you to redirect your resources to new priorities, shuffle or bury people not in sync with you, and best of all, reorganizing establishes you as being in charge.

Reorganizing is an easy thing to contemplate. Be wary of the temptation, though. Senior political appointees, flag officers in the military, career managers and even presidents often employ reorganization as a substitute for leadership.

ADVICE TO BRIAN

While it may seem easy at first, reorganizing can be very difficult because employees do not want it, managers do not want it, and most importantly, Congress may not want it. Reorganization requires relentless attention and a battle plan.

Decide what changes you should make. In your early days on the job, you will not know enough about the organization to reorganize intelligently. You will need to call upon the old hands in your organization. For ideas, you must turn to the career civil servants, and they always respond. Year after year, in administration after administration, career civil servants are always willing to show their new bosses how to attack the castle.

After identifying ideas on how to proceed, focus on three questions. How will you make the reorganization happen? How will you overcome the inevitable resistance? Where can you find supporters to help you?

Finally, after developing your battle plan, you must find allies in high places in four groups: your employees, your bosses, officials at OMB and in Congress. As with all issues when you need support, potential supporters will ask at least two questions before they come on-board.

What's in it for me?

Will this cause a problem for me?

Answering these questions relative to the four potential support groups will provide some hints on how to obtain support for your reorganization.

28

PROBING THE WORLD OF POLITICAL APPOINTEES

Frank,
It seems you are wary of political appointees. It
sounds like they are sometimes uninformed and arrive
in government with their own interests rather than
those of the taxpayers. Nevertheless, I will have to work
with them. Can you tell me more about them, and give
me some advice about managing my relationships with
political appointees?

Presidents fill jobs to reward campaign supporters, to
promote their agendas, to build coalitions and to maintain
funding sources for campaigns.

Some appointees are qualified; others are not; but the White
House owes them for helping the president win the election.

Appointees to agencies important to the president's agenda
at State, Treasury and Defense are often better educated, have
subject matter knowledge, some agency experience, and prior

government experience in related work, and they are unlikely to have political backgrounds.

Conversely, when agencies are not responsible for the president's priorities, the White House will assign appointees more likely to have worked on the campaign and have a political history.

Less qualified appointees receive jobs in the social welfare agencies such as Labor, Housing and EPA. Some find themselves in public relations, press relations and congressional relations jobs.

Major donors receive prestigious ambassador assignments to Great Britain, France and Japan. The State Department's Foreign Service career officials fill the less prestigious positions, often in danger zones in the Middle East. The White House assigns other major donors to positions in Commerce and Justice for jobs in business, economics and law, jobs that pay well in the private sector.[79]

Working for political appointees can be difficult, but the experiences can be among the most rewarding of your career—it depends on the person and the respect they have for the career workforce.

There are good things and bad things to say about political appointees.

They can bring new ideas with a fresh perspective.

They can emphasize the president's priorities.

On the other hand, some political appointees are like the college star athletes making the transition to the big leagues. It takes time to get the hang of the faster pace, the different cultures and the new complexity.

Moreover, the scale of the issues faced by newcomers can be overwhelming, even for 30-year veterans of government service. The rules and policies are extensive. The personal system can be bewildering. These factors may cause some new political appointees to become paranoid and withdraw into a tight clique populated only by other political appointees.

Political appointees are different. They look like you and me and the people walking the streets in the cities and towns in the country. But, for one thing, they have stronger legs than most of us. They have sturdy muscles built from walking the neighborhoods and from knocking on doors during a campaign. Some have bigger bank accounts and a willingness to open their checkbooks and contribute to a would-be president. They have a superiority gene magically developed because the president appointed them and they successfully endured the clearance process.

Sometimes they make decisions for purely political reasons without giving due consideration to what is best for the agency or the taxpayers. They can make bad decisions trying to show support for what they think are the current priorities at the White House.

Political appointees have different motivations than others in government. When a career official sits down with a new boss to discuss an issue, he/she will be thinking of the facts and the merits of the case. Your political appointee, in addition to these factors, will be evaluating whether the proposed action will look good to White House officials.

There is still another difference. If a career official does a good job, does not leak classified secrets or badmouth the agency in the media, and does not grope a member of the opposite sex, a long career in the government is likely. Your political appointee boss, however, will remain in government only two years on average. As a senior executive, I had eight bosses at the political level in 23 years, but this three-year average is unusually long.

Anticipating about two years in office, your new boss will soon be thinking about his or her next job, most likely in the private sector. Your boss will want you and your organization to do work that will attract the attention of companies and bring favorable recognition from the White House.

All political appointees have power, and the president has the most. In addition, there are the other attractive benefits. For the president and cabinet heads and others with regulatory or spending power, captains of industry and heads of state will clamor for 10 minutes in the great one's presence. Then, there is one's name and quotes cited worldwide often hourly, in the newspapers, on TV, and to some extent in social media like Twitter and Facebook, although sometimes the commentary is not pleasant.

It is all very exhilarating and not to be relinquished without a fight. Many tools are available to retain power and to try to ensure a favorable legacy in history. These including lavish use of spin, which can border on lying, use of a supportive media to "translate" events for the public, and a vast cadre of political appointees whose first and foremost job is to get the "boss" re-elected and keep him in office for as long as the rules allow, or to try to change the rules if possible.

However, the time will come to move on. A few countries, including the U.S., have a rule requiring that power be passed on to someone else every few years, allowing another and his family, friends and close supporters to taste the nectar. Yet, for those leaving, the aftermarket opportunities for former well-known government officials can be attractive. As one example, corporate groups are willing to pay up to $100,000 for a 20-minute speech.[80] Famously, the Clintons became multimillionaires in 15 years as speakers after exiting the White House.

Then, there are the notations and footnotes in history books, flattering biographies and a few that are not, and best of all, one's own autobiography written by a paid employee, providing a quick couple of million dollars for insights from the ruling period.

As the post-government years pass, the opportunities slowly decline for speechmaking, writing op-ed articles in *The New York Times* and appearances on late night TV. Eventually, the once powerful fade, often comfortably, into history, until only researchers poking into times-gone-by care anymore. Henry Kissinger is the exception.

For former presidents and nationally known figures, the price for this acclaim and notoriety means that they will never be able to dress in old clothes, climb in their pickup truck, drive to the local Home Depot and wander the store in peace like most citizens.

There were 4,000 full time political appointee positions available to President Obama, and the number increases with each president. After the White House selects a person for a job, the process becomes long and complex, and Congress, playing politics if the job is one of the 400 requiring senate confirmation, can delay confirmation up to a year, if not permanently.

To ensure fairness and transparency in the White House appointment process and, more importantly, to avoid appointments that backfire later on the president, his political appointees must complete 60 pages of clearance forms before the hiring process continues. Despite this, after President Obama announced several senior appointments in his first term, media researchers identified some that had not paid their federal income taxes. His Treasury Secretary Timothy F. Geithner was the most prominent appointee owing money to the IRS.

Some political appointees sound like echo chambers for whatever they think is important to the president and his inner circle.

A Department of Agriculture speechwriter sent an e-mail to 60 undersecretaries, assistant secretaries and other political appointees providing stock phrases about how well she thought things were going in the third year of the Iraq war. She advised the officials to include the "good news" in their public speeches and suggested sample introductions to ease into the subject. For example, "Several topics I'd like to talk about today include the Farm Bill, trade with Japan, the World Trade Organization, and Avian flu, but before I do, let me touch on a subject people always ask about, progress in Iraq."

Once into the subject, she said, you can tell your audience, "We are helping the Iraqi people build a lasting democracy that is peaceful and prosperous," or any of several related phrases she provided.

The speechwriter said that the administration's talking points should be included in every speech made by agriculture officials. She sent along language used by the Secretary of Agriculture Mike Johanns and his deputy secretary, Charles F. Conner, in all of their speeches. She indicated that each political appointee should use the same language in their speeches. Each appointee, she said, must provide a weekly report summarizing the name of the event, the date and location of each speech in which they incorporated the language. She said she would send an account of each official's speeches each week to the White House.[81]

Can you imagine an audience made up of corporate farmers, agricultural lobbyists, agricultural suppliers, exporters, trade specialists, bird flu researchers, grant applicants and others interested in the specialized agricultural sector of the economy listening to a progress report about the Iraq war delivered by a farm official?

Some will say that the president has the right to use his

appointees in whatever legal way he wishes. That is true. However, would you rather hear about surgery from a surgeon? Would you rather hear about golf from a golf professional or a long-time golf instructor? Would you rather hear about war from someone involved in it rather than from an agriculture official?

Political appointees and party ideology lead to inflexibility. Political appointees sometimes make decisions harmful to the reputation of the White House. They may be positioning themselves for employment after their government service, or they may be seeking kudos from the White House.

A young NASA appointee stirred up a hornets' nest of scientists buzzing angrily all over government because of his efforts to keep the agency's top climate scientist from speaking publicly about global warming.

The backlash he created brought the case into media headlines for a few days, requiring the head of NASA to establish a policy of freedom of expression for scientists in the agency.

The young appointee was a college student in Texas when he quit school in 2004 to help with the Bush re-election campaign. After the election, he accepted an appointment in the Office of Public Affairs at NASA. There he established himself as a gatekeeper between the media and the agency's scientists.

In several interviews with *The New York Times*, Dr. James C. Hansen, the director of NASA's Goddard Institute for Space Studies in Manhattan, and several other career NASA public affairs officials and scientists complained about what they said were intensifying efforts by political appointees to control more closely their scientific lectures and Web presentations.

Dr. Hansen, a respected international figure, had worked for years on global warming and the Big Bang theory of cosmology. The Bush administration was very sensitive to discussions about these subjects, as were the administration's friends on the religious right.

Later, other NASA scientists and public affairs officers complained to *The New York Times* about additional instances in which Bush political appointees altered news releases or Web presentations based on political ideology. The appointee, defending himself in a discussion with a colleague, said, "My job was to make the president look good."

He said Hansen exaggerated the threat of global warming, casting the Bush administration's response to it as inadequate.

To stem the furor, NASA Administrator Michael D. Griffin issued a public "statement of scientific openness" to all NASA employees, saying, "We have identified a number of areas in which clarification and improvements to the standard operating procedures of the Office of Public Affairs can and will be made."

Griffin also said, "It is not the job of public affairs officers to alter, filter or adjust engineering or scientific material produced by NASA's technical staff."[82] [83]

How does this kind of thing happen?

A dedicated 24-year-old non-college graduate knows two things in this case.

His president opposes the theory alleging global warming and its danger to the world.

The administration supports religious groups denying evolution.

Acting on those two pieces of information, a junior political appointee could conclude his job was to keep a respected scientist's views from the American public.

There are hundreds of eager 20-somethings in every administration creating dilemmas for career officials, because they all give the impression they speak for the White House. Few career employees have Hansen's audacity to push back. Even fewer have the support of prestigious officials, as Hansen did, including the president of the National Academy of Sciences who spoke out on his behalf.

Another appointee Michael Chertoff, the Secretary of the Department of Homeland Security, after some months eventually accepted blame for his organization's poor performance during and after Hurricane Katrina. Senior government officials have discovered that it is easy and harmless to accept blame, since there is rarely accountability for poor performance. In fact, accepting blame and saying "I am responsible" defuses an issue and gets it out of the newspapers and off the CNN channel.

If there are charges of malfeasance, possibly criminal, there are five traditional responses of choice:

- *I do not recall.*
- *I was not aware.*
- *When I was young, they abused me.*
- *I am entering an alcohol treatment program or an addiction center.*
- *I am to blame, and I take full responsibility (while fully recognizing that there is no penalty).*

These may not generate the sympathy that offenders seek. Current political figures have discovered a new and better response:

I apologize, I apologize to my family, I apologize to the voters, and I apologize to the great nation that I am honored to serve. Moreover, I have checked in to a newly created addiction center for my newly created addiction.

If your boss gets into the newspapers for some alleged misdeed and if your boss's initial response is denial, wait and see if more details surface.

Observe whether the inspector general in your agency is investigating the case. If so, the report may lead to congressional hearings. If the FBI is involved, your boss could be dead meat, and criminal charges may follow. In any event, he is in for hell for at least 18 months while peers and the White House shun him. They do not want anything to rub off on them.

The FBI usually gets their man based on lies to them, to the inspector general, or to another law enforcement or investigative organization. Conviction is rarely due to the alleged deed. Lies get the conviction.

Two Suggestions for Political Appointees

First, political appointees should listen to their long-term career employees, who, of course, will try to promote their priorities; but they know how things work and how to get things done. In addition, they can:

- Introduce a new political appointee to important persons
- Help to identity the unseen potholes
- Advise the appointee where he or she can make their

mark in government
- Identify those who they believe the appointee can trust

In short, working with experienced career officials augments the skills of political appointees, allowing them to manage effectively and sooner in their new jobs.

The wisdom of this surfaced publicly early in 2011 when the Republicans took control of the House of Representatives. Determined to reduce the deficit and to bring fiscal sanity to Washington, some new members wanted to clean house, replace the 50 staff members of the House Appropriations Committee and bring in new staff. However, seasoned Republican members of Congress, other political experts and even some Tea Party activists said that replacing the Appropriation Committee staff would be a mistake, because the staff has the high level of expertise and institutional knowledge needed to help write the nation's laws and complex spending bills in the contentious environment that is Congress.

These staff members know the details of every account in every federal agency, knowledge that is not available from any other source, and it is certainly not available from elected Congressional members who must rely on these staffers. Similarly, senior career executives in the federal agencies have important institutional knowledge and can provide needed insights to political appointees.

Second, political appointees should not waste their time micromanaging the work of their career managers. Instead, they should identify "make a difference" objectives and work on those. Appointees should let their subordinate managers do what they are supposed to do and should not second-guess them unless there is a compelling reason.

Advice to Brian

Here are eight points to keep in mind about political appointees, even if you become one:

- Political appointees arrive in their new jobs with zeal and enthusiasm, but, and this is a big but, they are likely to see career officials as part of the former crowd, the crowd whose deeds they feel they must correct.

- Typically, appointees enter the government believing everyone remaining in it is a dullard, although they change their minds after a while, and normally they leave government with great respect and admiration for career civil servants. So be patient.

- Political appointees are a network unto themselves, whether their party controls the White House or not; and the network thrives even when the party is out of office, while awaiting the next election and the chance to regain power.

- Political appointees serve at the pleasure of the president and are in office primarily to carry out the agenda and priorities of the White House.

- Just like leaders in any other sector of society, some political appointees are highly qualified and try to make the organization more successful; others are not qualified; and some will rest on their political laurels earned during the campaign.

- In closed-door briefing sessions for new officials, speakers tell political appointees not to discuss political issues in the office or on government property, and career officials should avoid political discussions at work.

- Toward the end of their term, they begin worrying about their next job, which will be in the private sector in all likelihood. They may neglect their duties to the agency as they prepare to move on, or they may intensify their efforts to implement the outgoing president's goals as they sprint to the finish.

- With 15 months to go in his term, the Obama Administration created "The Leaders Delivery Network," made up of 25 officials representing 17 agencies involved in 23 of the 92 priority objectives to be implemented before the next president is in office. The officials will be exempt from the daily grind so they can each focus on one of the top priorities.[84]

Because of their short tenure in government, two years is the average, your political boss will be interested in making a mark in government. You can help in two ways:

If you are a career official, you can use your contacts in government and industry to put your boss in touch with people interested in the skills and experience he or she has demonstrated.

You can help identify an initiative, which can be prominent and successful during an 18-month period, to allow your political boss to exhibit an important, perhaps saleable accomplishment after his or her stint in government is over.

In addition, if you are a career official, be aware that political appointees are a network in which only political appointees are welcome at times. Be sensitive to the boundaries between political and career officials. Being outside their network is often a blessing. It can prevent them from using you to spread the political gospel.

I have counseled ambitious individuals to contribute $10,000 to each party and then ask the victorious White House for an assistant secretary of management position in one of the 18 major cabinet agencies, and you may want to do so later in your career if you have some extra money.

Unfortunately, the White House may have raised the bar higher when it appointed a woman as a recent administrator of the General Services Administration who, with her husband, a government official, contributed $226,000 to Republican campaigns and causes in the ten years before her appointment.

ADVICE TO POLITICAL APPOINTEES NEW TO GOVERNMENT:

You cannot create experience. You must undergo it.
—Albert Camus

29

CAN POLITICAL APPOINTEES RUN THE GOVERNMENT?

Frank,
Your concerns about the White House awarding
important government jobs as the spoils of an election
victory troubles me. While most political appointees
want to do a good job, can they?

In responding to your question, I suggest you consider Ernest Hemingway's advice. "Don't confuse action with motion."

Political science research demonstrates that federal programs run by political appointees perform poorly compared to programs managed by career employees. The main reasons are lack of background training and experience.[85]

Wanting is different from doing. Intending to do a good job is different from succeeding. Because political appointees placed in office by Presidents Bill Clinton, George W. Bush and Barack Obama have occupied all of the top positions in the Executive branch, it is reasonable to ask whether they had the background and ability to run an effective government. Here are four examples of individuals appointed to government jobs by Bush and two appointed by Obama whose credentials are questionable.

After the Hurricane Katrina disaster in New Orleans, members of Congress and the media questioned the qualifications of many George W. Bush nominees, including FEMA Director Michael Brown.

The hurricane revealed a sorry response by officials at the White House, the Department of Homeland Security and FEMA. Tens of millions of Americans and overseas viewers watched the tragedy unfolding on TV. We saw hundreds of people in chest-deep floodwaters struggling to reach safety while clutching babies and a few possessions in black plastic bags. When the cheerleader statements by politicians, as in Hurricane Katrina, do not ring true with what the public sees on TV, the credibility of the government and its appointees are in question. President Bush's praise, "Brownie, you are doing a heck of a job," is one example.

The New York Times reported on June 27, 2006 that, "among the many superlatives associated with Hurricane Katrina is this one: it produced one of the most extraordinary displays of scams, schemes and stupefying bureaucratic bungles in modern history, costing taxpayers up to $2 billion."

Under pressure from Congress and the media, the White House sacked Brown because of the poor performance of his agency during Hurricane Katrina. One of Brown's mistakes was to surround himself with political appointees while building a wall between them and career officials. The government does not work well when 4,000 political appointees isolate themselves from the 6,000 senior career executives, each possessing 20 to 35 or more years in a variety of government jobs.

With more than 4,000 jobs available to the White House to reward political supporters, some poor choices are inevitable. The George W. Bush administration attracted unprecedented attention because of the unusually odd choices he made for some high visibility, critical jobs.

He appointed David Safavian, who had only congressional and agency staff experience, to lead the government's top procurement policy organization.

Bush unilaterally elevated others to important posts, including Julie Myers, a young lawyer without law enforcement experience. The White House appointed her to replace a 25-year veteran and head the 15,000-person Immigration and Customs Enforcement agency, the government's second largest investigative force.

Harriet Miers was a staff secretary, a longtime confidant and gatekeeper to George W. Bush. He appointed her to eight jobs in her career, nominated her to become a Supreme Court Justice and later withdrew the nomination after howls of disbelief from the public.

Barrack Obama continued the pattern of appointing people with marginal skills especially into senior information and telecommunications jobs. Eyebrows lifted when the White House appointed two individuals with limited experience in small state and local governments to serve as the chief information and chief technology officers in the massive federal government.[86]

This trend continued in the Obama administration as senior career officials gave poor or failing grades to political appointees.[87] Of those responding to a survey:

- More than 30 percent gave overall "D" or "F" grades to Obama's political appointees
- Sixty percent gave Obama's appointees a grade C or lower for their functional expertise
- Almost 40 percent gave political appointees a D or F for their collaboration and communication skills with their staffs

Selected comments from the survey:

"Their role [political appointees] has increased, but their effectiveness, skill and knowledge have decreased."

They presume the "institution is an obstruction" and attempt to eliminate the organization.

Some "have a divide-and-conquer strategy, and there are way too many industry fingers allowed in decision-making."

The result has been "politicization of normal agency functions."

The US Comptroller General, David Walker, head of Congress' investigative arm, said, "There needs to be more emphasis on the qualifications of individuals that have key positions."[88]

Even political appointees agree the current process is uneven at best in recruiting talented people to serve. In one survey, only 11 percent of past appointees agreed that political appointees represented the best and brightest America has to offer. The majority of the political appointees participating in the survey said current political appointees are a mixed lot, some are highly talented, yet others lack the basic skills and experience.[89]

When the White House proposes a nominee who will become your boss or the head of your agency and the Senate will not confirm, you need not worry if the Senate bases its refusal on ideology. After all, *politics is politics.* However, be alert if the Senate alleges the nominee lacks qualifications. This person could be a real dud, and the road ahead can be difficult.

Unfortunately, a particularly unqualified person tends to be a screamer and aggressive to employees and clients once they taste the power of a high-level government job. Suppose your political boss is a screamer. This can be unnerving. It is time for you to be composed and diplomatic when the boss's face gets as red as volcano lava, the veins in the throat enlarge, and his or her emotional voice carries 100 feet down the corridor and into the elevator.

A small number of political appointees are screamers. Unleashed emotion usually belies insecurity. Many political appointees are in the biggest job they have ever had or will have. They can turn, unpredictably, on anyone working for them. Recognizing extreme emotion as insecurity may help you to collect yourself and respond constructively, versus screaming back in response.

Thankfully, I only worked for one screamer out of eight political bosses. Give it a chance if you inherit a screamer. However, if you soon think that you or your program will suffer because of the new appointee, it may be time to look for another job. Call upon your friends and former colleagues that you treated well in the past. Use the network of contacts in and out of the government, the network that you should be building every day.

ADVICE TO BRIAN

Each of my political bosses was a very different person with dissimilar backgrounds and personalities. I learned from each one of them, and even today, I appreciate the experiences I had with each of them.

I, and other senior career government officials will tell you that many political appointees are reasonably good managers. Moreover, they bring fresh ideas to the government, and they can challenge existing practices, a good thing from time to time. At the same time, many are washouts who deserve "British Lord-like" titles, not senior government management responsibility.

Brian, even if you are one, you may be concluding that political appointees are difficult to work with, and, yes, it can be true. The worst problems occur in the smaller agencies where the quality of the appointees placed by the White House is less than in the more visible agencies such as the Treasury Department or the State Department, although in recent administrations this is not always true. In the George W. Bush and Obama administrations, all agencies received their share of poor quality appointees.

I hope you get one of the good ones.

30

SEIZING THE OPPORTUNITIES AFTER A PRESIDENTIAL ELECTION

Frank,
There will be an election before I can fully implement
my program across the nation. What happens in that
period? Those who have been through one before may
be able to relax; but I will be concerned about the effects
that a presidential election can have on my program
and on me. Can you give me insights about what to
expect as the election becomes reality?

The period after the election between November and
March is one of endless rumors in the government. Agency
staffers speculate on who will be their new directors, what are
their backgrounds and reputations, and what will be their new
priorities?

There are two kinds of political appointees. Those in the
outgoing administration who need to continue working will leave
as soon as they can find a job, before the rush when many private
sector job possibilities still exist and while they have useful
contacts remaining inside government. Seven months before the

presidential election, it may already be too late to find good jobs outside the government.

The rare appointees are those who do not need to work because they are independently wealthy or because they will retire. These individuals will probably stay on the job until January 20 following the election when, by law, they must have previously tendered their resignation, which is accepted 99.99 percent of the time. A few political appointees assume their work is so important that the new administration will jump at the chance to retain them. Every agency has some of these misguided souls.

Nevertheless, the new people who worked to elect the incoming president will get the senior government jobs. I have seen some sad cases in which the White House shoved previously important political appointees out the door because they stayed too long.

THE NEW ARRIVALS

The first to arrive in agencies and take up their new posts are the cabinet head appointees of the top-tier agencies like the Treasury Department and the State Department. Lesser agencies like the Small Business Administration and the GSA may not see a new administrator until summer, nine or more months after the election. They in turn will interview others for jobs in their organization, although sometimes the White House tells them whom to select. After preliminary selection, the White House, the FBI and the Office of Personnel Management investigate new appointees. These reviews take time, a lot of time.

The George W. Bush administration worked for eight and one half months to get the president's cabinet and sub-cabinet confirmed by the Senate. In addition, when 9/11 occurred in New York City and at the Pentagon, ten months after the election, the administration had filled only 50 percent of the other political jobs while beginning the war on Muslim terrorists.

The public might think that delays in filling the top jobs in government could make the country vulnerable in the crisis; however, career executives are well equipped to run the government for extended periods without guidance from freshly appointed politicals. In fact, the government may function better for extended periods with career executives at the wheel.

Be aware—the White House normally does not give government jobs to the first wave of supporters fanning out across the agencies; this initial group is an advance transition team that will work in agencies for a short time to evaluate programs and develop information for the second wave of supporters, those who will get the actual jobs.

The first wave will also evaluate the career executives while scrutinizing the agency in the weeks after the election. You have to be out and about in this period, picking up crumbs of information here and there until you assemble a complete picture of what the transition team will propose about your organization and possibly about you. Even better, you might know someone on the transition team who could slip you an advanced copy of the team's report.

Long before the presidential transition, building strong relationships across your agency and throughout your industry is critical to the future of your program, and you. Do not forget to seek advice and build relationships with the hundreds of Non-Government Organizations (NGOs) community in Washington. The Council for Excellence in Government, the National Academy of Public Administration, and numerous state and local government associations are examples of such organizations.

Being able to communicate the value of your program is critical because there are so many major programs across the government. Those less well known and the unknowns get lost in the dust. The Air Force, for example, broke with tradition and spent taxpayer money to hire a public relations firm because they felt the American public believed they were not contributing much in the Afghanistan and Iraq wars.

ADVICE TO BRIAN

As fresh appointees enter government, you have an important opportunity to promote the innovative program you have been holding secretly, waiting for this opportunity. New appointees want to make their mark in their brief time in government, and their ears will be receptive to new ideas that support the ideology of the party, save money or solve long-standing problems.

However, timing is crucial. The third week after a new

appointee is in office is the time to step forward with your idea for a new program. Doing so in the first couple of weeks is a mistake, because many self-styled career entrepreneurs and industry executives are bombarding the new executive with ideas, complaints, self-serving briefings and more.

When you present your ideas, encourage your new boss to make them his own. You both can benefit; you get to see your ideas become reality; your boss makes a mark. Win. Win.

At one time, my deputy and I had an idea for an intergovernmental group composed of federal, state and local government officials. We envisioned a new organization to bring cross-government issues to the attention of federal program officials for a coordinated federal-state-local government solution. We quickly identified one problem. Individual federal officials were placing desktop computers in state and local agencies and forbidding their use on any other federal government task. Therefore, state and local officials had to manage several hardly-used computers, when one or a few would have done the job.

We had the idea for the intergovernmental group a year before the presidential election. We recruited officials from federal, state and local governments with a passion for working intergovernmentally. We held a few meetings to work out the kinks. However, we did not publicly announce the program during the remaining months of the outgoing administration.

It makes no sense to start a new program in the last year of a president's term when his appointees are bailing out of the government. Even if your boss is not rushing to leave, the chances are good he will be gone anyway within the year, so there will be insufficient time to implement a new program. More importantly, if the program was unfinished, the newcomers would view it as being a program belonging to the people they are replacing, making it eligible for cancellation.

FOURTEEN TIPS TO GIVE YOU AN EDGE DURING A PRESIDENTIAL TRANSITION

1. Brian, while you must assign staff to prepare briefing books, you personally should not spend much time on this job because the final products from your group

and many other organizations in the agency will be stacked too high to be read, and nobody will read any one of them cover to cover. Still, the material will help you to prepare for your first meeting with the new agency head.

2. Take every opportunity to educate new appointees until you know they understand your program. Any face-to-face meetings, whatever the subject, provide good opportunities to continue to educate your new boss about your program.

3. Transition is an opportunity since everyone starts fresh at ground zero. While there can be real tension during the first year, there can be many opportunities. This is a time to be watchful, on your toes, and ready to help. It is also a time to promote your program, yourself and your creative ideas for change, the main interest of most newcomers.

4. Many political appointees enter government with some distrust of the government and its employees. However, some quickly figure out that most government employees, especially the senior career officials, want the new appointees to be successful. They trust the career managers to do their jobs, freeing themselves to operate on the most important issues upstairs with the agency's leaders.

5. If you have been honest with yourself while examining your program, you will have corrected any soft spots. Yet, what should you do if the newcomers signal they are unimpressed with you or your program?

    Data documenting the value of your organization is the best cure when you encounter a disbelieving boss. There is considerable data available about government programs. However, data produced by companies such as the Gartner Group or the Forrester group should be used carefully and confirmed by other data sources if possible because these companies are also in the business of seeking government contracts. Try to produce your own data and use outside sources only to confirm your findings.

6. If the new people do not invite you to meet even though you manage one of their important programs, consider it a sign; call upon your allies and give them ammunition to intercede on your behalf.

7. There is only so much money available in an agency. If other program chiefs sense that you are vulnerable, they may disparage your program, attempting to pirate some of your staff, budget, other resources and possibly your entire program.

   If buccaneers challenge your program, you may find support from your boss; then again, you may not. You may find support from the agency budget office, although this is normally unlikely unless the budget chief believes Congress will be unhappy if your program is under siege.

   You may find support from the OMB budget examiner who probably understands your program as well as anyone in your own agency; however, the budget examiner may be looking for programs to cut to meet budget reduction goals set by the new White House.

   The inspector general at GSA once used Congress quite successfully when the new administrator tried to reduce his staff and budget.[90][91]

   Alternatively, you can speak to a Congressional staffer with whom you have a good relationship. Care is required because senior political officials in your agency dislike, even fear, their employees taking their agenda directly to Congressional committees. Nevertheless, you know the staffers on committees important to the agency better than the Congressional Affairs staff in your agency, or at least you should because your agency's Congressional Affairs people need to develop contacts for many agency programs, not just yours.

   However, should they place the handcuffs on you, there are alternative ways to convey the message that your program is under attack. For example, at a gala attended by 1,000 people in a big ballroom in a D.C.

hotel, you can truly answer a Congressional staffer's greeting—"Well, Brian, how are things going?"

8. Sometimes, you can reverse negative opinions about your program by calling on allies in government, Congress or industry, assuming you have been wise enough to build relationships in these communities. However, if you are not successful and the newcomers seem likely to kill you or your program, you should take the Band-Aid approach—tear it off fast. Accept the momentary pain; avoid the long drawn out drip-drip tortuous death. If they are going after you, go to your boss and declare, do not make me miserable, send me wherever you want, but do it fast.

9. If you conclude you are not going to fit with the new Administration, do not blame yourself. There will be times when the chemistry between two good people will be toxic. Career executives with new political bosses every two years on average will likely run into a bad chemistry situation at least once in a 20-year career. The key is not whether it happens to you, but how well you recover.

10. In the outgoing administration, an interesting period occurs after the presidential election in November for about nine weeks while the lingering politicals are still packing. I call this "open season," a time to make new contacts on the Hill, resurrect old ones and consider modest policy actions not possible earlier.

11. Several weeks after the election, you should anticipate a freeze—a stop-all-hiring order—to allow the new political appointees to make employment decisions according to their priorities. It happens every four years and sometimes more often. Employment freezes cause erratic decisions to purchase things, usually technology, and to hire contractors to get the work done with fewer government people.

   Anticipating the customary freeze, experienced career officials rush to fill as many vacancies as possible before the White House order that OMB normally delivers in a time and in ambiguous language designed to evade public attention.

12. Once the White House selects the new agency head, the system forbids the appointee from entering the building where he or she will work until background investigations are complete and Congress confirms the appointment. Until these actions are complete, GSA provides new appointees with modest office space.

   One location is on G Street two blocks west of the White House in an unpretentious building occupied by the Secret Service and other government agencies. New appointees, lonely at this time, are more accessible than they will be after their confirmation. Take advantage of the opportunity and schedule meetings with proposed office holders. Be persistent when you call. The proposed agency head may be down the hall getting a foam cup of coffee weeks before he or she will have three secretaries.

13. There is a virtual fence between political appointees and career executives as there is in the Department of Defense between military officers and career executives. The fence is not made of cement blocks, sensors and predator missiles; rather, it is an invisible fence. You can sense it by observing body language such as an abrupt shifting in the chair, or your boss' eyes suddenly going blank and dead like the mackerel on ice at the Whole Foods supermarket, clear signals that the fence is up and active.

14. When the new administration takes over, you are part of the old crowd. Although you may be a national figure with contacts in governments and industry all over the country, and possibly the world, you have to start anew to build a relationship with a fresh and often inexperienced boss. You may believe in the goals of the new boss and the political party, you may be a Hall-of-Famer, but you have to prove yourself once again.

   At some point, managing the transition will become your full-time job for several months. If the chemistry is good between you and the newcomers, you could have four good years until the next transition, unless your new boss leaves government in two years, the average stay of senior political appointees.

31
WINNING WHILE OUTSOURCING

Frank,
To get the skills needed for my new program, I will need to hire some companies to augment my government staff. I understand that the government term for this is "outsourcing." Is there anything special I need to know about it?

Outsourcing government jobs is an emotional issue that Republicans and industry officials worship, and government employees, unions and some Democrats generally detest. As the manager of one of the government's major technology programs, outsourcing will dominate your life for several years.

HISTORY OF OUTSOURCING

Outsourcing by the federal government is not new. The DOD, for example, has employed contractors since the American Revolution, when there was one contractor for every six soldiers.

Currently, the government relies heavily on the private

sector to provide commercial services. OMB Circular A-76 is the policy document that opens government jobs to private-sector competition. A-76 has evolved many times since OMB created it in 1966.

In addition to A-76, the Fair Act of 1998 requires each agency to publish an annual inventory of Federal Government functions that are not inherently governmental and thus are candidates for transfer to the private sector.

Traditionally, there are certain sensitive functions government employees must perform. Some observers think the following are, or should be, classified as inherently government functions:[92]

- Controlling prosecutions
- Commanding military forces
- Conducting criminal investigations
- Conducting foreign relations and the determining foreign policy
- Determining the content and application of policy and regulations
- Determining priorities for budget requests
- Directing Federal employees
- Directing intelligence and counter-intelligence operations
- Selecting or non-selecting individuals for Federal Government jobs
- Drafting of Congressional testimony and responses to Congress

However, Congress and the White House have not defined inherently government functions. Most Democrats, Republicans and those occupying the White House in recent decades have ignored the question about which jobs are the core jobs.

In its first year in office, the Obama administration for a short time encouraged agencies to in-source critical jobs. A year later, Obama's director of federal procurement policy settled on a single, historical definition of core government jobs from the 1988 FAIR Act, which defined inherently government functions as being those so intimately related to the public interest as to mandate performance by federal employees.

In his guidance letter implementing the new policy, the administrator of the Office of Federal Procurement Policy provided his insights, which government employees regarded as an inconclusive example of "it could be this, or it could be that."

Among nations emphasizing outsourcing government jobs, the United Kingdom has been the leader. Since Prime Minister Margaret Thatcher's reign in the 1980s, the UK has outsourced government jobs to focus on core business functions and to "get the government out of [that] business."

Connecticut was perhaps the first to outsource all of a state government's desktop computers, mainframes and telecommunications. In late 1998, the governor ordered the State's CIO, Rock Regan, to privatize the state's IT infrastructure. This was a bombshell to IT managers nationwide, and it resulted in a $1.35 billion seven-year contract to EDS. Regan became a short-term rock star on the speaking circuit because everyone in management positions in many governments wanted to learn what he did in Connecticut and how.

However, Connecticut cancelled the contract in less than a year due to lobbying from unions, state legislators, the state controller and resistance from several state government agencies.

Today, however, such programs in state governments are routine because of the ubiquitous deficits in the 2010-2012 period, and they are becoming routine in the federal government.

As time passes, the pendulum swings back and forth emphasizing outsourcing, then de-emphasizing outsourcing. Depending on whether the Democrats, favoring work done by government employees, or the Republicans, favoring work done by contractors, control the White House, you may or may not find support for outsourcing some jobs or your entire program.

WHY GOVERNMENTS OUTSOURCE?

- To save money, they think
- To hire skills the government lacks
- To build a new industry in the private sector
- To get the government out of a particular business
- To hire bodies for wars to avoid a domestic and unpopular draft

- To transfer more jobs to industry that was supportive during election campaigns
- To avoid the government's personnel regulations, union pressures, procurement regulations and other headaches associated with managing government personnel
- To accommodate an ideology that advocates small government and a robust private sector.

The Expanding Role of Contractors

There has been an outsourcing boom in the federal government since Ronald Reagan took aim at what he felt was a bloated federal workforce and launched a drive to transfer government jobs to the private sector.

Every subsequent administration has embraced some form of Reagan's war on government. Clinton and Gore under their Reinventing Government program continued Reagan's work when they ordered that outsourcing procedures be streamlined, and then they slashed the federal work force to the lowest level since 1960, forcing agencies to shift more jobs to contractors, whether it was advantageous or not.

Today, contractors build ships, planes and helicopters. They develop and manage many of the information systems the government relies upon. Contractors collect income taxes, issue social service checks to the public, and provide weather data to the media and the public. Contractors manage disasters, provide health care and education to veterans, research diseases, and protect the meat and food supplies. The list is much longer.

By the end of the George W. Bush administration, the government had reached the point where there were no inherently government core jobs. All government jobs were candidates for outsourcing. The Department of Justice used contractors to provide litigation support. The Department of Homeland Security used contractors to supply the services of 20 lawyers. GSA employed 60 specialists from a private company to manage government contracting responsibilities, and IRS bought credit collection services from 10 companies.

The DOD and State use contractors to handle increasing

amounts of the nation's national security business, to provide security for key personnel and locations, including embassies, to feed and house the troops, train army and police personnel, and manage other contractors. Defense hired contractors to interrogate and torture prisoners. The State Department hired contractors to perform security and intelligence functions and sell democracy—once regarded as diplomatic functions.

Further, the IRS asked tax lawyers and accountants—those same officials that create tax shelters and exploit loopholes in tax law and regulations for corporations and wealthy citizens— to draft some of its new tax rules. Quoted in *The New York Times* on March 9, 2007, Paul Light, a professor of political science, said, "It's not the fox guarding the hen house; it's the fox designing the hen house."

Companies with their lobbyists and supporters in Congress advocate even greater use of contractors. Additionally, many government managers prefer to use contractors to avoid the frustrating federal personnel system.[93]

Companies like Boeing, Northrop Grumman and Lockheed Martin have the money to promote their products and, indirectly, advocate outsourcing of government jobs with full-page color ads in *The Washington Post*, in Capitol Hill publications such as *Roll Call* and *The Hill*, in *Aviation News,* the *Navy Times* and elsewhere. In one ad, Boeing advertised its AH-64D Apache helicopter as being the most powerful and effective combat helicopter in the world, a matter of little interest to most *Washington Post* readers, but it may have caught the eye of a few well-placed elected officials on the Hill.

New York Times columnist Thomas Friedman warns that the government is allowing a contractor-industrial–complex to grow in Washington with an economic interest in foreign relationships and warfare.[94]

How Many Contractors Does the Government Employ?

Contractors are an important part of the government team, but no one really knows how many there are. Paul Light, professor of public service at New York University, tackles this issue from time to time and estimates that there are about ten million contractors, outnumbering government employees by a factor of four, possibly five, to one. Moreover, the government anticipates additional and massive outsourcing in the future because of retirements and a shortage of certain skills, caused in part by presidential personnel policies since the Carter administration.[95]

On May 20, 2010, the nation's top procurement official, Daniel Gordon, testified to Congress that in his six months on the job, he heard numerous times that the number of contractors is out of control.[96]

To provide perspective on the extent of outsourcing in the federal government, contractors in 2009 accounted for 48 percent of the DOD war machine in Iraq and 57 percent in Afghanistan. In addition, roughly 80 percent of the State Department's budget went to contractors in 2008.[97]

At the same time, the number of federal employees in 2009 was the same as it was in 1963, although Congress created many new programs and the federal budget tripled in real terms in the intervening years. Contractors, doing the work of government, fill the gap.[98]

In recent years, without a military draft, the ratio of contractors in Iraq to uniformed soldiers was 1-to-1. In Afghanistan, the ratio became two contractors for each uniformed soldier in our all-volunteer military services.

Because, elected officials have weakened the government workforce in the past three decades, outsourcing government jobs is a necessity. Our complex, giant-size government needs contractors to get it all done.

The government has so many contractors that the national economy suffered when the 2013 sequester cutbacks reduced government spending. We know that outsourcing is big business, perhaps in the hundreds of billions of dollars annually. However, nobody really knows how much. There is no hard data, only some narrow, inconclusive studies. Perhaps nobody wants to know.

A REVIEW OF THE MAJOR COMPANIES YOU LIKELY WILL RELY ON FOR SUPPORT

A few large companies dominate the federal marketplace, and because of the size, scale, and budget of your program, you likely will be wedded to one or more of these companies for your entire term in government.

Consider these headlines from a single day chosen at random, recognizing that similar headlines occur every day.[99]

Boeing banks over $5.2 billion in Navy deals

Another day, another multi-billion dollar IT deal for Northrop Grumman

Four for L-3: DOD deals come in for Communications Giant

CSC wins $118 million Contract to Support Army Aviation Simulation Training

Northrop Grumman, CSC, Honeywell Win Defense Contracts

Booz Allen, Raytheon, Lockheed Martin Ink DOD Deals

ICF Earns Four Lucrative Deals to Support Head Start

Just three firms at the top of the military-industrial complex, Boeing Company, Lockheed Martin and Northrop Grumman accounted for $89 billion (16 percent) of the government's contract spending of $543 billion for goods and services.

Close behind were Raytheon, General Dynamics, L-3 Communications Holdings, United Technologies, BAE Systems and Science Applications International Corporation, collectively receiving awards of another $62 billion. Together, these nine firms obtained contract awards equaling almost 28 percent of the total federal spending with the top 200 contractors. This domination by a few top companies remains consistent in recent years and is impressive considering the thousands of companies selling or wishing to sell to the government.

These companies are heavily dependent on government awards. Lockheed Martin's total sales in 2010 were $45.8 billion to all sources, and $41.5 billion, or about 90 percent of its 2010 sales, were to the federal government, as they were in 2008. In 2014, Lockheed's total sales were $45.6 billion, and 79% were to the US Federal government. In a sense, these are federal agencies operating as profit-making companies.[100] [101]

The Boards of these companies reward their CEOs well for their work acquiring and managing government contracts. The CEO of Lockheed Martin, a quasi-government organization, for example, led Lockheed Martin for 8 years until 2013. His average compensation was $23.33 million or almost $140 million for the six-year period. [102]

The CEO of General Dynamics received $13 million, about 33 times the salary of the president of the U.S. and about 14 times the salary of each member of Congress and each of the top officials in the government.[103]

The main business of these companies is to produce weapons systems. Although weapons systems are generally very profitable in wartime, sales tend to decline somewhat in peacetime. In contrast, the information systems sector continues to grow every year.

To balance their revenues in peacetime, major weapons systems manufacturers buy their way into the information and telecommunications services marketplace by purchasing smaller, established firms or new companies with an important innovation. For example, weapons producer General Dynamics bought 30 companies between 1995 and 2005, becoming the fourth largest company serving the federal government, instead of the twentieth. Lockheed Martin in 2014 alone spent $898 million to acquire four companies with technologies complimentary to Lockheed's plans for growth.

Civilian companies also are active in investing in smaller companies. Cisco Systems, for example, prior to 2014, had already invested $2 billion in some 80 companies and 35 venture capital funds run by entrepreneurs.[104]

Because of their campaign contributions, other personal services and compatible ideologies, major firms have access to Congressional members and key staffers. They also have plenty of resources, including in-house and under-contract lobbyists, to fend off challenges from any source—whether it be questions about their business practices, performance under contract or proposed legislation.

In government sales for IT, systems integration and other professional services (not weapons systems) to the federal government, Lockheed Martin, Northrop Grumman and Boeing occupy positions one, two and three among the top 10, followed by Raytheon, General Dynamics and CACI International, occupying positions five, seven, and ten. IBM, an excellent technology systems provider, occupied only the fourteenth position among information technology providers to the federal government, well behind the quasi-government, weapons systems suppliers.[105]

At the same time, you should not believe that these and other companies have brigades of people more qualified than those in your agency because the experience level in companies is often limited as well. Frequently, companies supporting the government hire talented, but entry-level people and train them on a government contract at government expense.

Noting the difficulty, SRA International in its Feb-2007 Quarterly Report said:

> *"Additionally, it is difficult to hire and retain highly qualified individuals who have advanced technology and technical services skills and who work well with our clients in a government environment, especially those with security clearances. These individuals are in great demand and are likely to remain a limited resource for the foreseeable future."*

Briefly then, as a major systems program manager, you will likely partner with some of these companies. Here are some issues to consider.

Outsourcing can limit the government in three ways.

Outsourcing normally involves a long-term contract, seven years or more, during which the contract may not allow the government to consolidate functions to streamline the government.

Sometimes, severe and unnecessary contract termination penalties negotiated by the contractor may eliminate the government's ability to cancel a contract, as some government managers discovered while attempting to redirect failing programs.

When a function is outsourced, the government without in-house resources is unable to respond. In the Hurricane Katrina floods in New Orleans, the Army Corps of Engineers could not repair the levees until they found a contractor and negotiated a contract, taking time that the dislocated survivors did not have.

PROBLEMS WITH OUTSOURCING

After receiving shoddy products from contractors during the Civil War, President Lincoln established the National Academy of Sciences to provide truthful information about the quality of gunpowder and other materials delivered to the government.

In 1941, echoing a similar theme, Senator Harry Truman (D-Missouri) said, "I have never yet found a contractor who, if not watched, would not leave the government holding the bag."[106]

In recent times, Rep. Henry A. Waxman (D-California), chair of the House Committee on Oversight and Government Reform, discussing contracts in Iraq and in the Department of Homeland Security, said, "Billions of dollars are being squandered, and the taxpayer is being taken to the cleaners." [107]

David M. Walker, former head of the Government Accountability Office, an arm of Congress, said contractors often fail to deliver the promised efficiency and savings. He said you cannot expect private companies to look out for taxpayers' interests. "There's something civil servants have that the private sector doesn't. That is the duty of loyalty to the greater good— the duty of loyalty to the collective best interest of all rather than the interests of a few. Companies although, important to government operations, they have duties of loyalty to their shareholders, not to the country."

Congress, which generally favors outsourcing, may attack it if it will reduce jobs already in place in its districts. A report prepared by the Congressional Research Service in 2005 identified eight outsourcing bills, later signed into law. The bills placed limits on or delayed outsourcing plans. For example, Congress required the Pentagon to submit annual reports on anticipated savings before any additional jobs could be outsourced. These requirements had the desired effect—delayed outsourcing. However, the overall trend is to outsource more and more government jobs.

When Roger Johnson led GSA, he recognized that the government works with spinoff organizations created by the major corporations. The government, he said, does not have access to the talent in America's major corporations. Aside from companies such as weapons manufacturers that sell mainly to the federal government, other Fortune 100 companies create independent spin-off organizations, keeping separate books for government review.

Major suppliers to the federal government "are not really companies," said Peter W. Singer. "They are quasi-government agencies." Yet they are free to influence government decisions. Singer pointed out that Lockheed Martin spent more than $53 million lobbying and $6 million on political donations between 2000 and 2006. In a recent year, it led all defense companies with $25 million spent for lobbying defense legislation. In 2015, Lockheed Martin was in the top 10 of U.S. companies lobbying Congress.

Lockheed Martin, General Dynamics and other firms are able to keep unneeded arms programs alive long after the Pentagon has little or no need for the products forced on the military by the Congress.

At the same time, major hardware producers receive more money in contract awards than the Congress appropriates annually to the Departments of Justice or Energy.[108]

With millions of contractors performing thousands of jobs, there are going to be problems, especially in the very high dollar programs and those requiring R&D in our science agencies and in many DOD programs.

In 2008, government investigators charged Blackwater Worldwide Security guards working for the State Department for a shooting frenzy in Baghdad that left 17 Iraqi civilians dead.

In 2009, Wackenhut Service Company, owner of AmorGroup International, declined comment on a report by the Project on Government Oversight about the lewd behavior of its employees in Iraq. As reported on TV in the U.S., the guards hired to protect government officials held parties where they urinated on themselves, drank vodka which had been poured over their bare buttocks, while the men fondled and kissed each other, and paraded around virtually nude.

Wackenhut's firm recruited the guards from Nepal, where wages are low. Most could not speak English, although their job was to protect the United States embassy and the 1,000 diplomats, staffers and Afghan nationals working in Iraq.[109]

During the second Iraqi war, there were at least 50,000 private security contractors in Iraq working alongside American troops and officials. In some cases, companies recruited these workers from the ranks of mercenaries in Chile, Nepal, South Africa and other countries.

One of many stories coming out of Afghanistan and Iraq was about Shane Schmidt, a former Marine who served two tours in Afghanistan. Later, Triple Canopy, one of the larger contractors in Iraq, hired him after he left the Marine Corps. He accused his civilian boss of randomly shooting at and perhaps killing civilians in Baghdad. He said that working in Iraq was a lot like going to war with the Marines, except there were fewer restrictions. In an interview with Steve Fainaru, author of *Big Boy Rules,* about the lawlessness of contractors working in Iraq, he said his company briefed him to take a shot if he ever felt threatened.[110]

Contractors exploit a murky legal status. Under the Geneva Conventions, contractors are noncombatants. However, many contract personnel in Iraq served previously in America's military. As civilians, they trained Iraqi security forces, and in that role, they sometimes killed Iraqi civilians.

 The government investigated employees from at least two military contractors—CACI of Arlington, Va., and Titan of San Diego—for their role in the alleged torture and sexual abuse at Abu Ghraib prison.

The CACI contract in particular drew attention because the Pentagon did not award it. Rather, the civilian agency, the Department of the Interior, negotiated the contract to provide computer network solutions, not for the prison guards and interrogators that the Defense Department hired.

Noteworthy is that companies are not subject to the same accountability rules as government agencies. For example, companies are not subject to the Freedom of Information Act.

Major companies supplying products and services to government often have more power than government contracting officers do. Sitting across the negotiating table from a government-contracting officer are companies so big, almost nothing can get their attention. With several billion dollars in annual sales and a declining number of competitors, a major company can respond quickly and powerfully if its interests are threatened. In 24 hours, to protect its interests, it can muster several in-house lawyers for litigation, hire lobbyists for publicity or to confuse the issue, and employ perhaps ten more specialists on contract at $100,000 a week to start work immediately.[111]

In addition, major companies have access to senior political officials in agencies that government contracting officers seldom meet, even once. Because of generous campaign contributions and their ability to provide perks, such as (until recently) the practice of providing seats on corporate jets, major companies have little trouble opening doors to lawmakers and their key staff members.

As a result, agency contracting officers often find themselves outgunned and on the defensive. Agency policy prohibits them contacting the media to explain their decisions, and they lack similar access to Congress except through agency political appointees who may or may not be willing or able to provide support. To compete with the resources of a major company, one part-time agency lawyer, a generalist, might be the only support available to the government-contracting officer. Major suppliers often have more firepower resembling an armed brigade facing a government contracting officer standing alone.

DOES OUTSOURCING SAVE DOLLARS?

The short answer is that no one really knows, because while the OMB, the president's budget office, identifies at-risk systems in contracts already awarded, it also promotes outsourcing and makes predictions about savings, but it does not follow up after outsourcing takes place to validate savings or identify cost overruns.

Here are some perspectives on the question of outsourcing savings.

Rep. Henry A. Waxman (D-Calif.) pointed out that Middle East and African contractors signed by the United States military charged $25 million to repaint 20 police stations. The governor of Basra in Iraq claimed local firms could have done the work for $5 million. Of course, the larger question is why the military is spending taxpayer dollars to paint Iraqi police stations.

Considering the prices paid by the government to contractors for computer personnel, it is questionable whether OMB's projected savings of $12,500 for each of the 400,000 jobs it claims could be outsourced is realistic. One firm doing routine performance management studies for a government agency was paid $270 per labor hour. This is an annual fee of $486,000 for one person for one year (1,800 hours, or 36 hours a week for 50 weeks) of routine work. The government could hire three employees and pay their salaries and benefits for the amount paid to this firm for the equivalent of one contractor.

In another example, the State Department awarded a defense-oriented firm a $545.7 million follow-on contract, extending the original contract to continue police training in Iraq. In the 22-month contract, the company was responsible for recruiting about 800 civilian police advisors to help train the Iraqi Police Service and law enforcement officials in the Minister of the Interior and in the Department of Border Enforcement. The cost for developing each of the 800 civilian police advisors, presumably including the actual training provided, computes out to $682,000 each—in a country in which the 10-year war reduced employment and jobs to almost zero.

In a decade, according to the Commission on Wartime Contracting in Iraq and Afghanistan, the Defense Department and the State Department have wasted more than $30 billion and possibly another $30 billion in contracts and grants in Iraq and Afghanistan, the latter a country where 42 percent of the people are unemployed and 36 percent have a daily income of less than one U.S. dollar.[112] At the same time according a to a senior CIA official, we triggered massive corruption in Afghanistan, a primitive country, with a mostly illiterate population, a tiny farming economy, a tribal leadership and few national institutions.[113]

Off-shoring jobs to workers in other countries, another form of outsourcing, is attractive to U.S. companies because Administration policies restrict them from hiring immigrants with special engineering and scientific skills, skills reportedly in short supply in the United States. Another roadblock is the years-long delay required before the government grants the security clearances needed to work on many government programs. These policies lead to more (rumored) offshoring of government jobs to countries such as China, India and Malaysia as the skilled labor pool in the US allegedly shrinks.

As leading U.S. companies such as CISCO, GE, IBM and Microsoft continue to establish major research laboratories and to transfer computer and software research jobs overseas, it is likely that foreigners will work on U.S. government programs. They have the scarce and lower-cost talent that U.S. companies covet.

In addition, be alert to the changing landscape in outsourcing. Consider, for example, Watson, IBM's artificial intelligence question-answering system that has the potential to do the jobs of hundreds of thousands of analysts in the government and many more elsewhere. [114]

Watson runs on about 2,500 parallel processor cores, each able to perform up to 33 billion operations a second. It competed in February 2011 and trounced two expert humans on television's Jeopardy in the follow-on to the 1997 match when IBM's machine, Big Blue, defeated the world's reigning chess champion.

Futurists Arnold Brown and Martin Ford forecast a different version of government outsourcing, predicting that robots, networks and other forms of non-human electronic decision-makers will routinely substitute for humans in the future.[115] [116]

ADVICE TO BRIAN

While there can be problems with outsourced contractors, there are many instances in which contractors do an outstanding job, especially in lower dollar, less complex programs. And the government could not do its job without thousands of contractors. Therefore, outsourcing is here to stay. As Tiger Woods said many times in his career, "It is what it is." How then can you, as a high-level program manager, navigate the outsourcing process to ensure that the outcome will be successful? Here are five recommendations.

Plan for and expect the worst. In the history of federal, state, and local government, many attempts to privatize major government functions failed in part or completely for three reasons:

- Because of the complexity of the job

- Because the job required emerging technology still in need of further development
- Because of poor estimates about the risk and potential savings[117]

Decide how much you can outsource while retaining enough expertise to manage the contractors. You should retain certain functions in-house because your contractor in his drive for profits, stockholder value and executive bonuses may trump the objectives of your program and the terms of the contract.

Retain your contracting flexibility and the right to introduce new technologies and replace large numbers of contractor personnel if new technology would allow it.

In addition, maintain the right to fine-tune goals and milestones as you and your contractors learn while working to meet the goals of the contract. Encourage your contracting officer to incorporate these flexibilities into the contract.

Study the practices in leading countries, especially Australia, Great Britain and Singapore. Ideology and politics, not business reasons, dictate many outsourcing decisions in the federal government. In other countries, Singapore for example, common sense and good management drive outsourcing decisions, according to Wu Choy Peng, the former CIO.

Before we sign the contract, we identify every possibility in which things could go wrong, she said. There must be no surprises after signing.

We monitor contractors very carefully each month. Any slippage can result in a penalty to the contractor. You must not let things drift because problems will only get worse, she advises.

If you do not build in a measurement process before contract award, "savings" will be difficult to quantify.

Finally, recognize that you will have to outsource your billion-dollar program. Be wary and anticipate problems. Recognize that the contractor's lawyers and procurement experts could outgun the often-overworked personnel assigned to you, so study the proposed contract terms and conditions to identify items that could be detrimental after award.

Attention to these recommendations will help you to excel in outsourcing. In addition, if your contractor is missing milestones, do not delay action hoping and trusting that the contractor will be able to reverse a deteriorating situation. Delay in big systems complexity rarely solves performance problems. Singapore, often the leader in electronic government, sets the standard by facing up to contractor performance problems quickly before conditions get worse.

Brian, do the same.

32

WORKING WITH CONGRESS

Frank,
I recently read this quote from former Congressman
John Dingell.

> "We in Congress are tearing our country
> apart and weakening the foundation established
> by great leaders. I am ashamed of our recent
> record. I am disgusted with our performance,
> Republican and Democrat alike. There has been
> failed leadership and worse, failed following
> within the ranks—and we owe the country far
> better."

This is discouraging for those of us in government.
How do you keep perspective and stay motivated?

Congressman Dingell's comments represent exactly what
many people feel about our Congress. It is a pack of scallywags,
as an old Irish grandmother would say. It is usual to find some
bad ones as you might find in any group of 535 Americans.

The American public does not hold Congress in high regard. For example, a 2013 Pew Research Center survey reported that seven in ten Americans have a "very" or "mostly" unfavorable opinion of Congress. This is the worst rating in the 30 years that Pew has been asking the public about their opinion of Congress. In an earlier survey, only 17 percent responded that Congress is doing an excellent, or even a good job.[118] [119]

In early 2015, just before the beginning of the new Republican-dominated Congress, the public reported a dim view of Congress and both political parties. Just 22 percent expressed a favorable opinion of Congress; positive views of Congress have remained below 30 percent for more than three years. [120]

Nevertheless, you should develop a working relationship with congressional staffers on your appropriation and oversight committees.

Focus on those individuals that have influence over your agency and your program. Some individuals in Congress know more about how the government fits together and how it works than most officials in a new administration. There are many knowledgeable and visionary congressional officials and staffers in Congress, and they likely will know more about your program than you will know in your first few years in your job.

Rohit Kumar, a senior GOP staffer for the Senate Minority Leader, is one such individual. At age 39, with 13 years on the Hill, he conceived a way to sell a $700 billion bank bailout bill in 2008 when the country's financial system was collapsing and the Democrats and Republicans were at odds on the path to take. He also figured out how to let conservatives raise the debt limit while they simultaneously voted against it in 2011 when the nation was days away from default.

The Washington Post described Kumar as one of the nuts-and-bolts guys that congressional leaders trust to negotiate details with the other party, draft details into law and explain them to elected officials before they vote on legislation for the nation. When he left government, influential officials in both parties and at the White House described his departure as a great loss to Congress and the government. Moreover, there are many others like Rohit Kumar on the Hill, equally unsung, but critically important to the functioning of the government.[121]

Appreciate the power of the members of Congress and their staffs. In the Executive branch, working in a large and powerful agency, it is easy to forget the power of Congress and the knowledge that resides on the Hill.

After President Clinton appointed Roger Johnson as administrator of the GSA, Johnson made the customary courtesy calls to congressional leaders and to those members with some influence over GSA. One of his visits was to Tom Foley (D-Wash.), Speaker of the House. Johnson spoke his prepared remarks, including the issues facing GSA, and some broader issues, including reinventing government, a major program of Vice President Al Gore. Foley continued to work on the papers on his desk and never looked up when Johnson entered Foley's office or when he discussed his prepared list of issues.

When Johnson finished, Speaker Foley looked up and said:

"You didn't have to go through all that stuff. . . . I know exactly who you are and what you are up to, and if you think that some rich Republican businessman and those children at the White House are going to tell me or the Congress how to run our affairs, you have another think coming! I run the House, and the sooner you and Gore understand the separation of powers, the better off you will be. Thank you for the visit."[122]

In another example, Johnson concluded that the Brooks Act caused the government to pay higher prices for computer technology. Then he began to speak frequently in public about his conclusions and the need to amend the Act. Months later, when he went to the Hill to testify to the House Subcommittee on Government Operations, chaired by Congressman John Conyers (D-MI.), Congressman Jack Brooks (D-Texas), with 40 years of service in the House of Representatives, showed up apparently to even the score and asked for the opportunity to speak.

Brooks said a certain Republican computer executive, a newcomer to Washington, had the sole purpose of turning control of the Federal procurement process back to unscrupulous computer companies, thereby undermining his efforts to protect the American public. Brooks went on to make the following remarks.

"Mr. Chairman . . . you and I remember another Orange County, California Republican who came to this town about 20

years ago . . . and I know you remember what happened to him
. . . . We sent him packing back to California . . . . Today we
have another Orange County, California Republican who does
not belong here, and we are going to send him back also . . . .
However, there will be one difference, Mr. Chairman: President
Nixon was able to fly in a fancy government plane back home—
but not Mr. Johnson. No big plane for him; I'm going to make
sure that he has to ride back on a bicycle without a seat."[123]

TIPS FOR WORKING WITH CONGRESS

You may need Congressional members and their senior staff
to help defend you and your program from challenges when a new
or re-elected president takes office.

In the first month after new political appointees arrive in the
agency, some industry folks with a serious dislike of government
regulations will schedule appointments to brief the new head
of agency. In my case, they complained about the Brooks Act
and the authority it gave GSA over procurement of information
technology in the government. If the CEO of a Fortune 100
company called for an appointment with the head of the agency,
he got it and quickly, and used his time to recommend changes
in our procurement regulations. Senior government officials in
other agencies subject to GSA's authority would take a few shots
as well.

Brooks's staff had been through this routine many times in
almost four decades. Their response would be to invite a new
administrator and his senior staff to Brooks's chambers for a
private meeting. Brooks could be fiery and enjoyed a fight. In an
initial meeting, he could be courteous, but everyone at the meeting
understood what the congressional representative wanted.

Either Brooks's chief of staff or his chief investigator, Jim
Lewin, would follow up later by telephone, making it clear the
chairman hoped GSA would help the Brooks committee to
eliminate the waste, fraud and abuse they saw in the government.

If necessary, they would then schedule a public hearing on the
Hill to question the new administrator and his immediate staff
about their commitment to reduce waste, fraud and abuse in
the computer and information sectors in the government. Since

there are always plenty of examples of these three problems, such hearings are entertaining for the press and painful for new political appointees and the agency managers responsible for the failing systems.

The Social Security Administration provides an example in which Congress was the savior of a senior career official, threatened by a political appointee. The chief actuary of the SSA assesses the solvency of the Social Security program. Congress created the actuary's office and gave him independence from the SSA commissioner who might want to spin the data about the solvency of the Social Security fund for political purposes. Tension developed, and the commissioner tried to limit what the actuary said in public, but the actuary resisted.

The commissioner implied that the actuary was insubordinate. The actuary, with 37 years of service, pushed back, stating, "My goal is to maintain the absolute independence and integrity of the actuary's office. We do not countenance any influence of any type on our assumptions or our prognostications. Our estimates may not always be right, but they will never be biased."

Learning of the tensions between the two officials, chairs of powerful committees in Congress, with absolute power over SSA's budget, spoke loud and clear to the commissioner that he was not to reassign or demote the actuary.

The chair of the Ways and Means subcommittee on Social Security said, "Steve Goss personifies the meaning of public service. He is viewed broadly in the halls of Congress as a vital asset—a trustworthy source for confidential and honest analysis on which Congress relies to make sound policy decisions." Two additional and powerful Congressional chairs made similarly strong statements in support of the actuary.[124]

The commissioner had two options to wound the actuary. He could withhold end-of-year bonuses from the actuary; and, secondly, if he gave the actuary three successive poor performance ratings, he might be able to fire him for cause. However, in view of the support given the actuary by Congress, those actions might seem petty, and the commissioner might find the budget of SSA appropriated in a way that reduced the commissioner's options to manage the agency.

As the new GSA leaders prepared to testify before the Brooks Committee, my staff and I provided background materials and helped to draft their testimony. This gave us an opportunity to show our stuff and to develop relationships with the new leaders of the agency; and should your program be under attack, seek similar opportunities.

Although Congress can help save you and your program from precipitous action by new political appointees, you have a major responsibility in such a case.

The congressional committee responsible for creating your agency can be a great help and an important ally. At the same time, your agency pays your salary, has a right to expect you to operate above board, and alert senior officials early on to emerging problems likely to affect the reputation of the agency.

We elect candidates into political office hoping they share our values and will make good decisions. However, once in office, they often make decisions in ways we did not anticipate. When you work with political office holders, you can never be sure about their motivation, goals and perspectives about you and your program. Just be sure that you do not think you know what they know and how they are thinking.

Congressional members change their tune in various ways after voters put them in office.

- They can make decisions and vote for the good of their district, not the country.
- They can vote according to the platform they ran upon before the election.
- They can vote according to the polls of the voting public, whose opinions can be fickle or uninformed.
- They can vote in ways they hope will get them re-elected.
- They can make decisions and vote for the interests of special friends of their political party.
- They can vote influenced by money, benefits and future job opportunities hinted at by potential employers.

In real life, elected officials make decisions to hold hearings, support or fight agency regulations, and vote for legislation based on any or all six of these possibilities. Elected officials are flexible, if nothing else, when responding to the challenges and opportunities of the moment. What they say publicly, what they really feel and how they react in their official position are normally at odds with each other.

Here is an example of likely deception by a Congressional representative on behalf of his district. Ron Piasecki was one of our senior managers at GSA. At a staff meeting he reported about a Congressional hearing that he said had gone well the week before. Piasecki told us Senator Lightfoot (R-Iowa) praised GSA's performance at the hearing and in other public venues. This was important because Lightfoot was in charge of GSA's appropriations committee and played a leading role in determining whether the agency survived.

Iowa took a big step forward well in advance of any other government and wired the state with the most advanced telecommunications facilities available using federal money. The goal was to allow the state to provide improved education services to its citizens. After Iowa installed the system, state officials "discovered" they had a great deal of excess capacity. They asked the federal government to help Iowa's officials find reimbursable users to help pay for the operation of Iowa's new network. This was a reasonable step in view of the electronic traffic flowing between Iowa and the federal government.

Piasecki later reported that GSA and Lightfoot were working nicely together on the "Iowa Network." Twenty million dollars flowed into Iowa's network through GSA in an arrangement made the previous year by Lightfoot. Later, GSA senior officials were shocked to learn that Lightfoot had not allocated new money for the network; rather, he required GSA to redirect funds from its existing programs to subsidize the state network in Iowa.

The lesson here is to avoid dragging your agency into the pet projects of leaders in Congress. While you may think you are building an important relationship, Congressional leaders often search for ways to fund an initiative in their district. Too often, Congressional officials will find a way to make your agency pay from its existing funds rather than negotiating with their peers in the appropriations process.

Should you bring your agency into one of these arrangements you can be sure your boss and other agency managers will not think highly of you. Your reputation and ability to work in the political environment as a senior government official will deservedly suffer, as if you dragged an animal three days dead into the room.

Resisting Congress can be fatal to your career unless you are willing to negotiate. If Congress really wants it, and be sure they really do, try to compromise. Do not say "no" flat out and refuse to negotiate. Propose an alternative solution that will achieve their goal and maintain your program. The idea is to stay in the game, keep talking and cut the best deal you can for your program.

Before the Cuban missile crisis in the early 1960s, the government relied on AT&T to provide long distance telephone service for civilian agencies, the White House and miscellaneous Defense organizations. During the crisis, with telephone lines jammed, President Kennedy could not get a line to make a call outside the White House to obtain an assessment of the situation; nor could he direct the use of government resources in response to the crisis.

The result was to build the original Federal Telecommunication System (FTS). Brooks (D-Texas) placed the first call over the system on February 14, 1962. He called an assistant administrator in the Federal Aviation Administration's Los Angeles office. Speaking to the press after the call, Brooks said the service was fast and the cost was one-half the former commercial rate.

Eighteen years later, in 1980, FTS was out of date and costly. The commissioner at the time, Frank J. Carr, assigned several successive managers to try to assemble the government's requirements for the next 20 years. None was successful until Bernard Bennington accepted the assignment. Bennington built a consensus in GSA and in the agencies served by FTS for his approach to modernize FTS and provide the U.S. government with digital fiber-optic network capabilities, including voice, video, e-mail and high-speed data communications services.

After several years of intensive work by Bennington and his staff and shortly before GSA was ready to sign the contract, Brooks decided the award for FTS 2000 should go to the two finalists, AT&T and Sprint. Bennington resisted Brooks' decision, concluding it was wasteful for the government. Carr supported Bennington. Brooks demanded the administrator, Carr's boss, replace both men, and they were finished at GSA. When Bennington flat out resisted Congressman Brooks's demand to award the system to two contractors, he may have been right considering the government's requirements and the industry structure at the time. Today, however, GSA routinely awards to several contractors to meet the needs of the successor to FTS 2000.

It is vitally important to develop relations with congressional staffers with appropriation or oversight power over your program. This relationship needs to be more than a surface relationship; it needs to be deep enough so there is trust between you and the staff members. With trust, you can speak the truth as you see it even if it is not what the staffers want to hear. Easier said than done, you say. Here are some ways to do it that have worked for others.

An annual golf outing is a possibility. You can schedule it at a local public course. Pebble Beach is not necessary.

One federal official organized a weeklong field trip each year for key congressional staff so they could learn first-hand the results of the program their committee had authorized. During the trip, the congressional staffers had an opportunity to talk with the field managers of the agency program and to the users of the program, allowing the congressional staff members to make their own assessment of the value of the program.

One morning in California, the Executive branch people and the congressional staffers rose early for a quick tour down the famed 17-mile drive along the spectacular coastline from Pacific Grove to the famed Pebble Beach. Before sunrise, they bought pastries and coffee in Carmel. They were back at work by 8:30, having ensured their early morning trip was not at taxpayer expense.

On these trips, the group eats all meals together, and they get to know each other socially. Activities such as these can build trust, valuable to each party in the future back in Washington.

New officials appointed by the White House may forbid their senior career officials to have further discussions with their long-term contacts in Congress for three reasons.

They want to be in control and protect what they feel is their turf.

They have different objectives than the Congressional committees which oversee your agency's programs.

They feel that numerous people talking to Congress provides too many and sometimes conflicting messages; and this last concern is legitimate.

In such cases, it will be dangerous to go to the Hill. However, there are numerous opportunities to develop relationships or to share concerns through mutual friends, at Christmas parties, at retirement parties, at formal galas, in church, during golf outings and while speaking together on panels at one of the many conferences in Washington each day.

If Congress wants to use your program to deliver pork to their district or to the district of a Congressional colleague, you can attempt to negotiate.

Senior officials in all agencies will occasionally find themselves on the Hill trying to stop awards of pork through their agency budgets and programs. Even though you can demonstrate the disadvantage of bringing home the bacon to their district, Congressional officials may award it despite your best efforts. At this point, accept it. Congress controls the money and decides what to do with it.

The GAO developed a series of questions they feel Congress should ask agency program managers during hearings on the Hill. They are included here so that agency managers can be prepared to respond to such questions in testimony before Congress.[125]

Does a program's mission statement match the agency's statutory authority? If not, does it demonstrate that laws should be updated or even revised?

- Is another agency doing similar work? If so, are the two agencies working together to make the programs complementary?
- Does the agency's management plan reflect coordination with other agencies?
- Are the agency's goals and priorities consistent with Congress' priorities? If not, why do the differences exist, and can they be resolved?
- Are the program's strategies clearly linked to the agency's higher-level goals?

- How is the agency measuring progress?
- Has the agency been meeting its own performance targets?
- Will the performance targets enable Congress to meet its oversight responsibilities?

ADVICE TO BRIAN

Quietly develop working contacts and long-term allies with staff officials in Congress so they will be willing to help your program and your agency when you need their support. A career manager with good contacts in Congress developed over a period of many years is an asset for political appointees new to government, and they should use these contacts with confidence, not fear.

Enlightened and confident political appointees will use long-time agency officials with well-developed contacts to handle most issues arising between the agency and its Congressional appropriators and overseers. They reserve themselves or the agency head, the top dog, for the toughest issues, requiring a face-to-face meeting with the committee chair.

Senior congressional staffers can help you to sell the administration's initiatives if they feel you are being honest in your explanation of the program's business case and goals. They are more likely to believe a person with whom they have had prior good experiences than a new White House ideologue with a PowerPoint slide presentation.

Follow three steps.

Keep the Congressional Affairs Office in your agency informed. They may use your information in discussions during the agency head's staff meetings, which they, not you, attend. Importantly, they will receive feedback from the top boss, and later, they can share it with you.

Invite senior Congressional Affairs officials to your meetings on the Hill.

Even better, ask them to schedule the meeting on the Hill after you have greased the skids with congressional staff members.

33

Using Regulatory Authority to Change a Program's Direction

Frank,

Okay, I understand that working with Congress can be a full-time job. Are there other ways to get things done without waiting for Congress to pass a law? Earlier we saw how the White House and Congress implement change. What about me? Will I be able to use the power of rules and regulations to further my program? Is this a possibility?

Yes, you can issue a federal regulation if your organization is one of the many agencies with regulatory power. A little background at this point will help you in the future.

More than one hundred federal agencies have economic, environmental, safety, health and other regulatory power under law.[126] In one year, they issued 2,926 final rules with the power of law, while Congress enacted 138 laws in the same year. In addition, to enforce their regulations, agencies conducted 939,000 adjudicatory proceedings, while federal judges conducted "only" 95,000 adjudicatory proceedings including actual laws in 2007.[127]

In industries based on technology and in the technology industry itself, companies move faster than the government can regulate, so the government is often playing catch-up. This may require writing new regulations, amending older regulations; or it may simply require enforcing existing regulations.

The many sectors in the economy regulated by the government may surprise you. Here are a few.

Agriculture
Environment
Food and drugs
Banks and banking
Occupational safety
Commerce and foreign trade
Patents, trademarks and copyrights
Commodity and security exchanges

You can access federal regulations on the Internet at regulations.gov. You can also use this site to search and review original regulatory documents, as well as comments submitted by others.

Government laws and regulations have several purposes:

- Control behaviors in society
- Maintain competition in each market
- Punish enemies of the current administration
- Protect consumers from companies that grow too powerful and treat the consumer in an abusive way

For example, President Obama used the regulatory power of the SEC to investigate Standard & Poor's after the firm downgraded the credit of the U.S. in August 2011 and created a political problem for the president. S&P, demonstrating unusual courage, ignored earlier private arm twisting by the White House and the Treasury Department and decided that the size of the U.S. debt justified ignoring the government pressure. The brave people in S&P took on the legal and regulatory power of the government despite the possible future consequences.[128]

The interests of industry and government are not the same, despite those who talk about a partnership between these two sectors of society. Companies seek greater dominance in their marketplace and more profit. Their natural goal is to control 100 percent of their market. The government seeks to limit a single company's dominance while protecting the interests of the American public—at least this is the goal some of the time.

The trick is to find the right balance. Too much regulation can doom an industry sector. Too little regulation, or regulations not enforced, can benefit the bottom line of companies, but bring pain to the American public.

Our country goes in cycles with tight regulations for years followed by long periods of loose and unenforced regulations.

We have been in the latter period since the early 1980s, when corporate leaders in America sought and over time obtained greater independence from government regulations in banking and finance, environmental practices, labor practices, discrimination and other facets of American life. Corporate leaders argued that government should get off the backs of industry, repeal regulations and let the nation's corporations proceed more freely to create the wealth they promised for the nation.

They found a sympathetic ear in President Ronald Reagan, and change began and continues. Government regulations were either repealed or barely enforced. New laws aimed at unions limited their ability to balance the ascendance of corporate power.

All went well for a while, at least for the corporations; but three financial crises occurred in a twenty-year period.

In the late 1980s the Savings and Loan industry collapsed after operating for a decade under the new freedom granted by the White House and Congress. Seven hundred and forty-five financial firms failed, and many more teetered on the edge of failure, requiring massive bailouts organized by the government and funded by the American taxpayers.

Then in 2001, the dot-com bubble burst, wiping out many fledgling companies with unrealistic dreams of Internet business. Rapidly increasing stock prices, unrealistic predictions about future profits, individual speculation in stocks and widely available venture capital encouraged many investors to overlook traditional price-to-earnings ratios in favor of the power of new technology to create riches.

Again, in 2007 in another financial crisis, housing prices collapsed, requiring the federal government to bail out many legendary firms, particularly banking and financial management companies on Wall Street.

Leading up to the housing bubble in the U.S., people with no documented employment and little income could obtain a large mortgage, for example, $500,000, and then get a home equity loan for a new vehicle, a cruise or college for a child.

Many associated with home mortgages, including real estate agents, settlement attorneys, lawyers, mortgage companies, banks, Wall Street investment houses, Fannie Mae and Freddie Mac, benefitted in a somewhat unregulated market by not asking questions about whether the mortgagee really qualified for these loans and whether there was any possibility they could make the payments; and many could not and did not. All parties associated with home mortgages happily took their cut from each approved mortgage, ignoring the problems they were creating for their fellow citizens and the country.

Wall Street, which had long derided federal government regulations, turned to the government in the market crash in 2008, because only the government could save Wall Street from its excesses. One estimate of the cost to the taxpayer through 2009 was $4.28 trillion dollars, more than what was spent on World War II, adjusted for inflation.[129]

To sell the bailout programs to the American people, the government claimed the companies saved by the bailout programs would repay significant amounts sometime in an unspecified future, and some did.

The five largest firms on Wall Street, previously unregulated, disappeared, or their character was materially changed. Conditions forced Bear Stearns to sell itself at fire sale prices to J.P. Morgan. Lehman Brothers filed for bankruptcy, was divided into three pieces and sold. With the federal government working behind the scene, Merrill Lynch sold itself to Bank of America, also at fire sale prices. The government temporarily nationalized AIG to save the world's largest insurance company, which itself insured many of the products of Wall Street's giants. Goldman Sachs and Morgan Stanley had near-death experience, necessitating revival by the federal government, which allowed them to turn themselves into regulated banks, becoming in the process eligible for government insurance programs backing investors.

Fannie Mae and Freddie Mac, owners of half of all the mortgages issued in the U.S., came under tighter federal control despite the efforts of their many well-paid lobbyists and friends in Congress. As they faced collapse, the federal government ploughed billions into Fannie Mae and Freddie Mac, and the U.S. Treasury placed them into conservatorship in September 2008, assigning the Federal Housing Finance Agency (FHFA) to oversee the two organizations.

Fifteen months later, in December 2009, as their balance sheets continued to degrade with ever-larger amounts of red ink, the Treasury announced it would provide unlimited funds to ensure these government giants dominating the mortgage industry would not fail. The concern was that failure of Fannie Mae and Freddie Mac would reduce the value of the housing inventory of countless banks, raising the possibility of the failure of hundreds, if not thousands of banks.[130]

In 2012, Treasury Secretary Geithner proposed a slow process that would kill off the big government mortgage operations. We need to "substantially reduce the government's footprint in the housing market," said Geithner.[131] In 2014, both were profitable, and the pressure to reduce the footprint was easing. In 2015, killing off the two giants had not happened, although discussions continued across Washington.

However, regulations are powerful and can be beneficial to the American public on a case-by-case basis. Once issued by an agency, other affected agencies and industry must follow them, as they must also follow laws, assuming that the issuing agency follows up and enforces its rule, not always the case. If there is follow-up, the government may level criminal charges when regulated parties do not respect the rules. Additionally, companies may sue if a competitor does not follow a regulation and gains an advantage.

Do you remember the 2006 cases of E. coli sickness contracted from contaminated California spinach? Some 50 cases of sickness broke out in nine states. It fell to the FDA to identify the source and to reassure the public that things were, or soon would be, under control. The FDA, working with the federal Centers for Disease

Control and Prevention in Atlanta, discovered the source of the poisoning. FDA then issued regulations to industry producers of fresh spinach and guidance to consumers to halt the spread of the outbreak, prevent another and by its actions encourage Americans to resume eating spinach.

Despite FDA's important role in protecting the health of the American public, companies and elected officials constantly bring pressure on the FDA to speed up its product reviews, to lighten up on inspections and to write accommodating regulations. Some members of Congress have deliberately kept FDA weak, reducing its ability to review products, thereby allowing companies more freedom with their products.

For years, Congress has kept the FDA budget smaller than necessary while freely adding new responsibilities. The Bioterrorism Act of 2002, for example, saddled FDA with new duties related to the protection, safety and security of the nation's food and drug supply. However, the agency's budget remains tiny compared with its responsibilities, on par with some rural county school systems.

Consider that FDA performed 50,000 food inspections in 1972 and only 5,000 in 2006. At this rate, the FDA inspects each U.S. food processor about once every 10 years. Inspection of an overseas food producer, the source of much of America's food, is a remote possibility, as likely as a Martian spaceship landing in your front yard.[132]

Foreign manufacturers produce most of the raw materials for our drugs, and FDA rarely inspects them. If you think FDA is inspecting your pacemaker, heart valve, microwave oven or morning vitamin, forget it; not a possibility.

Soon, gene therapy will merge with nanotechnology and robotics, creating medical solutions and unintended consequences. Ahead is the day when the majority of our foods and vegetables will come from as many as 130 other countries, including some with dubious leadership and major social problems. The public faces great dangers if Congress continues to favor profits for American importers and technology behemoths instead of public safety.

In the transportation sector, the National Transportation Safety Board investigates accidents involving planes, trains, boats and cars and proposes ways to avoid them. Lacking enforcement power, the board works with agencies that do have the power to implement the board's recommendations.

However, there is a tradeoff between public safety and the cost to the carrier or industry. If the board's recommendation would cost the transportation industry money, some 2,000 registered lobbyists spending $243 million in 2009 worked on behalf of the industry, not to kill the proposal because the recommendation was sound, but to muddle and confuse the debate and delay any resolution, perhaps indefinitely.

For example, the FAA has been considering NTSB's recommendations to prevent icing on aircraft wings for 30 years, while more than 700 people died in icing accidents. There are other examples in the transportation industry in which delayed regulations resulted in deaths.[133]

Even when there is no resistance from industry or unions, issuing a new regulation can take five years. To make it more difficult for his agencies to exercise regulatory authority provided by Congress, President George W. Bush issued an executive order in January 2007, placing political appointees in charge of all regulatory activity in each agency. The new order required regulatory officials in all agencies to obtain approval from this official in their agency before beginning work on a new regulation.

In addition, the OMB's Office of Information and Regulatory Affairs (OIRA) reviews and approves any agency's regulatory activity with a potential annual effect of only $100 million or more on the public, ensuring that OIRA reviews virtually all of the government's proposed regulations.

The Union of Concerned Scientists believes this authority allows OIRA even more latitude to delay endlessly proposed regulations intended to protect the American public. Another White House effort to bring independent regulatory agencies under the control of OIRA caused some 50 prominent organizations to protest that such action was not in the best interests of the American public.[134]

The Clinger-Cohen Act nullified regulatory policies in IT and telecommunications, which GSA had carefully built up in 34 years, and replaced them with a series of always-evolving processes and policies. Did Clinger-Cohen cause improvements in the delivery of major systems? Well, it all depends on the measures you choose. In general, things are no better or worse in the delivery of complex systems. Today, the high-dollar systems fail in part or completely with regularity, as they have for 40 years.

Enacting regulations or legislation to control a selected industry's activities is never an easy battle. Industry employs lobbyists and lawyers to fight for regulations they want and fight even harder against those they do not want, as President Obama learned when revamping the nation's health delivery system. Pharmaceutical companies, health insurance companies, hospital management companies, their lobbyists and others in the fragmented health industry ganged up to limit the reach of the president's proposed plan. Moreover, even after a bill passed, some continued to work to repeal it.

In other cases, companies often seek and get a national regulation to trump regulations and laws passed by state governments. It is easier for companies to influence one short-term political appointee in Washington than multiple officials in 50 state governments.

Alternatively, if a federal agency proposes a hard-hitting regulation, corporate representatives will switch sides to defeat the proposal by campaigning for states' rights and state, not federal, regulations. Corporate officials will invoke the Constitution and the wisdom of our Founding Fathers as they lobby for state, not federal regulation. On a case-by-case basis, it suits their financial interests to play one level of government against another.

Each administration manages the regulatory process to ensure that regulations conform to the party's ideology and to the demands of its campaign supporters.

Presidents attempt to control regulations in several ways by appointing people who are:

- In synch with the president's sentiments
- Totally opposed to regulations in general
- Sympathetic to an industry they will regulate
- Indecisive, wary of hard work, and bureaucratic infighting

George W. Bush made an appointment very much in harmony with his sentiments when he gave a recess appointment to Susan Dudley to lead the Office of Information and Regulatory Affairs (OIRA) after the Senate refused to confirm her. Dozens of interest groups opposed her nomination, believing she was deeply hostile to regulatory safeguards. In addition, they suspected she brought a radical agenda to an obscure but incredibly powerful office.

One of those groups, Citizens for Sensible Safeguards, emphasized Dudley's previous opposition to regulations to control arsenic levels in drinking water, require air bags in cars and inform the public about industry-produced toxins in communities.[135]

Presidents have another important tool to use when developing regulations to implement new laws created by Congress. When a president signs a new law created by Congress, he may object to its contents. Then he will issue a *signing statement*, which revises the intent of Congress. The signing statement gives the president's administration flexibility to implement the new law, often in ways that will cause Congress to howl. Signing statements accomplish three things:

- To claim that the law is constitutionally defective, enabling the president to be interpretive when implementing the law
- To redefine vague terms to provide him and his administration additional flexibility during implementation of the law
- To use the signing of the bill to mobilize political constituencies

George W. Bush used signing statements to challenge some 1,200 provisions of 172 laws that he signed. This was twice as many as all of his predecessors combined. President Obama continued to use signing statements, although not as many as President Bush.

Obama used his earlier signing statement to avoid the requirements of a law in the case of the release of Army Sgt. Bowe Bergdahl by the Taliban. In return for the release, Obama freed five Taliban terrorists from Guantanamo Bay prison. In this controversial decision—Bergdahl went missing from his colleagues under mysterious circumstances, and the Taliban held him for five years—Obama referred to his signing statement and ignored a provision in the 2014 National Defense Authorization Act requiring the Secretary of Defense to notify relevant Congressional committees by at least 30 days before transferring anyone from Guantanamo Bay.[136]

Here are three examples when the George W. Bush administration used questionable judgment to enforce its legislative responsibilities.

The Minerals Management Service allowed drillers to fill out their own inspection reports, leading to disastrous oil spills.

When banks began to provide home loans to borrowers with poor credit and no money for a down payment, the Office of Thrift Supervision in its regulatory role endorsed the approach, as did other federal regulatory agencies, contributing to the six-year financial crisis that began in 2007.

The SEC and the Financial Industry Regulatory Authority, the industry-run watchdog for brokerage firms, probed Bernie Madoff at least eight times in 16 years and could not identify fraud. Yet, as the case broke in 2008, Madoff admitted his fraud. FBI agents described the 30-year Ponzi scheme as the largest financial fraud in U.S. history.

Note also that the George W, Bush White House and the Republican congressional leadership in the Obama administration kept the SEC weak and understaffed, limiting the ability of the agency to pursue investigations.[137]

Let us look at what can be the weakness of the regulatory process implementing laws to protect the American people. The Dodd-Frank Act, known as the Wall Street Reform Act, the biggest overhaul of U.S. financial regulations since the 1930s, contains more than 90 provisions that require SEC rule making and dozens of other provisions that give the SEC discretionary rulemaking authority. Congress passed this law responding to the collapse of the nation's financial system following the absurd practices of Wall Street and all financial institutions as they created the credit bubble that burst on the scene in 2007, affecting almost every person and organization in the country and some overseas for a decade.

Congress gets kudos from the public when the president

signs an act into law amid media hype. Later, when it is time to implement the new law, Congress may not provide the resources to do the job. This was the situation in Dodd-Frank because Congress did not provide reasonable resources to the SEC, keeping their financial industry campaign contributors happy, providing yet another example of spin at the highest level and ensuring a win-win for all parties except the investing public.

During the George W. Bush administration the SEC budget was frozen or cut between fiscal years 2005 and 2007, and it did not return to the 2005 level until 2010, where it has remained, ensuring that the SEC could not truly regulate the nation's financial industry.

In the Madoff case, the second Bush administration was selectively unwilling to enforce regulations, and Congress was unwilling to provide adequate resources to the enforcement responsibilities of the SEC. Were these actions a factor allowing Madoff to swindle so many for so long?

SEC Chair Mary Schapiro testified in 2011 that the agency needed about 780 people to implement and enforce the Dodd-Frank reform law—and it needed more of the latest technology to compete with such things as the hedge funds use of advanced technology and algorithms. Until we have the resources, we can write the implementing regulations, but we will not be able to enforce them, she testified. "No matter how strong the rules are, we will have non-compliance" [unless we can enforce them].[138]

As the Republican Party took control of the House of Representatives and the Senate in 2015, many in the party vowed to overturn Dodd-Frank so that Wall Street and financial institutions could return to the freedoms they had prior to 2007 when the economy collapsed.

For almost thirty years, the government patronized Wall Street and corporate leaders with easy money and limited regulation, and it "got off the back" of corporate America, resulting in three economic fiascos in a short period of two decades. These cost many Americans their jobs, their retirement nest eggs and, in many cases, a large portion of their savings.

ADVICE TO BRIAN

In my organization regulating technology acquisitions, we often issued guidance, rather than a new regulation. Guidance is easier, faster to develop and simpler to issue than a new regulation. Guidance is the best approach in a fast-moving field when a major issue surfaces, requiring a quick response by the government. Later, when government officials understand the issue in all of its dimensions, they can draft a regulation.

If the problem you are trying to solve requires a regulation, expect to spend one to five years from the point where you sit down at your keyboard until all parties approve the regulation and you publish it in the Code of Federal Regulations. Then again, your regulatory work may be destined for a dark corner in a seldom-opened closet.

I leave this discussion reminding you of two final points. You can sometimes treat government policies cavalierly. However, do not ignore regulations. They have the power of law unless a sitting president opposes regulations and government officials do not enforce regulations already on the books, which often happens with Republican presidents.

The highly political world of federal regulations should convince you to seek a job in a non-regulatory agency; and it should sensitize you to the problems you will face implementing regulations to guide companies and protect the public as you place your new system in operation.

34

USING POLICY AUTHORITY TO CHANGE DIRECTION

Frank,
Aside from reorganizing and issuing regulations,
are there other ways that I can make major program
changes?

Yes, you can initiate change by issuing a policy decision, although it will not be easy if the policy will affect other agencies or companies.

One example reveals the complexity of policymaking. The good news is that it is hard work to create a government-wide policy, and that is as it should be.

Many federal agency managers are policymakers. In the GSA, we had the authority to help disabled federal employees to obtain the same desktop computer technology as everyone else. In the early days of graphical user interfaces (GUI)—the technology that lets us intuitively and easily navigate our computer and cell phone screens—was a real issue. Judge Leonard Suchanek, Chair of GSA's Board of Contract Appeals, himself blind, told me on several occasions that 80 percent of the disabled people in the country are unemployed, and those with jobs are underutilized.

When a contingent representing blind federal employees in Massachusetts travelled from Boston to meet with us, they gently chastised us for not using our legislative authorities to ensure that workers with vision impairments could use computers with GUI interfaces, the same as all other government employees.

In this case, the software manufacturer, for whatever reason, had not been a good citizen. Two years earlier, in a quasi-hearing, which Suchanek and I co-chaired, company officials said they were aware of the problems blind employees had with their software. They assured us they would solve the problem, but obviously, they had not followed through on their promise.

GSA, as a regulatory agency, always operated behind the screen, never seeking publicity. However, GSA had a big stick: We could prohibit the company from selling its software in the federal government, as Massachusetts itself was apparently prepared to do. However, as always in GSA, we preferred to use our authority as a last resort; negotiation was our preferred route.

In this case, we had recently contacted the company representative in Washington to express our displeasure, since the company after two years had not fixed the problem. Our next step was to meet with other company officials, those with authority to fix the problem.

At times like this, companies try to steer you to their public relations and Washington liaisons. Sometimes it is okay to work with these officials. Sometimes, it is not. In this case, these officials were not decision-makers and could only carry the message back, possibly with spin, to someone else higher up in the company.

We wanted a specific corporate commitment to solve the problem and a quarterly plan to develop the needed accessibility products in the software. We did not want to wait until they had a single, all-in-one, final solution that could take years. We wanted intermediate solutions as evidence of progress. If not, we could, as a last resort, freeze the company out of the federal market. Today, it is inconceivable that a government official could stop a leading manufacturer from selling its software to federal agencies. At the time, it was quite possible for three reasons.

Our legislative power in GSA was secure.

There was a high level of interest in the country and in the government to address the problems of the disabled in society.

The disabled community itself was large and sufficiently organized to create a public protest. For example, the hearing-impaired community once demonstrated on Capitol Hill when it felt Congress was ignoring their needs in emerging technology. Congress quickly enacted legislation and assigned my office a role in implementation.

At the time, the company and most software manufacturers operated as if Washington did not matter. Later, in 1998, the Justice Department got their attention with a massive anti-trust lawsuit. Today, the company has a major presence in the nation's capital, with lawyers and lobbyists representing their interests. The company now makes generous campaign contributions.

While we were not directly successful in our efforts to ensure timely accessibility for the blind, there are some important lessons to learn from this experience.

Senior policy officials with government-wide responsibilities have so many issues to address, they cannot cover them all equally well. In this case, Suchanek and I let too much time pass after first talking to company representatives. We had a good plan of action, but companies with only one major issue with the government can outlast government officials occupied with many issues. If the employees from Massachusetts had not asked us to put pressure on the company, we might never have returned to the issue and pushed the company to live up to the promises they made two years earlier.

While we brought attention to the problem, the company solved the problem on their schedule, not ours.

FOUR POINTS TO CONSIDER BEFORE TAKING POLICY ACTION AGAINST A COMPANY

Carefully choose the time to act—timing is critical. Do not expect much support from the White House if you take action against a major company shortly before a presidential election.

Evaluate whether you have the time to see the issue through to the end, considering all of the other issues you need to manage.

Send measured signals rather than taking precipitous action likely to cause the company to rush into an ill-conceived attack from which they will be unable to back down later when they have time to consider an appropriate response.

Measured signals could include discussing the issue with an industry association. The association can provide useful insights into the market sector, and its representatives will carry your concern to the selected company, allowing its officials time to conceive possible corrective actions.

A second measured signal before going public is to schedule a private meeting in your office with company representatives to emphasize the government's increasing concern.

Line up support before firing the first shot if forceful action is still required. Support could come from other companies harmed competitively by the company against which you plan to take action. Better yet, a committee in Congress which has been tracking the issue could provide the support you need. In addition, you will need support from your boss because when the going gets tough, you will need your management to hang in there with you. However, you should not count on this.

35

INTRODUCING PROCUREMENT, A PRIMER FOR PROGRAM MANAGERS

Frank,
Would you talk some more about procurement and
the various requirements and minefields I should be
watching for?

Procurement, also called sourcing, is the acquisition of goods and services by government from companies.

Goods procurements acquire products such as computers and off-the-shelf shrink-wrapped mass-market software.

Service procurements acquire the personnel and other items needed to develop a new tax system, model a new weather prediction system, manage a computer data center and hundreds of other requirements.

Government sourcing is big business. It directly creates ten million private sector jobs, and it makes some people wealthy. Therefore, many try to get an edge in government procurements.

There are two phases to the procurement cycle.

In the first phase, the job is to get the contract awarded.

Agencies work energetically to award the contract on schedule. They will marginalize the rules within the limits of the regulation or law to make a timely award.

In the second phase, managing the contract after award, things begin to fall apart. Most of an agency's energy goes into awarding the contract on time. In managing the contractor after award, few agencies do a good job all the time.

Procurement regulations began in the Federal government in earnest during the Civil War when private sector suppliers sold moldy blankets and non-firing gunpowder to the government. American companies made fortunes supplying inadequate products during wartime. Congress and President Lincoln established the National Academy of Sciences in 1863 to provide objective, scientific information to the government.

The Federal Acquisition Regulation (FAR) governing federal procurement contains about 2,000 pages with hundreds of procurement regulations providing uniform policies for the acquisition of goods and services by the Federal government.

Three officials, the Secretary of Defense, the Administrator of General Services and the Administrator, National Aeronautics and Space Administration, jointly manage and update the FAR under authorities granted by Congress. They in turn delegate their authority to the Procurement Executives in their agencies.

Procurement is like getting married. At first, there is a lot of planning. Then the two parties sign a contract. After the big day, there will be disagreements from time to time, sometimes serious, requiring arbitration or judicial decisions.

Virtually, every new program in the government requires technology, normally obtained in major, high-dollar service procurements. You will find the procurement process to be frustrating, challenging and incomprehensible, and it can be dangerous to your career and freedom. There is much to know, and you will never know enough.

Once, when driving from Nice in the south of France to Monaco for an afternoon of sightseeing and a tour of the Casino, a woman clipped my right rear bumper, creating minor, almost invisible damage. She was Italian, and there we stood in the square with cars whizzing by on both sides, while we attempted to negotiate the proceedings that our insurance companies had taught us. We were both calm but struggled to understand each other. Hand gestures added to the confusion. An English-speaking American negotiating a minor accident in France with an Italian-speaking driver resembles situations you will face in federal procurement—government and contractors speak earnestly, but past each other.

To navigate through the mountains of laws, regulations and policies, you will need a true procurement specialist to sit at your right hand. In personnel language, these specialists are *1102s*. Be careful about your choice of a guide. The procurement policy official in each agency might be your first choice. This would be a mistake. These officials are by law required to be political appointees. Unfortunately, they generally are short on knowledge about federal procurement regulations. In some cases, the White House chose them because of campaign contributions or voluntary work done during the election campaign.

The Executive Leadership Conference outlined additional sourcing problems as follows:[139]

"Acquisition continues to be buffeted by forces often at odds with each other. The need for rapid implementation of innovative and creative IT solutions often conflicts with a relatively inflexible acquisition process."

Oversight bodies seek to ensure an open, fair and competitive process for the benefit of all, but their intense scrutiny has also hampered responsiveness.

The high cost of bidding and subsequent protests prevent many companies from competing in government procurements.

While you will never become a procurement expert, you will need to listen to those that are, but ultimately you will need to stop listening and make some decisions about the management aspects (not the regulatory aspects) of a procurement.

THREE CLUSTERS OF AGENCIES LEAD FEDERAL PROCUREMENT

DOD

The Department of Defense has 152,000 procurement officials and an extensive process-oriented training program designed to eliminate judgment. For the massive, worldwide DOD this may be the best approach.

Homeland Security

The sprawling Department of Homeland Security has procurement processes and many procurement officials in its 22 agencies. However, its political appointees that control the procurement programs remain on the job only an average of nine months. Short tenures are disruptive in long-term procurements, sometimes extending 10 years from concept development to the end of the contract.

It takes a minimum of one year for a newly assigned program manager to study and understand a complex, high-dollar program.

Two years are required to make significant changes and see them through to implementation.

Four years are required to make final changes and ensure the changes survive one's departure.

Political appointees in procurement jobs in Homeland Security should be required to remain on the job for 48 months. A 4-year commitment will weed out those simply seeking to include a high-level government job on their resume. In addition, a 4-year commitment signals to lower-level career officials that they cannot wait out the political appointee.

All other agencies

In the dozens of other agencies, procurement abilities are sometimes excellent, sometimes not.

Inconsistent procurement skills frustrate many newcomers, including retired military officers crossing over to civilian agencies after retirement. They are accustomed to a hierarchical, structured environment, which often eliminates judgment, not the frontier Wild West environment found in some recently established civilian agencies.

NEGOTIATED CONTRACTS VERSUS GSA SCHEDULES AND GWACS PROCUREMENTS

When the government needs hundred million-dollar and multi-billion-dollar systems, negotiated contracts are required. Companies fight hard for these awards because one major contract can sustain a company for years.

Negotiated contracts take months, sometimes years to award, and they are costly to bid. Fifteen million-dollar bid preparation costs are not unusual. Some federal procurement opportunities require a company to spend one hundred million dollars to develop a proposal and take a chance on winning a big one. Only a few companies have the resources to bid on the government's largest requirements.

The GSA Schedules Program (also referred to as Multiple Award Schedules and Federal Supply Schedules) offer an alternative to negotiated contracts. Over ten million commercial products and services are available directly from 18,000 preselected GSA schedule contractors or through *GSA Advantage!*®—the online shopping and ordering system. GSA negotiates prices, terms and conditions, relieving buying agencies of this burden. Use of GSA Schedules allows agencies to meet small business goals and comply with the various environmental and socioeconomic laws and regulations governing procurements.

Using these vehicles, agencies avoid the time-consuming requirements of negotiated contracts while receiving direct delivery of state-of-the-art, high-quality commercial supplies and services at volume discount prices. Agencies recognize the advantage of these vehicles. For example in 1995, 26 percent of procurement actions required a negotiated procurement, whereas in 2011, only 0.5 percent did. [140]

Negotiated contracts can require perhaps 450 hours of a procurement specialist's time for a plain-vanilla transaction. Several thousand hours can be required for the government's more complex systems acquisitions.[141]

Government Wide Acquisition Contracts (GWACS), managed by agencies such as the Department of Transportation, NASA, the National Institutes of Health and the Veterans Administration, provide additional alternatives to negotiated contracts.

Some GWACS are specialized. For example, the Veterans Administration runs VETS GWACS for veteran-owned firms. SEWP, managed by NASA, provides access broadly to hardware and services similar to, but is not as encompassing, as the GSA schedules contracts. Government and industry officials compliment SEWP as being as easy as the Marx Brothers' duck soup. In 2014, after being in business for 23 years, 97 federal agencies were SEWP customers buying $2.35 billion from 4,700 companies with some 2.7 million unique products available from SEWP.[142]

GSA Schedules and GWACS contracts are favorite choices for agencies because they are faster and allow lower transaction costs for the buyer and the seller. These procurement vehicles are available to all agencies and, in certain cases, to state and local governments.

Many companies survive because of their sales under the GSA Schedules and GWACS procurement vehicles. Without them, the largest companies would crowd out all but the Small Business Administration (SBA) qualified companies. In this sense, the GSA Schedules and agency GWACS are levelers of the playing field. In addition, they are the best choice in emergencies such as Hurricane Katrina when fast action is required.

GSA Schedules and GWACs contracts are licenses to hunt. Companies work hard to qualify to sell under these procurement vehicles. Then, they need to prowl in each agency to find the business. This can be expensive and difficult for smaller firms unable to employ sufficient representatives to market to the 128 federal agencies. As a result, only about 44 percent of the 5,000 companies on GSA's large schedule 70 receive awards in any given year. The other 56 percent receive no orders from the government

ANOTHER ALTERNATIVE IS THE SMALL BUSINESS ADMINISTRATION

All government contracts for supplies, equipment and services valued over $500,000 and all construction contracts over $1,000,000 must set aside some business for small companies. Large companies receive credits against legislative hiring quotas when they award business to smaller companies in the set-aside programs.

The goal of SBA's Disadvantaged Business Enterprise (DBE) program is to create opportunities for small businesses owned by Asians, Blacks, Hispanics, Native Americans, Pacific Islanders, subcontinent Asians, Women and other minority groups. In addition, there is a set-aside program for military veterans. Government managers can make quick awards to these favored groups, avoiding the time-consuming restrictions regulations placed on regular procurements.

In a program built on trust, companies self-certify themselves as small businesses, not always justified.

PROCUREMENT WORKFORCE PROBLEMS

Over the years, Democrats and Republicans alike have weakened the federal procurement community in three ways:

- By making it an upward mobility series in which people with limited backgrounds can progress
- By arbitrarily reducing the number of contracting officers and assistants
- By advocating the outsourcing of acquisition jobs that the government could use to train future contracting officers

The government has reduced the federal acquisition workforce by 50 percent, while the government's contracting workload increased 1,000 percent according to a senior DOD procurement official. The results of industry lobbying and political workforce decisions guarantee that contracting officials cannot do a good job in all cases; and a weakened, overworked procurement community gives companies a stronger hand during contract negotiations and contract management after award.[143]

Federal procurement officials negotiate and sign the contracts, committing the government to agreements often reaching hundreds of billions of dollars. However, procurement officials are not highly regarded by political appointees, who view them as back-office functionaries. For example, in one year contracts and grant awards swallowed 83 percent of the State

Department's requested budget, 82 percent of DOD's budget and 99 percent of USAID's budget.[144]

In addition, contractors perform 90 percent of the work at NASA and the Department of Energy. Yet, the procurement function in these agencies is located four levels down in the hierarchy with little or no access to agency leadership.

Peter Levine, general counsel on the Senate Armed Services Committee, suggested eliminating procurement abuses by rebuilding the workforce. DOD must restore the workforce to improve the management of government contracting, and it would take at least 15 years to do so, he said. There is no quick fix.

Levine also suggested eliminating abuses caused when agencies hire unqualified people. President Obama reversed recent presidents when he directed that in-sourcing become a priority, including in-sourcing of government contracting jobs. Progress was slow because people acquire contracting skills during a career, not overnight. Eventually, the administration gave up on in-sourcing as a priority.[145]

THE BID PROTEST PROCESS

Bid protests by companies can add a year or more to major acquisitions. Government procurement systems in the United States and in other countries allow vendors to challenge procurement awards when they believe government officials did not conduct an acquisition lawfully or in accordance with regulations or policy. The intent of the process is to bring transparency and accountability to government procurement actions.

Since Congress eliminated GSA's Board of Contract Appeals in 1997, the GAO hears all bid protests by companies. The GAO hears some 2,500 cases each year and rules in favor of protesting companies 20 percent of the time. In addition, GAO dismisses 20 percent of the cases on procedural rules or because a company withdraws its protest. Other protests are resolved through mediation before GAO reaches a decision.[146]

COMPANIES HAVE FOUR INCENTIVES TO PROTEST PROCUREMENTS

They may get a second chance to bid.

They may feel the agency treated them unfairly.

They have nothing to lose because there are no penalties.

Their bid protest costs will be reimbursed by the government if they win the protest.

In addition, companies currently under contract protest to delay an award so they can continue to work while the protest is resolved. In one case, the GSA continued to pay the incumbent contractor for three years while the same company kept the procurement tied up with successive bid protests.

In another case, the Transportation Security Agency awarded a $489 million contract to Computer Sciences Corporation in May 2010. Unisys, which had held the contract since 2002, protested the TSA action three times after 2008:

- When it failed to make the final cut of eligible bidders
- When TSA awarded the contract to CSC the first time in September 2009
- When TSA awarded the contract to CSC the second time in May 2010

While Unisys may have had legitimate reasons for their three protests, they were able to remain on contract receiving income for at least an additional 11 months.[147]

FEWER COMPETITORS FOR MAJOR GOVERNMENT PROCUREMENTS

Major companies continue to buy their smaller competitors, further reducing competition. Midsize companies with one billion dollars in annual sales to the federal government are too small to compete with the major companies. Don Orkand owned a midsized company providing IT services to the federal government for 34 years. He observed that medium-sized companies (up to $1 billion in annual sales) are caught in the middle and are being frozen out of the government market by the actions of the major systems integrators and by the set-aside rules giving special preference to small companies run by minorities, veterans, women and others. He told me that medium-size companies have three choices: grow substantially, sell out or eventually go out of business.

The biggest companies encourage the government to bundle their requirements into mega-procurements, which they alone have the resources to bid. This is not in the government's interests because when only a few companies compete, the likely result is higher costs and programs too big to fail. Proposed legislation in 2015 attempted to curtail the bundling problem.

Unfortunately, the number of major competitors declines each year, as the remaining majors digest their competitors and midsize companies. In 2008, for example, Hewlett Packard acquired EDS. Before the acquisition, EDS and its subsidiaries employed about 139,500 people worldwide, and HP itself employed about 172,000 workers. While HP was marginally in the services business as well as in product development, the EDS acquisition allowed HP to offer more services and compete with the services leader, IBM.

The result is one less major competitor available to compete for the billion-dollar systems jobs in the federal government. In a sense an old boys club—one official labeled it a cartel—is becoming a reality.[148]

POLITICS CAN PREVAIL OVER GOOD PROCUREMENT DECISIONS

In one example, the Air Force went through the required complex procurement process to buy the next generation of airborne tankers to refuel its long-range bombers and fighters. The Air Force awarded to Northrop Grumman apparently in part because it bid newer technology and more capability than Boeing. Boeing launched a multimillion-dollar advertising and public relations campaign and encouraged members of Congress from states where Boeing has manufacturing plants to weigh in on their behalf.

At the request of Congress, the GAO evaluated the case and concluded the Boeing protest had merit and advised the Air

Force to reopen the competition. Later, the Bush administration decided it would kick the can down the road and let the incoming Obama administration handle the politics of the matter.

There are two things to remember about this Air force case.

There are thousands of pages of acquisition policies and regulations. In considering a bid protest, it is easy to find some "Is" not dotted and some "Ts" not crossed.

The GAO, in its reviews for Congress, normally does not evaluate the merits of the government decision—in this case, whether the Air Force made the right decision to meet its needs for a long-range refueling tanker. GAO simply reviewed whether the Air Force followed each of the thousands of process requirements in the federal regulations and in this case concluded that the Air Force had not dotted all the "Is" and crossed all the "Ts."

TEN TIPS TO HELP YOU NAVIGATE THE PROCUREMENT PROCESS

1. As the manager of a planned major system, you can change the direction in the planning phase, but in the later stages of the procurement, the contracting officer assumes control, relegating the program manager to the bench. Therefore, you as the program manager should work hard in the planning phase to help build the proper requirements and flexibilities into the acquisition.

2. Avoid the negotiated contract route. It takes too long, and vendors usually protest, extending the time to complete the procurement. If your staff recommends such an approach, overrule them. Tell your staff to give you a plan using GSA Schedules, GWACS contracts or the SBA set-aside programs. For more than 20 years, many government managers have used these flexible programs with great success.

3. You will encounter many fearful or unqualified people in your agency. Some on your own staff will counsel the best action is no action. Reaching closure in the form of a signed contract with these advisors will probably be impossible. In desperation, you may

decide to take over, authorize it yourself and "ram it through." Do not do it. You do not know enough to avoid falling through the trapdoor into trouble

The media can be helpful in publicizing your program and objectives. Allow time and resources to work with the media. Note that the Air Force and the Navy employ public relations firms to get their message to the American people. The Air Force did it first because they felt that the American people were not aware of their contributions in Iraq and Afghanistan.

4. The military uses Hollywood to project a positive image. Films like *Top Gun* proceed only after the military approves the script, ensuring that the film will place it, and war, in a positive light. Then, the Pentagon makes available aircraft carriers, planes, tanks, troops— anything needed in the film—at negligible cost to the filmmaker. In *Top Gun,* for example, the Pentagon reportedly charged the filmmaker just $1.8 million for use of its aircraft carriers, planes and other resources.

5. Your political bosses will invariably run for the hills, leaving you alone under the spotlight at the first sign of trouble, such as a bid protest or a *Wall Street Journal, New York Times,* or a *Washington Post* investigation. If this occurs, and you should expect scrutiny because billion-dollar programs interest many players, your best option is to close ranks with your career officials who have the experience and contacts to bring clarity to the situation. If you blame your staff, look for a scapegoat, or try to rewrite history, the game is over at halftime. You lose by four touchdowns.

6. Bring patience and endurance to the table. Procurement, especially a negotiated procurement, is tedious and frustrating because of the endless rules. Hardly anyone knows or understands them all. There are always surprises. Congress meddles while introducing new laws, conducting committee

hearings and sometimes applying indirect pressure on specific procurements. Companies bring their own pressure to the process and may try to get you fired if you are going in a direction they feel is not in their interest.

Awarding bonuses to companies is a sensitive area and one in which you may feel pressure from your contractors. The GAO (GAO-06–66) reported that the Department of Defense paid about $8 billion in award fees without regard to contractor performance and failed to appoint performance monitors in more than a third of the cases GAO reviewed. This documents longstanding Congressional concerns that agencies award bonuses to companies despite poor performance.

7. If you recommend award bonuses only to good performing companies, you will be pressured by other companies in any way they can apply it, including questioning your credibility. Anticipating this, you must never provide any ammunition to companies, which they can later use to pressure you. Get too close socially, accept favors such as tickets to sporting events, lunches or dinners, or other small favors, and you compromise yourself. Meet with your contractors in your office, not theirs, but mainly listen. Keep the relationship businesslike. Shun the social until you leave the government.

8. Avoid a major grand design system requiring a negotiated contract. These can be enjoyable in the planning stage because as a senior program manager, you will receive a lot of attention from the trade press like *Government Computer News* and *Federal Computer Week*, and there will be many invitations to speak at the many forums for the Washington, D.C. technology crowd. However, numerous of these billion-dollar grand designs do in fact fail in part or completely. Press your staff to build systems in an incremental manner so you can redirect the program as you and your staff gain experience each step of the

way; and noteworthy, this became government policy in 2014. Also, be selective in accepting invitations to speak in public. Keep yourself and your message special.

9. How should you respond when a major company protests a contract award made by your staff? Encourage your contracting officer to fight it as long as is realistic. Recall, however, some agencies have fought for a year or more while their requirements remained in legal limbo. Eventually, they often give up and divide the award between the company they selected and the protesting company.

10. Do not expect too much from your agency lawyers. They work many issues, not just technology, and are very busy. They are generalists trying to respond to a wide variety of legal issues facing your agency. In addition to your issues, they must deal with issues raised by Congress, companies, and grantees, non-profit associations representing industry, individual taxpayers, and even employees. These keep your agency lawyers hopping.

ADVICE TO BRIAN

Peter Drucker summed up an important truth when he said in response to an interviewer's question about new management techniques, "The young people today expect to see business run by theory, knowledge, concepts and planning. But then they find it is run like the rest of the world—by experience and expediency, by who you know, and by the hydrostatic pressure in your bladder."

At the end of the day, experience rules in the federal acquisition process. As a program manager, you do not have it and never will have enough. At the same time, you have important responsibilities. You need access to people with real knowledge and the experience, judgment and courage to help you get it done in the minefields of federal procurement. Find the experience on your staff or hire it.

Also, do what you can to help your contracting officer to hire sufficient qualified people.

36
RECKONING WITH CONGRESS, LOBBYISTS AND POLITICAL APPOINTEES DURING PROCUREMENTS

Frank

As you said earlier, I will need to do one or more major procurements to hire contractors to help me develop the system. You also mentioned that congressional members might weigh in on issues that might involve jobs in their district. Can I expect pressure from Congress during my procurements? If so, how should I respond? Also, what about lobbyists? How might they get involved? And, what can I expect from political appointees? I know they will want to help.

CONGRESS CAN BE A PROBLEM

Periodically, Congress will produce a reform bill, hoping to "fix" the procurement system.

Congress meddles in selected procurements to bring employment or other benefits to their home district.

Congress may intervene if prompted by a lobbyist representing a company that contributed to campaign coffers.

Congress may tack an earmark onto existing legislation requiring your program to benefit a favored company or a Congressional district, circumventing the traditional budget process.

Periodically, congressional members will howl about some action taken by an agency contracting officer. A tired, but still favorite theme is to bemoan the number of sole source procurements, many of which are legitimate considering the circumstances necessitating the award.

In emergencies like Hurricane Katrina, sole source procurement authority allows rapid response. A full-negotiated procurement with time allowed for the routine bid protests will likely take two years. When the government uses its rapid response procurement authority in an emergency, Congress often second-guesses contracting officers' decisions a year or two after the emergency has passed.

Congress can be disingenuous when it wails about the national debt while simultaneously forcing waste onto the government in three ways:

- By forbidding DOD to close unnecessary military bases or by working to prolong the decision for years
- By forbidding DOD to cancel a failing program in order to save jobs for voters in their district
- By requiring the military to buy expensive weapon systems it does not want or need to create or maintain jobs in their congressional district.[149]

In 2007, the Federal Emergency Management Agency was trying to dispose of 41,000 trailers and mobile homes, purchased for Hurricane Katrina survivors. In a hasty purchase, at an average cost more than $18,000, the government bought these at the wrong time and for the wrong purpose, considering the proposed locations in flood plains.

When FEMA made these purchases, the Recreation Vehicles Dealer Association and the Manufactured Housing Industry lobbied Congress to forbid FEMA to resell the trailers and SUVs to the public when they became excess property. These industries had sold their products to the government in an emergency while successfully lobbying for a law forbidding the government from reselling them to the public when the government no longer needed them. Congress agreed and prohibited later resales directly to the public.

In addition, Congress continually heaps new laws, resulting in new regulations and policies on top of the thousands that already exist, all promising to ensure the taxpayers' money is well spent. While it is possible that these help in some way, no one really knows. Opinion, not fact, is the basis for any conclusions about Congress and its procurement rule-making adventures.

POLITICAL APPOINTEES CAN PLAY A DISRUPTIVE ROLE IN PROCUREMENT

Current legislation requires political appointees to be in charge of procurement in agencies. Normally you would expect these officials would have solid experience in the complex world of federal procurement. This is rarely the case. The White House appoints supporters to these jobs whose main qualifications are that they helped during the campaign, or contributed money, and will adhere to the party line. Although they can learn to speak procurement, they are like a high school football star, suddenly transported into the National Football League, the major league.

In the George W. Bush administration, the White House appointed an individual lacking any procurement experience to head the Office of Federal Procurement Policy in OMB, the top procurement job in government.

Later, the administrator of the General Services Administration appointed an individual to head GSA's Office of Acquisition Policy, one of the top four procurement jobs in government that set policy for the entire government. The person selected had no procurement experience and remained in the job only one year.

A few years later President Obama appointed an individual with no acquisition experience to the same government-wide policy job in GSA, although his qualifications were time spent on Obama's staff on the Hill and the support he provided during

Obama's campaign for the presidency.

He defended his lack of procurement qualifications, noting that his job as he saw it was to lead an office rather than to work down in the weeds. Signaling his intent to be above it all, he astonished many who view this $500 billion annual program supporting a community of more than 2,000 firms to be critical to the federal government and industry.[150]

Political appointees mess around with procurement and often attract attention for their indelicacies from five interested third parties, including the press and media, the Inspector Generals, Congress, the FBI and whistleblowers. There is a virtual trapdoor in the center of their new government office waiting for political appointees to stumble and descend into the darkness of the nation's judicial system.

It can happen because the federal procurement process is not intuitively obvious. In the private sector, there are some standard and legitimate practices forbidden in government. It is easy to see why political appointees get impatient and make mistakes.

For example, political appointees, new to the job, often want to hire a consultant to provide recommendations to improve the organization. The new government official naturally contacts a known consultant, probably a colleague from previous jobs when both worked in the private sector. This can be trouble. The government system requires full and open competition for jobs over $25,000.

In Frustration, the Political Appointee Has Choices

Try to find another procurement official willing to provide a different interpretation to the rules—unlikely, but not impossible.

Another choice is to make a series of awards for $24,500 just under the limit. This works for a while, but after two or three contracts with the same consultant, people get the picture, complaints arise, and the story finds its way into the newspapers, drawing the attention of the White House.

Or, one can ignore the rules, yank responsibility from the agency procurement official, and sign the contract as an Administrator of GSA did, only to suffer congressional criticism later.

Finally, the appointee can complain about the federal procurement system and try to bring about change—highly unlikely.

Follow the rules.

Lobbyists Influence Federal Procurements

When a company's interest is threatened, lobbyists use three techniques:

- Make an issue so complicated no one can understand it
- Prolong the discussion by introducing topics on the margin, diverting attention from the central issue, and creating so much confusion that Congress moves on to other issues
- Claim that the company's actions will create more jobs

With the vast amounts of money available from government spending and with the power that government has to write the rules, companies realize that they must invest in Washington politics. When they do, it leads to hiring a well-connected lobbying firm and former government leaders—*the practice known as the revolving door.*

Even before the British Petroleum blown-out well in the Gulf of Mexico created a disaster in Louisiana, Texas and Florida, the oil and gas industry called on its army of 600 lobbyists in Washington to hold off a rush of government proposals designed to crack down on the industry.

Three out of four of these lobbyists formerly worked in the government as lawmakers, congressional staffers and presidential appointees. Included in the total of former government officials lobbying for the oil and gas industry were 18 former senators and members of the House of Representatives and platoons of former congressional staffers who had specialized in writing legislation controlling the oil and gas industry earlier when they worked in government.[151]

When Toyota was in the headlines and in the eyes of Congress due to sudden acceleration cases, the automaker hired Rodney E. Slater, the former Secretary of Transportation under President

Bill Clinton, to head its North American Quality Advisory panel, which assists the company with quality and safety issues. Two former National Highway and Transportation Safety Administration officials in the Department of Transportation, formerly with the agency's Office of Defects Investigation, managed the federal investigations for Toyota. Toyota officials praised their work, saying that it saved the company as much as $100 million.[152]

When President Obama decided to upgrade fighter jets in Taiwan instead of providing the more advanced F-16C/D jet, Taiwanese officials employed former congressional officials to pressure the president, attempting to force him to sell the newer, more advanced weapon to Taiwan. Former Republican Senators Alfonse D'Amato (R-N.Y.) and Frank Murkowski (R-Alaska) and former Republican Representative Vito Fossella (R-N.Y.) were among the lobbyists on the Taiwan payroll. D'Amato, former chair of the Senate Committee on Banking, Housing and Urban Affairs, and his firm contacted members of Congress 44 times about the F-16 sale, and his firm was paid $250,000 in 2011. The lobbyists claimed that the United States was caving in to the Chinese bully by not selling the advanced jets to Taiwan.[153]

The number of registered lobbyists in 2010 was 12,986 with $3.49 billion in revenue.[154]

In 2009, lobbying revenue reached a record high of $970 million for a single three-month period as Congress debated the heathcare legislation proposed by President Obama. In addition to these sums, trade groups and individual companies spent heavily on television ads, grass roots organizing around single issues, and other activities to influence government policy.

Former Speaker of the House and presidential candidate in the 2012 election, Newt Gingrich, founded a think tank focused on health transformation in 2003. The Center collected at least $37 million in eight years from major healthcare companies and industry groups because the center offered benefits and special access to Gingrich and "direct Newt interaction." The Center closed in 2012 when Gingrich failed in his bid to secure the Republican nomination for president, causing clients to anticipate a loss of influence in the near future.[155]

In addition, lobbyists are a rich source of funding for

lawmakers eager to remain in office with the benefits and power it offers. Today, running for office requires large amounts of money, unless one is independently wealthy, as are many in the Senate.

Lobbyists have become indispensable to politicians, serving as advisors, fundraisers, even serving as finance chairs of their political campaigns. In addition, lobbyists often advise political action committees how to donate their funds ($510 million of $1.7 billion rose in 2014) to political candidates for best effect.[156]

In an interview with Robert G. Kaiser, Leon Panetta, then Director of the CIA and later Secretary of Defense, observed that lobbyists are in the driver's seat. "They basically know that the members have nowhere else to turn" for the money.[157]

Sen. Chuck Hagel (R-Nebraska) said when we need $20 million to $25 million, we go to a committee of 25 lobbyists and say, "Okay, you guys, each of you have to come up with a million dollars . . . So we go to them for that fast money."[158]

Procurement can open the door to big bucks so expect the big boys in companies to have an interest, but at the same time, the law enforcement folks will have an interest in their interest.

ADVICE TO BRIAN

You may not be able to do much about congressional meddling, but you can assist new political appointees by helping them link up with an old hand who knows the rules and can provide guidance to help navigate the complexities of government procurement.

Lobbyists normally operate at a level above you, and you may not be aware they are involved. However, if you sense pressure, you may conclude that lobbyists are involved.

You can push back against the power of lobbyists by providing information to your supporters in government, Congress and industry, assuming you have been wise enough and able to build relationships in these communities. As you call on your potential backers, provide them with information they can use to defend your program.

Do not forget to seek advice and build relationships with the Non-Government Organizations (NGOs) community, as described in Chapter 18. NGOs know how to weigh in on issues that interest them.

37
Six Reasons Help Explain Why Major Programs Fail

Frank,

The press reports that my system will be the most costly system ever attempted by the federal government. In addition, the press is reporting that most high-dollar systems fail in part or completely. Why is the record so bad? What can I do to ensure that my system is successful?

Asking why major systems fail with regularity in the short history of the computer industry is like asking why there are no more .400 hitters in major league baseball. Both are too difficult.

The federal government has a great deal of money to spend, and it spends about $80 billion of it on information and communications technologies (ICT); this increases about 3 percent each year. Not included are two other major pots of money spent on ICT:

- Appropriations to intelligence agencies, including the National Security Agency (NSA), some law enforcement functions and funds spent on classified DOD programs.
- Grants to state and local governments and other organizations processing parts of the federal government's nationwide systems

Sometimes the government gets value for its money—sometimes it does not. Systems fail in several critical respects: cost, budget, functionality and user satisfaction. While numerous mid-level and low-dollar contracts provide good results, many very expensive programs fail with hundreds of millions, even billions, of taxpayer dollars wasted. If you doubt me, Google *failed federal modernization programs* and skim the first 100 hits. For more information about reasons for failure, search the GAO reports and the Inspector General sites at each agency.

David Powner, the director of IT management issues at the GAO, in the June 15, 2015 issue of *CIO* said that the federal government has wasted billions of dollars over the years on failed IT acquisitions. Among other recommendations as GSA did in the 1980s, Powner stressed the importance of breaking large projects into smaller, more manageable pieces. Anne Rung, administrator of the Office of Federal Procurement Policy, implored agencies to adopt modular design, indicating it could help vendors as well.

The Rarified Air of the "Big Deal" is Captivating

Yves Rossy flew through the Swiss Alps for about five minutes using a jet-powered wing suit, reaching a speed of 186 miles per hour. *The Washington Post* quoted him as saying, "I am my own biggest danger now."[159]

"There have been times where I had to say, 'Okay, that was too far,'" said Rossy, known as the Fusion Man. "It is typical human behavior. You always want to do more, to achieve this super ability to fly. However, if we were really meant to fly, we would have feathers instead of hair."

Without any outside pressure, agency managers often adopt the grand design approach. Although they can think about a gigantus solution, write about it and hypothesize it, talking is not doing, doing is not achieving, and motion, including running from meeting to planning meeting all day every day, is not achievement.

What drives government managers to propose ever larger, ever more complex systems when there is such a sketchy history of success? Maybe it is because of human nature. As Rossy points out, we always try to outdo what we or others have already done.

What makes us think we can do better developing a complex government system than Microsoft, with its 10,000 employees, which took five years to develop a single system, Windows Vista, a very unpopular product with users?

What entices us to reach for higher levels of complexity than is prudent or achievable? One reason is that it is easier to plan systems than it is to develop, implement and operate them. A friend from college days invested early in Dunkin Doughnuts franchises. After years of baking donuts and managing minimum wage personnel, he was doing quite well. He owned two homes— one on the beach and another in a fashionable suburb—and a little red Jaguar coupe.

He preferred putting the deals together for additional franchises rather than running the store. For my friend, it was more stimulating to seek out sites for new stores, arrange the financing, work with designers and meet officials at corporate headquarters.

It is human nature to gravitate to the big deals in government because in the planning stage they are more fun than the day-to-day work. There are the speeches, the media interviews and the many opportunities to talk about how great the future will be. Planning the deal is important work, and it is an exciting period. Nevertheless, eventually you have to bake the donuts.

GOVERNMENT SYSTEMS ARE HUGE, COMPLEX, UNIQUE AND VERY DIFFICULT

Author Scott Rosenberg , co-founder of salon.com, writing in *The Washington Post,* said that although computer hardware, including PCs, have increased in capability as their prices have tumbled, software for government applications is unique and often needs to be developed from scratch. "It's still written, painstakingly, line by line and character by character; essentially, it's all made up. Software straddles the wide-open realm of the imagination," he wrote. "So far, it has proved uniquely resistant to engineering discipline."

Without such discipline, he said, "Software teams get lost in what are known as 'boil-the ocean' projects. These are vast schemes to improve everything at once." As users, he said, "Idealistic software developers love to dream about world-changing innovations; meanwhile, as users, we wait and wait for all the potholes to be fixed."[160]

Consider the complexity of FAA's newest modernization program, NextGen. This is a satellite-based navigation system that FAA plans to implement by 2025, although, under pressure from Congress to show earlier progress, the FAA will focus on progress they could make by 2018.[161] [162]

NextGen is not your normal billion-dollar information system. In addition to all the advanced technology that needs to be integrated at many sites, new GPS–based navigation systems must be installed in aircraft, and airlines are skeptical about these proposed cockpit upgrades. In addition, FAA's air traffic control facilities will need new tracking systems, monitors and software. Then, decisions need to be made on a user-by-user, location-by-location basis for new takeoff, landing and in-flight navigation procedures at 600 commercial airports, 377 terminal facilities, 21 enroute air traffic facilities, and possible upgrades in some 23,000 unmanned buildings and broadcast towers in the United States. This is a complex project.[163]

There is Seldom a Penalty for Failure

The DOD has an informal career development policy to transfer senior officers from program management responsibilities every two years. For example, the untidy F-35 Joint Strike fighter plane program will have 10 successive military program managers in its estimated 20-year life, effectively removing each of them from responsibility for the massive delays and cost overruns.

In addition to personnel decisions, Congress substitutes rules and detailed direction in its laws, effectively releasing people from their program management responsibilities. Reviews of federal highway projects took an average of two years in the 1970s. In 2011, they took eight years. Congress wrote the 1956 law authorizing the interstate highway system in 29 pages. The law revising the welfare system in 1996 filled 251 pages. The Volker Rule of 2014—one part of the Dodd-Frank law— regulating U.S. banks from proprietary trading and speculative investments is more than 950 pages. [164] Congress in the Dodd-Frank law vastly complicated the regulatory process to the point where nobody is at fault when speculation by banks affects customers.

Lockheed Martin, a major weapons manufacturer, won a contract in 2005 valued at $317 million to create a modern archive for electronic records. Six years later in early 2011, the GAO reported that the program was behind schedule and would eventually cost $1.2 to $1.4 billion. Furthermore, the agency's inspector general reported that when the system is implemented, searchers will only be able to search based on the subject line, not the body of the document.

GAO delivered an obscure explanation of the reasons for this failing as the result of "weak oversight and planning" by the agency. No official in the Archives paid a penalty for this failing program and for the 400 percent cost overrun, nor did Lockheed Martin. The Archivist, responding to the GAO report, agreed with its findings but disagreed with the future cost estimates. [165]

In one example of the lose-one, win-another climate of no accountability in federal government contracting, the Air Force awarded Accenture a $79.5 million contract for a new accounting and finance system—just a few weeks after a fellow defense agency, the Marine Corps, pulled the plug on a similar contract with the same contractor.

The Marines said Accenture failed to deliver substantial documentation in support of the system's detailed design review. The company also did not comply with cost, schedule and performance baselines, and risk assessments for the next phase of the program, so the Corps called a halt and fired the contractor. None of this mattered to the Air Force, which acted as if the Marine Corps experience did not occur.

In the government, acknowledgement of failure is easy, brief, and opaque and often serves as an introduction to the successor and more expensive multi-hundred million or billion-dollar replacement proposal. The failed program will slide silently, almost unnoticed, into a seldom-to-be referenced history.

CONGRESS AND UNINTENDED CONSEQUENCES

When Congress implemented a fee-for-service budget for the Immigration and Customs Enforcement (ICE), an agency within the Department of Homeland Security, it did so with good intentions that immigrants, not the American taxpayers, should pay for processing applications for U.S. citizenship. The outcome provides yet another example of the unintended consequences of congressional legislation affecting hundreds of thousands of people.

In the late 1980s Congress decided that immigrants should pay for the cost of citizenship examinations, not the American taxpayers. In the first year, this revenue source accounted for 10 percent of the agency's budget. Over time, however, user fees have crept up and now provide about 90 percent of the agency's budget. Moreover, the longer an immigrant remains in the pipeline, the more revenue the agency receives. While the agency could prescreen applicants and weed out ineligible candidates at the outset, this would reduce the revenue the agency receives from applicants in the pipeline. Therefore, the agency did not have an incentive to implement efficiencies such as prescreening, resulting in one more unintended consequence of Congress's directions.

The number of cases awaiting resolution before the Immigration Courts reached a new all-time high of 325,496 in February 2013, according to data obtained by the Transactional Records Access Clearinghouse (TRAC). The backlog has continued to grow despite a 2011 review initiated by Director John Morton designed to reduce the backlog and wait times for pending cases. In fact, the backlog increased 9.3 percent and the wait time increased to 553 days compared to 489 days when Mr. Morton's review began. The average wait time approaches 1,100 days if you are attempting immigration from a small country such as Armenia.

Major IT modernization programs continue to fail with great regularity. Immigration management, an e-gov issue, as well as a political issue, has been out of control. The backlog of applications for green cards stood at one million in 2000 and 2001, and because the Homeland Security frequently redefines its counting system, it is difficult to tell what the backlog is today. Nevertheless, a best guess suggests it remains in the millions as the following implies.

In 2010, the Department of Homeland Security did not allow applicants for green cards to submit their applications until three months before the expiration of their temporary green cards, yet the department's goal for processing green card applications is six months, so most applicants spend months with expired green cards.

In addition, Homeland Security commonly loses applications and fees and misreads applications. Contacting the service to correct mistakes requires a fee of several hundred dollars and months of waiting.[166]

DHS in immigration enforcement has a monopoly provided by Congress, and like most monopolies, its performance is poor.

MEGA-INTEGRATORS CAN CREATE PROBLEMS

The very large systems integrators supporting the government favor bigger projects because million-dollar systems or marginal upgrades to existing systems are not large enough for their multi-billion dollar appetites.

There is a more subtle reason for mega-integrators to push for bigger projects: larger projects squeeze out the midsized contractors that could provide competition.

If an agency manager adopts an incremental approach offering a better chance for success than a grand design, the mega-integrators can fight the decision in two ways. With lobbyists on the payroll and by making campaign contributions, they have access to congressional officials to make their case and possibly claim that the agency manager does not understand current technology and is exposing the government to needless costs. Mega-integrators may claim that the system could be operational sooner and cost less if the government manager took the grand-design approach they recommend.

Congress often listens to major companies more readily than to agency officials, and if company officials sway the congressional representative, he and his staff will promote the more ambitious approach and pressure agency officials.

Another tactic is to protest the planned acquisition relentlessly. Facing the prospect of lengthy delays while the successive protests are resolved, agency managers may capitulate and do what the mega-integrator wants in order to get the program moving.

Grand Designs Are Beyond the Current Ability of Managers and Technology

"Big-big," giganotosauris, describes the United States government's approach to problem solving.

Each new generation of government managers hears the mythical sirens calling them to the rocky shoals of grand designs. It is hard to resist the temptation to develop programs that push to the edge of emerging technology while amassing all possible requirements, including those that government and industry officials barely understand.

You could write a book about the Department of Homeland Security's SBInet, the FAA's efforts to modernize air traffic control systems, the IRS's tax systems modernization project, and other failed programs from recent decades. In fact, former IRS commissioner Charles Rossotti did just that when he wrote *Many Unhappy Returns: One Man's Quest to turn around the Most Unpopular Organization in America.*[167]

Large, bundled requirements became popular in the early 1980s, but a few years later, it was evident the approach failed. My fellow GSA manager, Larry Cohan, his staff and I wrote a report called "*An Evaluation of the Grand Design Approach to Developing Computer Based Application Systems,*" in September 1988. We distributed 14,000 copies of the report in response to requests from all over the world.[168]

We encouraged systems managers to take an incremental approach, building systems in small sections to allow relatively easy revisions to the plans as the project proceeded. It was not necessary or possible, we said, to plan every detail of a project 10 years into the future before getting started.

While it seemed, and still does, to be very logical, we hit resistance. GAO sharply criticized managers adopting the incremental approach, claiming it was not appropriate to spend taxpayers' money without a detailed long-term plan, perhaps extending out 10 or more years. After seven years, grand designs were back on the table. I chalked this up to a fundamental weakness in the otherwise valuable GAO review process. Its auditors focus on whether agency managers follow established management processes although adhering to process does not mean the project will succeed. It can even cause harm, as managers overlook emerging problems while trying to follow the templates imposed by OMB, GAO and oversight officials in their own agency.

In 2005, the pendulum swung again, and GAO was opposed to Grand Designs recommending that agencies ensure that a minimum of 80 percent of the government's major acquisitions deliver useful functionality every twelve months; and their research indicated that less than half of the investments that GAO examined met this standard. Continued tracking of this important measure in future years has great potential to improve the management and success rates of complex IT investments.[169]

The government admits to investing some $80 billion annually in ICT. Each year agencies launch about 30 new complex and unique acquisitions valued from $100 million to $2 billion or more. Unfortunately, there are no roadmaps to guide managers attempting to manage these expensive programs.

Governments rarely learn from their mistakes, especially when a new manager takes over with a fresh slate and little knowledge or interest of the factors that caused his predecessor to fail. As a result, these large, complex systems often run into repeated trouble with slippage in schedules, cost overruns and poor service to the end user.

In the government culture, the typical way to deal with problem systems is to reassign the manager, develop a new plan, promise success five years down the road and duck out of the limelight until new problems inevitably surface.

The 10,000-employee Patent and Trademark Office (PTO) began an ambitious program in 1982 to bring automation to patent examiners. Six years later, the parent agency, the Department of Commerce, concluded the program was in serious trouble. It formed a review team of senior government officials, which made many recommendations to get the program back on track. These led to some improvement.

In August 1994, twelve years after the modernization program began, GSA in its Brooks Act oversight role concluded that the latest PTO modernization program had derailed. The program was late, and it was going to cost $900 million instead of the original $400 million. There were obvious problems.

Only 100 of the 1,800 patent examiners had touched the new system after 12 years and $400 million in expenditures.

It took 10 minutes just to log on to the new system, and then the system was agonizingly slow.

Components of the system were not compatible and could not communicate with each other, requiring patent examiners to log onto two different computers to use the system.

GSA suggested a Time Out to senior officials in the Department of Commerce and to the Patent and Trademark Office. Time Out means four things:

- Stop further procurement actions
- Initiate an assessment by an independent organization, one that is not hoping for new business in the program after the current contract expires
- Consider cancellation of the program
- Rebuild a consensus with Congress, GSA, and OMB and other organizations with an interest in the program

Commerce, PTO and GSA officials including myself met in late December at the request of Commerce and PTO officials. The new program manager of the PTO system was unprepared, evasive and combative. In addition, he and his staff gave conflicting answers to our questions. This behavior reinforced our belief that PTO belonged in Time Out.

A series of meetings spread over a few months followed until PTO and Commerce agreed grudgingly to make some changes, but they never made the major changes necessary to do the job right. They were more interested in continuing in their current direction.

How did this modernization play out? The answer is that modernization did not occur. The modernization program did not give PTO's examiners the tools to do a better job. In fact, the results were disastrous, as we shall see.

Twenty-seven years after the PTO modernization program began and 15 years after GSA suggested a Time Out to allow PTO officials to rethink their approach to modernization, David Kappos took over in 2009 as the new director at Patent and Trademark. In his official biography, he stated that PTO had a backlog of more than 770,000 patent applications, "...long waiting periods for patent review, information systems regarded as outdated, and an application process in need of reform." In addition, he said PTO was often taking more than three years to provide a final answer to a patent application.

In an interview, Kappos said, "Imagine in the commercial world any service provider where if you sent the service provider money and a request for service and they said, thanks, we'll get back to you in three years, you'd say that is insane, unacceptable."[170]

Unfortunately, the PTO case is not unique.

In 1982, the Federal Aviation Administration declared an emergency and obtained approval and funds to modernize the Air Traffic Control System. Since many of the decision makers in government fly frequently, safety is a fine horse to ride. FAA systems are the most complex in the nation in or out of government; FAA, despite outdated tools, handles more traffic than any other country in the world, and the American flying public has been safe in the skies.

The Advanced Automation System (AAS) was the centerpiece in FAA's program to modernize the aging air traffic control system. The goal was to provide new and upgraded systems, including advanced tools for the traffic controllers, new and better communications networks, and new applications systems.

In June 1988, IBM won a hard-fought competition. The amount of the award was $3.5 billion. IBM's job was to design and implement three new functions to control aircraft:

- Enroute across the country
- In the immediate vicinity of each airport
- On the ground at each airport

Four years later, the program was in trouble, and FAA issued a warning to IBM because a 12-month delay was projected and estimated costs had risen 34 percent to $4.7 billion. Despite a strong commitment by IBM, including the takeover of the program by the president of IBM's Federal Systems Division, the situation steadily grew worse.

In March 1994, FAA announced additional cost overruns, raising the estimated total to a range of $5.9 to $7.3 billion—69 percent to 108 percent— over original estimates. FAA forecast a delay of 31 months. In just 12 months, the program slipped an additional 19 months despite IBM's commitment.

With the magnitude of the problems now visible, several key managers in FAA retired. Others received involuntary transfers to field locations. FAA took the usual steps to correct a serious systems problem: change managers and develop a new plan. As we later saw, this action did not solve the problem in this case, as it rarely does in other failing systems.

The problem began in the early 1980s when FAA configured an unusually complex and unnecessary Grand Design. The agency paid the price, as did most other organizations then and now, in and out of government pursuing Grand Designs.

The government scrapped it in mid-1990 for the usual reasons: large cost overruns and schedule slippages. The estimated project costs had soared to $7.6 billion, and the project was seven years behind schedule. The FAA announced that $1.5 billion of the $2.6 billion, already spent, had produced useless products.

The project was probably doomed on the drawing board by an unrealistically ambitious plan. "It was basically a big bang approach, gigantic programs that would revolutionize overnight how FAA did its work," said Pete Marish an analyst at the General Accountability Office.[171]

Subsequently, FAA divided the system into smaller segments, abandoning the Grand Design approach.

Not all major government modernization systems in past decades have failed partly or in total. AWIPS, the heart of the National Weather Service operations, is one of many successes. It is a complex system, which integrates meteorological and hydrological data, including satellite imagery, radar data, surface observations and numerical modeling. All sectors of the media, especially TV stations, use the AWIPS products to provide daily weather information and to warn the citizens of impending danger from such forces as hurricanes and tornados.

ADVICE TO BRIAN

In summary, recognize that major systems fail in part or completely for several reasons, and be sensitive to these as you proceed with your major system.

There is little recognition that government systems are huge, complex and one of a kind, and risky.

Some initiatives are too complex for current technology, software and management tools.

Congress and the White House set unrealistic goals in a crisis to demonstrate to the American public that they are in charge and the public should relax, not fear.

The big deals are attractive, almost fun, in the planning stage, reducing caution.

Since there is seldom a penalty for failure, risky proposals can win undeserved acceptance.

Inexperienced officials, including CIOs, congressional representatives and political appointees, often endorse risky proposals by lobbyists and companies.

Grand designs. when encouraged, routinely fail in part or completely.

38
MANAGING THE HUNDRED MILLION DOLLAR PROGRAMS

Frank,
Now that I have had some time on the job here, I am
starting to get a sense of the scope of my project. As you
know, it is going to be a big one. I will have a little time
to prepare before we get started, so what can you tell
me about managing such complex projects?
What special skills will I need beyond the traditional
project management skills? What ideas do you have to
help me manage my billion-dollar system?

Managing complex, high-dollar technology programs is not
an easy task, as governments around the world have learned.
Consider what United Kingdom officials concluded in their
report called *Transformational Government 2006.*

Delivering success in the public sector is tough, and the risk
of failure is often high. The diversity and complexity of the public
sector, the scales, and security requirements of its operations,
and the need to respond to policy change and legislative

deadlines make it difficult for Information and Communications Technology (ICT) managers to develop the information systems and the distribution channels needed in government.

FOUR CASE STUDIES

Case studies involving the IRS, Cedars Sinai Medical Center, the FBI and the Washington Hospital Center provide important lessons for managers of major information systems.

The Internal Revenue Service

When the president appointed Charles O. Rossotti as commissioner of the IRS in 1997, he knew the agency had already experienced several failed attempts to modernize its systems, and he concluded that the IRS's decentralized organizational structure was the cause. As he recalled:

"When I came to IRS, I actually put off some of the IT work to deal with structure issues. There was a matrix system in place, and there were nine service centers and forty-five district offices. I do not think we could have succeeded with that structure. Each region was a mini-IRS with its own computer center and e-mail system. Therefore, we did reorganization first. Take [our Integrated Collection System] ICS for example. What we have [now in 2008] is not a fantastically great system, but it is a much better tool than we had eight years ago, in part because everyone uses the same system. Before, there was no standardization, too much fragmentation and we could do nothing because of that fragmentation. Everyone in the regions was doing IT their own way, and there was no consistency. It took two and one half years to change the structure, and now we have a centrally managed information system. Now, modernization is still a big challenge, but it is doable. With the previous structure, it would have been almost impossible."[172]

This case study demonstrates that culture and structure will either allow or prohibit a modernization program to succeed.

After Commissioner Rossotti restructured and standardized IRS, his team conceived the Business System Modernization program, and even with his organizational changes, things did not go well for several years.

The centerpiece of the BSM program is CADE, or Customer Accounts Data Entry, a system to replace the Master File legacy system, which stores taxpayer records on magnetic tape. IRS has upgraded the Master File periodically over its 50-year life, but updating a taxpayer's record required passing up to 200 million records to get to the right one, which can take a week.

IRS hired Computer Sciences Corporation, which assembled a team of Bearing Point, IBM, Northrop Grumman, SAIC and Unisys to manage the modernization program. Because of the previous failed IRS modernization programs, a concerned Congress kept IRS on a short leash, requiring annual progress reports. The GAO also reviewed the program each year.

The first phase of the CADE System to provide direct access to each taxpayer record was due in December 2001, but the Computer Science Corporation's team missed the date, and subsequent due dates were rescheduled several times. In 2008, ten years after IRS hired Computer Sciences Corp., the GAO reported that CADE was able to process only 15 percent of the year's 200 million tax returns.

In 2009, IRS concluded they could not fully implement the program before 2018 and possibly 2028 and suspended further work under CADE to explore a new strategy. IRS then continued to use the old legacy system, processing magnetic tape as it had done after several failed modernization programs in earlier decades.

Despite the difficulties with CADE, the BSM program provided hundreds of deliverable products over the years. In addition, IRS finally declared a version of CADE operational in 2013.

Charles Rossotti was unusually qualified, as were the IRS contractors representing major international systems firms. Clearly, the IRS and contractor teams had impressive experience, but CADE was 12 years late, suggesting that some of the federal government's complex systems may be too complicated for current technology or management practices. Industry officials may disagree, but the record of billion-dollar failures suggests that systems complexity and immature technology contribute to the many major systems failures. Too-big-to-fail concerns should apply not only to America's major financial institutions, but also to the government's billion-dollar systems initiatives.

Before we extract the lessons learned from the IRS modernization program, there are three other examples of failed programs, out of dozens that I could mention, all offering important lessons for systems managers.

Cedars Sinaí Medical Center in Los Angeles

A full-blown staff rebellion of several hundred doctors forced the center to shelve a $34 million medical records system after only three months in operation.

The medical practitioners refused to use it because it did the opposite of what good technology should do: it made their jobs more difficult. A task that once took three minutes at the patient's bedside suddenly consumed 30 or 40 minutes. One doctor asked, "Who has five extra hours in a day when we already work 80 hours in a week?" Hospital officials implied the medical staff was at fault, asserting that they might wait for more tech-savvy doctors to join the hospital before trying to implement the system again.

I have heard this excuse for 40 years. "We need to wait for the next generation." However, waiting never saves a failed grand design. The next generation is never the savior of a system users do not want.

Washington Hospital Center in Washington

After spending $8 million on a patient records system, the WHC threw in the towel and cancelled the contract with a Fortune 100 company. Then, the in-house support staff at the hospital quietly, over time and at a modest cost, developed one of the most advanced systems for managing patient care in this country.

The system collects patient records, including X-rays, charts, and laboratory results from hundreds of incompatible sources. It stores these records in a single database and produces a complete up-to-date medical history for each patient when requested by an attending doctor.

The system evolved over eight years and spread throughout the hospital as more of the staff demanded access. Georgetown University Hospital, the National Rehabilitation Hospital in Washington and four hospitals in Baltimore now use the system.

To build and implement this successful system called Azyxxi, the developers did none of the things we do in the government. There was no cross-hospital task force, nor was there a detailed needs analysis or a long-term capital budget. There was no request for proposals, no campaign to obtain buy-in from the staff and no money budgeted for training.

Later, the WHC employees received a federal grant to create a regional health information system and link all of the medical records of the hospitals, labs and doctors' offices in and around the District of Columbia. *Washington Post* columnist Steven Pearlstein concludes you do not need a lot of money, a grand plan, a contractor, bureaucracy, regulations and process to bring health care into the information age.[173]

The Azyxxi development process could be a model for the federal government. The government's multi-step approach to major systems resembles an Army Bradley Fighting tank with its sheer brute, graceless force; and it often leads to failure, lawsuits and large penalty payments to ousted contractors.

In summary, the Washington Hospital Center faced uninvolved and unconvinced users and uncertain requirements after several years with a leading contractor before in-house staff took over and began to build the system. They did not use the Grand Design strategy that the government often requires. Rather, the in-house developers created and assembled the system piece by piece in an iterative approach, allowing the developers to make changes, if necessary, before beginning the next module.

The Washington Hospital Center, using a practice common in the 1960s, successfully employed their own in-house analysts with deep knowledge about how the medical staff did their work. Some federal agencies, unsuccessful using the lead integrator approach, know that using in-house staff can be a better solution in some circumstances.

The FBI
When 9/11 occurred, the fragmentation of the FBI's case files impeded investigative efforts, exposing the agency's lack of standardization to the public.

The FBI intended that the Virtual Case File (VCF) system would provide a single entry point into its patchy, silo-based, separate information systems used to track its cases. The FBI terminated the system in March 2005, after spending five years and at least $170 million with no results. VCF was a grand design, requiring an all-at-once launch, making debugging and correcting errors almost impossible until the entire system went on-line for use by agents.

The FBI then launched a new more expensive program called Sentinel, a six-year $305 million program with full operation due in 2012. In its second try at case management, the FBI adopted the incremental approach to develop Sentinel, dividing the system into four parts, each containing a number of smaller segments. The plan was to deploy these segments incrementally, providing the opportunity to learn and to make mid-course corrections before implementing the next piece of the total system. The Treasury Department's inspector general reviewed Sentinel several times and in late 2009 concluded that it provided a reasonable chance of success, although the Phase 1 implementation slipped 10 months, with program costs estimated to climb to $451 million, a 50 percent increase.

Two years later, the inspector general reported that the FBI had spent $405 million of the $451 million. However, only two of the four phases were complete and the contractor delivered on schedule only four of 18 processes, and the more difficult work was still ahead, the inspector general said.

While the FBI said that it could complete the remaining phases for an additional $20 million, the MITRE Corporation, hired by the FBI to assess the project, reported that another $351 million would be required. The FBI program management team, ignoring the delays and cost overruns in this ten-year attempt to modernize its case management files, responded in the typical program management manner style, stating that the IG did not recognize the many changes they had made and that 5,000 users accessed the system at least weekly.[174]

One of the significant changes FBI made was to take over the management of the program from its prime contractor Lockheed Martin in 2010. The FBI reported that a rough time and cost estimate to complete the program by its contractor was not acceptable, prompting the agency to announce that it would use in-house employees and its major software providers to complete the program.[175] With in-house leadership Sentinel got back on track becoming operational across the agency on July 1, 2012, allowing its agents the capability so sorely needed since September 11, 2001.

A SUCCESSFUL FAA TELECOMMUNICATIONS SYSTEM

Sometimes, systems run into trouble, and its managers take it on the chin from a variety of sources. Agencies usually slog on while changing managers and threatening the contractor while trying to sound optimistic when reporting to Congress and other oversight bodies. Sometimes things work out, but at a higher cost than the original investment. Managing the government's major developments is not for the faint of heart.

Not all major systems fail. The FAA's attempt to overhaul the systems used by air traffic controllers to communicate with pilots is an example of a successful complex system.

FAA's National Airspace System connects 3,800 facilities, providing some 22,000 telecom services. It supports voice and data, short range, long range and weather data, as well as air-to-ground and ground-to-ground voice communications.

The purpose of the FAA Telecommunications Infrastructure (FTI) program was to reduce operating costs by consolidating nine telecom networks into one system operated by Harris Corporation. FAA intended the proposed FTI network to consolidate all of the pieces and patches added over a 30-year period into one modern standard telecommunication system to support 40,000 employees servicing 87,000 daily flight operations.

FAA awarded Harris a contract for the potentially multibillion-dollar project in July 2002. It quickly slipped off track, and as costs escalated and deadlines slipped, accusations and countercharges of poor management began to fly. Three years after the work began, less than 4 percent (622) of the old system's telecommunications circuits had migrated to the new system, according to the Professional Aviation Safety Specialists (PASS) union. By December 2005, 815 circuits were operational, an additional 1 percent. FAA finally said the transition was complete in April 2008, six years after the agency signed the contract.

Since completion, the system failed only a few times for a day or less. However, given the complexity of the system and its crucial role in servicing the flying public, the FAA and its contractor Harris Corporation deserve an A- for their work on this program.

NINE MANAGEMENT LESSONS LEARNED FROM THE FOUR CASE STUDIES

Brian, the Internal Revenue Service modernization program, the Washington Hospital Center patient records system and the FBI Sentinel system provide important lessons for managers of complex systems.

1. Do not begin a complex system until the organization structure and culture can support it. From IRS we learned that centralization and reorganization are difficult and can take two years and serious internal battles. At IRS, management had to revamp the massive decentralization of resources and authority before the Business System Modernization program had a chance to succeed, and even then, it was a hard slog.

2. The top person in the agency needs to be knowledgeable and committed. Charles Rossotti at IRS had probably the best qualifications of any executive joining government before or since to lead the modernization of a complex system crucial to the nation.

3. Top down system decisions not involving the expected end user will produce a system that users may not want and may resist until the organization scraps the system and its investment, as the experiences at Cedars Sinai Medical Center and the Washington Hospital Center (WHC) revealed.

4. A methodical, incremental approach—building a segment at a time, allowing for course corrections and changes in direction—may take longer initially, but in the end it is the shortest distance from concept to full implementation, as demonstrated by the WHC example and the FBI experience in the later stages of the program.

5. The all-at-once, Big Bang, Grand Design approach to major systems development is a prescription for failure, as it has been in most major systems development programs in the short sixty-year history of computer-based information systems. Modular systems development as we learned from the FBI's experience with the Virtual Case File and Sentinel systems can help avoid failure, but if it is contained within a grand design envelope, failure is likely. Modular development became the Office of Management and Budget's government-wide policy in 2014.

6. In some cases, an organization's in-house staff is better prepared than the staff of a systems integrator to develop a system that the clients will use, as demonstrated in the Washington Hospital Center case.

7. In a troubled system, the success or failure of the program will depend on the rating the overseers give the manager. If they have confidence, they will grant time to fix the problems; if not, the program is in jeopardy. As a program manager, you must impress them by providing target dates and metrics they can track and by ensuring that you meet your targets.

8. Schedule slippage may not be fatal. The FAA schedule slippages and cost overruns were unfortunate, but not fatal. If your program slips, acknowledge it to the auditors, investigators, congressional representatives and staffers, and get the program back on track, recognizing that good management and a willing, skillful contractor can save some, not all, failing programs.

9. As manager of a complex system, you must stay more than the average two years. As indicated, the successful FAA network example took six years to complete, although it experienced potholes along the way. Be prepared to spend several years managing your project through to completion. Leaving in two years—as the average political appointee does—is disruptive.

In companies and governments all over the world, there are hundreds of systems that failed completely or in large part. You can learn from each, but you will not have time to review more than a few. You can do no better than to spend time studying the Internal Revenue Service, the Washington Hospital Center, the FBI and the FAA experiences.

Fortune does not reserve calamities solely for the federal government. The Texas State Health and Human Services awarded a contract to Accenture Ltd. in 2005 with an estimated future value of $899 million over five years. The purpose was to determine eligibility, provide enrollment assistance for government services and operate a call center. The following year the government scaled back the goals of the contract, but complaints of poor service and denial of benefits to those who were eligible for benefits caused the government to terminate the program in 2007, only two years after awarding the contract.

Two Mississippi state agencies sued American Management Systems, now part of CGI Group Inc., over a troubled tax system. The initial $11.2 million-dollar contract called for AMS to deliver 36 applications, but after numerous technical problems and schedule delays, the state's tax commission and the Department of Information Services filed suit, seeking about $1 billion in damages. AMS settled, agreeing to pay Mississippi $185 million in a 13-year period. Subsequently, AMS paid about $23.5 million, and its insurers paid the remaining amount.[176]

PROCESSES TO HELP MANAGE IT INVESTMENTS

There are a number of processes designed to help make good investments of your IT budget. These include Earned Value Management (EVM) analysis of IT investments under development. The intent is to monitor regularly the performance of projects to provide early warning of projects that may not be meeting cost, schedule or performance goals, allowing mid-course correction to bring the development effort back on track. See OMB policy on IT Investment Baseline Management (OMB Memorandum M-10-27).

Another important process is OMB's Exhibit 300, which establishes policy for planning, budgeting, acquisition and management of major information technology (IT) capital investments.

Exhibit 300s are companions to an agency's Exhibit 53. Together, with an agency's Enterprise Architecture program, they define how to manage the IT Capital Planning and Control Process. Exhibit 53A reports the funding of all IT investments within a Department. Exhibit 300A provides a detailed justification of major "IT Investments." Exhibit 300B helps manage the execution of those investments through their project life cycle and into their useful life in production.

Another useful process is five-stage framework from GAO, providing a method for evaluating and assessing how well an agency is selecting and managing its IT resources.

See GAO GAO-04-394G, March 2004, INFORMATION TECHNOLOGY INVESTMENT MANAGEMENT, *A Framework for Assessing and Improving Process Maturity.*

Ten Building Blocks for Managers of Hundred Million-Dollar Programs

Let's summarize this information into action steps you can follow as you take control of your billion-dollar program.

Assess yourself. Do you have all of the skills needed to run a hundred million-dollar program?

Project management courses do not teach the advanced skills needed to manage a major modernization program; experience matters because learning on the job is expensive and it can damage your reputation. In addition to the traditional management skills taught at schools and learned in smaller projects, managers of complex, expensive government systems need to be seasoned and skilled at managing by negotiation and inspiration.

In addition, these managers will face challenges in the following situations:

- Working with Congress, its staffers and White House appointees
- Testifying before hostile legislative committees

- Responding to critical administration and congressional auditors
- Responding to the probing of national media organizations
- Reorganizing in the face of union resistance
- Using policy and regulatory authority despite resistance from companies and other agencies

If you lack these skills, and most do, you may find them hidden away in your organization. Otherwise, hire from elsewhere in the government.

TREAT LEGACY SYSTEMS AS AN AGGRESSIVE BEAR IN MATING SEASON

The phrase *legacy system* defines a system developed years ago, a system that continues to operate an important government responsibility. Social networking tools are interesting communications tools for government and society, but they will not run the Air Traffic Control System, the Social Security benefits systems or the thousands of other systems the government and the public have relied on for decades.

All legacy systems represent the aggregation of decades of work by several thousand folks, many now long gone, taking their irreplaceable knowledge with them. Many legacy systems still grind day after day, doing important, productive work for their agencies. They contain thousands of complex programs and millions of lines of often poorly documented code, but they get the job done. They are very complex and may be close to impossible to replace.

Before you attempt to replace one, be certain you understand what they do so you have a decent chance of succeeding without bringing the wrath of the public down on your agency if the replacement system performs erratically and upsets daily life. My advice regarding legacy systems is to modernize incrementally; do not undertake an all-at-once replacement. Your young children will have children and possibly grandchildren before you might see the successful replacement of a complete major legacy system.

PLAN FOR THE UNEXPECTED

"To . . . not prepare is the greatest of crimes; to be prepared beforehand for any contingency is the greatest of virtues," wrote Sun Tzu, an ancient Chinese military general, strategist and philosopher.

As manager of a government program that millions of Americans rely upon, you will want to have an up-to-date Continuity of Operations Plan (COOP) to prepare for emergencies, and you should update it yearly by brainstorming with a group of officials with diverse experiences in the emerging world. Try to anticipate a broader range of possibilities than might have been necessary in the past. You also should identify the costs—in dollars and in public confidence—if you are unable to provide the traditional services the public has learned to expect.

Immediately after the terrorist attacks on the World Trade Center and the Pentagon on Sept. 11, 2001, John Ortego, director of the government's National Finance Center in New Orleans, reviewed his plan to move almost half of his staff overnight to alternate sites in either Chicago or Philadelphia to keep the center running after a catastrophic event.

John later observed that during 9/11, roads in major cities in the country including New Orleans were jammed, the government shut down air traffic, and communications were largely unavailable. In these conditions, his plan was defunct. It is a lesson many have learned in a catastrophe. Plan for unwanted surprises.

ATTRACT AND CULTIVATE A TEAM OF ADVISORS

Go with experience. Seek input from the wide range of sources available to you. As a high-level official, closed doors will open for you, and many well-placed people will want to help you. Your job is to select people with valuable insights while avoiding anyone with a shallow understanding or someone just trying to sell you a product or service. You should create a bench of about 20 trusted advisors to provide counsel as various issues arise.

KEEP SYSTEMS INTEGRATORS BEHIND THE FENCE

While you will need an integrator to manage the services of the several companies supporting your program, be careful not to ask the integrator to do the jobs that you and your staff should perform.

Reinstate the balance of power, if needed, between your managers and your contractors. There are dozens of responsibilities one could choose to assign to the government manager or to contractors. However, the government manager is responsible for the success or failure of the program and for evaluating the performance of the contractor(s). Do not allow the contractors to assume government responsibilities, even if it seems expedient.

As the manager of a major program, you may want to hire an independent assessment company to assess the risks to the government before and after signing the contract. However, be careful not to hire an assessor that will partner in the future with the company whose performance you want assessed today. One way to predict future liaisons is to review their business partners in the past five years.

You may want to call on your agency's audit resources, the inspector general, or you may want to convene an independent team with experienced officials from other agencies. The Government Accountability Office reviews can be helpful in assessing the real status of your contract. Your careful analysis of the systems integrator and his team does not imply distrust; it is just smart business.

CONSIDER SOCIAL NETWORKING TECHNOLOGIES TO PROMOTE TRANSPARENCY

Sometimes systems fail because government and industry officials either ignore or suppress early warning signs of impending crisis. Social networking technologies offer new and simpler paths of communication to close the gap between operations and modernization managers and the many layers of subcontractors, possibly 100, responsible for key aspects of major government systems.

DEVELOP AN ELEVATOR TALK FOR USE BY YOUR BOSSES AND WITH THE MEDIA

You will need a three-minute talk highlighting the goals of the program, progress to date, and numbers and percentages describing progress and benefits of the program. Managers and the media do not want mountains of detail. The media wants sound bites for use on the evening news. Busy agency heads want catchy highlights for staff meetings with the head boss or for meetings at the White House. They will assume you have the backup material.

BE ALERT TO GAMING BY CONTRACTORS

Although not illegal, gaming in procurement creates headaches for the government. Gaming causes your opponent to think you are doing one thing when it is just a feint and you are really up to something quite different. As in life, things are not always what they seem to be. One example is the practice some companies employed to bid engineers and computer programmers to the government for $15 to $20 per hour when the companies actually paid higher salaries for those labor categories. If the government client asks for these skills bid at the unrealistic labor rates, the contractor may respond that they are not needed on the current job. Companies are able to take this position when the contract assigns them the responsibility to design the system.

Another example of gaming occurs when a company bids a ridiculously low price to supply products such as desktop computers to an agency. After the government signs the contract, the company expects newer computers to be available in the market and expects the agency's users to demand the newer technology. The bet is won when the older low-priced, loss-leader computers are never delivered, and the newer, high-priced computers with good profit margins are substituted.

When you observe gaming before an award is made, work with your contracting officer to place a time out on the program, close the loophole, build in an anti-gaming fix and restart the acquisition from the beginning.

Government managers employ gaming as well because they need approval for their proposed program from their boss, the budget people in their agency, OMB and congressional appropriators. Both parties may then independently "low ball" the bid, manufacturing a number they think will sell.

The government manager does so, attempting to improve the odds of obtaining approval of the program. The contractor does so, expecting to win an award and later to convince the government to modify the contract with new, more costly requirements.

Work with Your Contractors to Seek Solutions for a Failing Program

All parties should learn from mistakes when things do not go well. Avoid the blame game unless your contractors drive you to it, and they may. U.K. officials recognize that contractors are not always the sole reason for failing systems; the government also causes problems. Recognizing the range of possible pitfalls, the U.K. has had two initiatives:

A "Strategic Supply Board" brings CIOs from government departments together with managing directors of companies (not marketing representatives) to discuss the systemic problems they face together.

Another UK initiative required the government agency and its lead contractor to sign a "Joint Statement of Intent" identifying the mutual objectives of the two organizations and the methods each will use to achieve those objectives.

Be Firm and Place a "Time Out" on Troubled Programs

Today, when programs are in trouble, the default choice is to slog on, hoping things will improve.

As the contract evolves, the government managers and their integrator may observe serious problems. Often, however, it is not in the interest of either to highlight the problems and take action. Typically, managers on both sides minimize the seriousness of the problem, hoping that things will get back on track before the next program review, often in 90 days.

Sometimes, procrastination works. Sometimes, it does not. Rumors begin to circulate that the project is going off the rails, and by the time someone finally blows the whistle, it is much harder to fix the problem, or a fix is impossible.

Postponing disclosure is in the interest of the contractor. The longer he can hang on, the harder it is to evict him. Delay is attractive to the government manager as well, providing more time to keep the program out of the spotlight.

But the best approach is to call a Time Out, allow experienced people with no financial interest in the program to take a fresh look and make recommendations to management, the agency and the contractor.

All involved generally benefit when there is a common understanding and acceptance of the true status of the program.

HOLDING YOUR OWN IN THE BLAME GAME

If your program is failing and the blame game begins, be wary. Companies are experts at the blame game. Department of Defense officials have perfected their responses as well. Program managers in civilian agencies, especially political appointees, are less adept at the game.

If it is a failing DOD contract, expect the DOD to respond with its classic *slow roll* defense. Its officials will agree, yes, the project has some problems. However, they likely will say they were aware of problems and plan to establish a board of eminent private sector chieftains and prestigious scientists to provide suitable recommendations to the Secretary, Congress and the White House. It may be at least a year before the promised board comes into existence and holds its first meeting. By then, the watchdogs may have lost interest, or the agency managers will have solved the problems.

Civilian agencies do not have DOD's resources to dispense stipends and travel to attract prominent figures to serve on evaluation teams. It is more common for civilian agency managers to deny the existence of any problem, thereby provoking pushback by oversight officials.

Contractors rarely accept responsibility for poor performance. When many eyes fall on a troubled government contract, contractors may attempt to place the blame on the government managers, claiming they were slow to make critical decisions or that they changed the requirements after awarding the contract

Large companies have allies in Congress because of campaign contributions or because the corporation has employees in the congressional district. Companies will provide position papers to the congressional representatives which lay the blame on the government managers. Concerned about sources of future funds for the next political campaign or jobs in their district, the congressional representative may question government managers, possibly challenging them during public hearings on Capitol Hill.

Members of Congress can also use the GAO and agency inspectors general to investigate failing systems. Most IGs are excellent and provide fair evaluations, but some are incompetent or politically motivated. In some cases, the government manager never has a chance to explain the agency's role and its actions.

In addition, the complex federal procurement system encourages failures, and it is true the government consciously tends to underestimate the costs of a system in order to obtain approval. This encourages, even requires, companies to underbid, to support the lowball estimates provided by agencies. Then, after the government awards the contract, the costs escalate, and the blame game begins.

If Congress assigns GAO to examine your program, there are certain moves you should take. As noted previously, if you are on the receiving end of a critical report, your best course is to admit the problem and declare you were aware of it and that you have already begun to correct a bad situation. In addition, if you have done so, you can announce you have beefed up your risk management procedures and have hired an outside contractor to monitor agency and contractor performance. Promise a new assessment in six months, a year would be better, while assuring your critics you expect to have everything back on track by then. Then, make sure it happens, or update your resume.

Also, update your snappy elevator talk, program metrics and a limited amount of spin, to be available for media interviews and for use by your bosses.

Advice to Brian

While there are many ways to spend your time, not all will be productive. You should repeat to yourself each day that the only objective worth pursuing is to help develop and distribute information to meet the emerging needs of your agency and the needs of the public that your agency serves. Nothing else matters.

Policies, standards, architectures, training, conferences and committees are simply burdens if you cannot develop the right systems on time and on budget while meeting the real needs of your agency and the public.

Review the nine lessons learned from the four case studies and employ the ten building blocks discussed in this chapter, and you will improve your chances for success as you lead the development of a complex, costly system.

39
FENDING OFF CHALLENGERS TO YOUR PROGRAM

> *Frank,*
> *My staff is telling me that there are people in the government that dearly wish to see my program sent to the dustbin. In addition, perhaps ominously, several companies want to meet to propose "innovative goals" for my program. While new ideas can be helpful, changing the goals developed by others after much debate in the last two years would be problematic at this point.*

Be aware your program may change the balance of power between agencies and among competing companies, motivating them to pressure you to redesign the fundamentals of your program to accommodate their capabilities. Sometimes they succeed, sometimes they do not.

Combating those who want to kill your program or steal your resources is light years beyond the lessons trainers teach in Project Management 101. To protect your program, you must be prepared to spend major time making and working with supportive contacts.

Challenges Can Come from Several Directions

Numerous, powerful sources can challenge any federal program. Here are two that can be real threats.

Other federal agencies may work behind the curtain with their congressional authorizing and appropriation committees, attempting to reshape or sink your program because it will invade their turf.

Similarly, companies will want to win your contract because the revenue stream will be healthy for a decade or more. To improve their chances of winning, they will work with their lobbyists, congressional committees and the media to try to reshape your program. In addition, if they have a contract with an agency and yours would replace theirs, they may attempt to derail your program.

There are Three Other Sources of Concern

Peer government managers who covet your resources will be watching for signs of inattention among your supporters.

Political parties and non-government organizations will be active when their political, religious or philosophical agendas conflict with the goals of your program.

White House operatives and political appointees in your agency may plot to kill your program for political or ideological reasons. If they are effective and you are not vigilant, you may never notice they have "done you in."

When Fighting Back, Answer Two Questions

Did Congress or the White House create your program? If Congress created the program, and especially if the members overrode White House objections to do so, Congress will be your primary ally.

On the other hand, if the program is a presidential initiative, you can expect the political appointees to be helpful, while Congress may cause trouble by withholding funds, eliminating program authorities, or by holding public hearings, disparaging you, and your program.

Officials in Congress and the White House have access to channels of information you will not have, and they have more influence. Keep them informed if they are approachable, so they can develop responses to each new challenge to your program.

Which organizations could support your program? Many organizations and individuals try to change the direction of government programs to obtain a competitive advantage or simply because they see a "better" way. There are political groups, trade associations, advocacy organizations and lobbyists for every issue. Identify those likely to be on your side and develop relationships.

For example, Tech America (formerly The Information Technology Association of America) supports federal government contractors by working with Congress, providing information, and by attempting to influence legislation. Gay rights groups support programs doing research into a cure or provide late-stage care for HIV patients. Breast cancer patients lobby for more research for their disease. Seniors and organizations such as AARP support programs benefiting senior citizens.

Your supporters will counter those attacking your program. You cannot win a sustained fight with competing agencies and companies by yourself.

Two Approaches to Build Support for Your Program

Mark Forman, the Administrator for Electronic Government and Information Technology in OMB, was the first government-wide CIO.

As the originator of E-government, he recruited more than 100 officials from various agencies when he organized the federal E-government program—called *Quicksilver*— early in the George W. Bush administration. Quicksilver was a project to baseline federal IT programs and identify redundancies to cut costs and increase the efficiency of services provided by Government to Business, Government to Government and Government to Citizens.

He and his project lead, GSA's John Sindelar, enlisted 80 federal political appointees and senior career officials, 16 state government CIOs, and the President's Management Council to contribute to the U.S. birth of E-government. Involving many high-level officials and establishing committees are two ways to build support for your program.

However, these will not work indefinitely. Soon after the initial meetings, people will drift away, and fewer and fewer people will attend your meetings. Anticipating this, tell your group at the outset that you favor a sunset date when the work of the group will end. Then, if you must, you can organize another group for another six-month period.

Once you have built an active group of supporters and officials interested in what you are doing, use one of the numerous web-based private meeting tools so your supporters do not have to travel to participate in each meeting.

For more than a decade, the country of Estonia has what *The New York Times* called a "space-age cabinet," using collaboration software to let the cabinet members "meet" from their individual offices.

When they meet together in session, they debate and cast their votes on their laptop computers. Estonia's CIO said if he can get the heads of governments to sit down in front of a computer to do their real work, he has achieved buy-in for other e-gov initiatives; and you, Brian, can do the same for your program by making it easy for potential supporters to participate with you.

ADVICE TO BRIAN

When challenges to your program appear, call on existing allies, and develop new ones to provide support. Also, work continuously to fine tune your performance metrics and your elevator talk to provide your supporters with information they can use on your behalf.

Measuring results is not easy. Unlike the private sector, which deals in profits and losses, performance metrics can be difficult to identify for agency programs. Nevertheless, unless you are able to demonstrate real results, your program will be vulnerable to those motivated to sink or reshape it.

Early on, identify the results that auditors expect your program to achieve, and decide how to measure them. Obtain baseline measurements before you begin so you can demonstrate before-and-after results to your agency's leaders, Congress and anyone else targeting your program.

It can be hard work fending off challengers to your program. Spend the time to ensure that you are not shown up in a showdown.

40
RESPECTING THE
INSPECTORS GENERAL

Frank,
I see that Inspectors General are powerful. The one
at General Services Administration in 2010 and 2012
was able to drive out two administrators in four years.
I assume that the IG in my agency will be scrutinizing
my work. What can I expect?

Currently, social networking, smart phones, tablet technology, 4g telecommunications, mobile and cloud computing, data analytics, and virtualization are allowing almost everyone in the world to become connected and to access most of the world's unclassified information.

Beyond these winners, it is difficult to pick the emerging technologies that will endure 10 years from now. Yet, Social Security Administration officials found it necessary to push back against an often-typical Inspector General report recommending that the agency develop a long-range plan and commit to current technology for a decade.

SSA officials responded strongly to the IG, convinced that the incremental approach allowing flexible investing as technology evolved was a better approach to meet the agency's requirements: "We do not believe it is wise to commit now to specific expansions or refinements of agency electronic services in future years, given the constantly evolving need of the agency and our customers." In addition, they said, we adjust our plans according to the satisfaction of our customers and our available resources.

Inspectors General and others in the government audit community do much good work. However, many continue to favor long-range plans and grand designs despite the uncertainty associated with rapidly emerging technologies. In periods of rapid change, agencies need the option to work with short-term exploratory projects before committing for the long term.

One example of the incremental approach during this period originated in the Veterans Administration where the chief information officer, Roger Baker, organized a pilot test of 1,000 Apple iPad tablet computers in October 2011. He anticipated that doctors on the move in hospitals would access patient records using the tablets while discussing patient care issues with nurses, families and the patients.

Baker foresaw the possibility that the graphics properties of tablet computers would display heart monitor results and blood chemistry charts. Patients in remote areas could be loaned tablet computers to support home telehealth programs. Did these forecasts work out? Some did. Will Baker's projections of up to 100,000 tablet computers in the VA happen? Maybe not. Did the program provide lessons and ideas that will lead in directions not yet anticipated? Yes, for sure.

Not to lean too heavily on the oversight community of Inspectors General and others in the audit community, but we should ask them a question. Should the VA have developed a long-range detailed grand design for the use of tablet computers and then set out on a 10-year program to buy 100,000 tablet computers instead of the pilot, incremental approach they elected?

When discussing Inspectors General and auditors, one needs a balanced picture. Law requires government agencies to maintain inspectors general programs to investigate, evaluate and combat waste, fraud and abuse in government programs. However, some government officials attack the program.

An op-ed in *The Washington Post* illustrates the challenge. Written on April 4, 2007 by the former head of acquisition policy in the federal government, he condemned inspectors general, and he declared an unhealthy situation has emerged because the IG culture has undermined public management and that this is bad for good government, he claimed.

Representatives of the contracting officer community complain that IGs create a climate of fear and recommend that the government rein in the IG community.

An identical view in 2015 claimed that cases previously settled as routine administrative mistakes are now regarded with suspicion and often of criminal wrongdoing. Many officials apparently are reluctant to speak out for fear of drawing the attention of the IGs. "No one oversees the IGs," one government official said. The result is that procurement officials and others are reluctant to speak with the vendor community, a problem in the IT world where the government relies on the vendor community to provide the resources for the government programs.[177]

On the other hand, the Inspector General in the Energy Department reported that his office has 200-250 criminal investigations ongoing at any point in time, and 60 percent of those deal with potential fraud in government-issued contracts. Shouts to restrain Inspectors General in favor of greater latitude for contracting officers can overlook real problems.[178]

A strong and independent inspectors general program is necessary in this day of billion-dollar programs managed by fewer, but larger companies.

Many critics of IGs lack an appreciation of the ongoing waste in major contract awards. Increasingly, big systems managers in government are political appointees lacking an understanding or the ability to relate to the many missions and programs of the agency. Moreover, appointees are often initially hostile to career employees, ignoring their 20 to 30 years of experience. Rather, they rely on contractors who have their own agenda not easily detected by inexperienced White House appointees sitting across the table in a partnership discussion or in a negotiation.

Relying solely on contractors ignores the hundred million and billion-dollar contracts failing with regularity in the US, the UK and other governments. The Inspectors General, along with agency auditors, are often the only ones paying any attention. Examples include successive failed modernization programs in the IRS, the FAA and the many failures in the DOD, to mention just a few. Billions of taxpayer dollars have gone down the drain over decades, while the problems with these huge contracts continue to this day and will into the future.

In most cases, contracting officers are ineffective to do much about this scandal. They do not have access to key officials. They often lack sufficient resources, power or the time to do a superior job in all cases.[179]

In this environment, the agency inspector general is an important resource. Attacks by George W. Bush administration led to the 2008 Inspectors General Reform Act in which Congress, offended by the attacks, solidified the roles and responsibilities of federal IGs. As part of the new law, Congress established the Council of the Inspectors General on Integrity and Efficiency (CIGIE).[180]

The CIGIE 2013 Progress Report to the President listed the achievements of the IG community.[181]

- Handled about 5,865 suspensions or debarments of companies
- Issued 7,618 audit, inspection and evaluation reports
- Identified $37 billion in potential savings agreed to by agency program managers
- Led the way to 6,705 successful criminal prosecutions
- Processed nearly 619,400 complaints received on telephone or online hot lines

Advice to Brian

Sometimes IGs can arrive at the wrong conclusions. Nevertheless, they provide important transparency in government. You can expect that your agency IG will be looking carefully and frequently at your program and its progress, or lack of it. In addition, the GAO will be doing the same, probably every year. While no program manager wants to see a published report critical of his program, the information in the report may provide new and helpful insights.

Inspectors General and auditors perform a critical function. They present reality, whether it is success or failure. Only IGs and auditors can do this job. They help protect the government from waste, fraud and abuse. If they focus their resources on your program, respect their power and their recommendations.

At the same time, if they come knocking on your door, the reality is that they can stay forever until they find something. If you face an IG inquiry, you can spend a fortune on legal services to defend yourself. As recommended earlier, rely on the insights of the old hands in your organization. In addition, work selectively with individuals on the 20-person advisory group you created to deal with the complexity of your task.

41

UNDERSTANDING CHIEF INFORMATION OFFICER JOBS

Frank,

I am learning that there are hundreds of CIOs in this government. Particularly, there is the national CIO, the Department CI, and numerous CIOs in agencies including my own agency. Can you tell me about these folks? What do they do? What authority do they have? Will they be involved in my work? Should I consider them as friendly?

Although you are not going to be a CIO, you should understand their place in government, their responsibilities and the limitations of their position so you can work effectively with them. Moreover, someone might offer you a CIO job in the future.

THE FATHER OF CIOs

Have you heard of Andy MacDonald, the first government CIO in the world? He conceived the position in 1993, convinced the government of Canada to create it and then assumed the job.

Before taking the role, he was Canada's chief financial officer. In that job, he observed that there were heads of IT in each department and agency, but noted that none was taking a whole-of-government view.

When I tracked him down at the World Bank several years ago, he told me he got the idea for a government-wide CIO position from his membership on *The Research Board,* an international think tank headquartered in New York City. Membership is by invitation only and is restricted to chief information officers of the world's largest corporations.

MacDonald was the only government member of the Board, although not a CIO at the time. I knew him as a strong, imposing, knowledgeable, no-nonsense man with charm. In addition to being the first, he may also have been the second government CIO in the world when he relocated 10,289 miles to fill a similar position in the Australian government.

Making the switch from CFO to CIO, though, was a dash of cold water for him. As Canada's chief financial officer, he had control of the budget and real power. When he tried to exercise similar power as the CIO, he met stiff resistance from Canadian program officials; and in Australia, he found the resistance even more ferocious. He grew to believe confrontation and conflict are the destiny of change agents, including CIOs, in any organization. Thousands of government CIOs worldwide followed in Andy MacDonald's footsteps. He broke new ground, and many after him have had success and failure.

CREATING THE CIO JOB IN THE FEDERAL GOVERNMENT

While MacDonald was serving as Canada's CIO, the Clinton administration and Congress wanted to change the power structure for IT management in the federal government. Paul Brubaker, then serving as a senior staff member in Congress, reviewed the Canadian and Australian experiences and drew from them when he drafted the Clinger-Cohen Act, creating CIO positions in Federal agencies.

Early expectations for the CIO as a change agent were high. From the outset, Congress anticipated that CIOs would identify better ways to manage government using advanced technology.

However, the results have been less than expected, but there is continued hope.

The Clinger-Cohen Act created CIOs, but it did not specify skills needed for the jobs. Yet, when Congress created the chief financial officer position in 1990, it delineated a rigorous skill set, written right into the legislation. As a result, agencies select qualified people for CFO jobs, but not always do they do so for CIO jobs.

John Sindelar, formerly the deputy associate administrator for government-wide policy at GSA, concurs. He feels the omission of skill requirements for the CIO position was a fatal flaw in the otherwise relatively successful Clinger-Cohen Act.

CIOs and Control of Spending

CIOs in 2015 reported varying control over their agency's IT budget. Some CIOs reported they control up to 50% of the budget; others reported much less control.[182]

The Clinger-Cohen Act of 1996 required a CIO office in every federal agency, but it did not include a specific provision giving CIOs control of the money. Sources that drafted the Act say this outcome was part of a power struggle with chief financial officers opposed to transferring spending power to CIOs. Traditionally, control of the budget is a CFO responsibility because these officials are theoretically better able to manage investment decisions.

Control of IT spending could be important to CIOs. "Congress would have loved to add more authorities for the CIOs, including budget authority, when it passed the Clinger-Cohen Act," said Drew Crockett, deputy communications director for the Government Reform Committee. "However, since Clinger-Cohen was such a huge burden to pass, Congressional members and staff at the time felt they could get no more into the bill." Crockett said, "Budget authority for CIOs has been discussed on and off for years, and we continue to explore ways to strengthen the CIO function."[183]

There are two other ways that agencies give CIOs a voice in the IT budget process, according to Jim Flyzik, former CIO at the Treasury Department.

- Allow CIOs to approve spending, but keep the true control of the funds with the officials responsible for the program
- Give CIOs informal authority to make final "go or no go" decisions to an agency's or to a department's proposed information technology

Another solution to budget control is to give department level CIOs full control over spending on infrastructure and enterprise-wide applications and software, while CIOs in agencies and in lower level organizations would retain budget control for their mission applications.

For years, the question has been whether CIOs should have more control over their agency's IT budget. Some CIOs say yes. Others say no. Those who say no, we do not need it include former CIO leaders Karen Evans, OMB, Vance Hitch, Justice Department, and Dan Matthews, Department of Transportation. More recently, Lisa Schlosser, representing OMB, provided insights similar to others in years past.[184]

"My experience is that you don't need to sign off on every dollar spent on procurement; but what we do need to do is have a seat at the table when strategy is being established, when a budget is being put in place, when the priorities are being laid out, [when] the organization is going to invest in in terms of technology."

On the other hand, those with control over spending emphasize it makes a big difference in the results they can achieve. Patrick Pizzella, the Labor Department's CIO, had budget authority because he also was the department's assistant secretary for administration and budget. Wearing these two hats, Pizzella said, "[They] allow me to see the IT spending issues very early on and allow me to pre-allocate resources as appropriate."

When Alan Balutis became the Commerce Department's CIO, he was also the director of management and budget. "I went through four years of having the full budget formulation and execution authorities as well as being the CIO. . . . A strong voice with real authority is a key arrow in the CIOs quiver," said Balutis.

Fortunately, for those CIOs without direct control over an agency's IT budget, they have access to two other tools. In 1996,

Clinger-Cohen mandated a Capital Planning and Investment Control process chaired by the CIO. This tool integrates strategic and operational IT planning with the processes for the selection, control and evaluation of IT investments. While CIOs do not have the final decision for IT capital investments, the Control process gives them a degree of influence that varies in many cases.

A recent OMB tool, PortfolioStat, provides CIOs with insights into the money flow. The tool requires agencies to build a baseline, focus on duplicative spending and improve transparency into infrastructure investments. According to the Tech America 2014 survey, some CIOs report it is valuable. Others say that it has had little impact, or it is too early to tell.

OMB's Exhibits 300 and 53, discussed in Chapter 37, provide additional insights and help manage IT investments.

Factors Limiting What CIOs Can Accomplish

There are many difficult, almost impossible jobs in government. The CIO job is one of those.

Government leaders do not recognize that a strategic level CIO job in a major federal agency may be too complex for any one person to perform successfully.

CIOs often are short timers. In a recent four-year period, 26 percent of CIOs participating in a survey said they were in their job less than one year; and another 21 percent responded that they were in their job between one and two years, indicating that almost 50 percent had limited time in these high level jobs in some of the largest, most complex and often contentious organizations in the world.[185]

New CIOs often do not know the business of the agency. CIOs need to know the business of their agency's programs from the bottom up, the grassroots level. Consider any large sector such as taxation, health or social services. These are complex fields, and you cannot suddenly parachute in and expect to be effective. You must make a major investment of time to learn the business.

CIOs make as much or as little difference as their Secretary or Deputy Secretary care about the CIO role. It may be that the cyber security problems will cause agency leaders to seek the CIOs counsel, but can they deliver when they and their staffs generally lack solid cyber credentials?

A high percentage of CIOs are academically unqualified for their jobs. *FCW*, in a survey of 25 CIOs, reported that management and administration degrees far outnumber engineering and computer science degrees. In addition, there were no doctorates or PHDs in engineering or computer science among those surveyed, and none held degrees in cyber security.[186]

Some CIOs do not have advanced management skills. The CIOs that agency heads are most likely to invite into the inner circle have advanced management skills, including leadership, negotiating, lobbying and mediating skills.

CIOs face resistance from executives responsible for managing and modernizing the programs that run agencies. These program administrators are rightfully suspicious of change proposed by a relative newcomer in a CIO position, especially when Congress approved their own multi-year program plans only after long and tough negotiations in their agency and with OMB. In addition, these program officials often have good congressional connections that approve the money for their programs and can ensure deflection of any thrust for change from an agency CIO.

Agency heads are interested in solutions to current problems, especially those on the front page of *The Washington Post, The New York Times* and *The Wall Street Journal,* which the White House notices. The pressures of attending to the new and emerging crises partly explains why agency heads do not focus on CIO issues or possibilities, which, by nature, are long-term, back room, invisible to most and rarely a quick solution to today's crisis. However, this may be changing.

In 2015, the CEO of Target and the Director of the Federal Office of Personnel Management were fired because hackers broke into their files and stole millions of personnel and customer records. As a result, the Boards of many companies are emphasizing cyber security. Clearly, the executive suites are learning that their jobs are at risk if hackers successfully penetrate. Going forward, inattention to cyber security will be costly in terms of job security.

In this environment, the C level likely will turn to their CIOs for leadership. But, will they be able to deliver? Protection from hackers is a highly technical challenge.

Scientists in the Department of Energy call plutonium the world's most dangerous material. Askold Boretsky formerly with Acquisition Solutions Inc., disagrees. He says "administronium"—the administrative processes necessary to run an agency— is the most treacherous, because policy officials can go overboard, sap the energy of its most vibrant people and divert them from real work.

CIOs are heavily into process activities while forming committees to develop standards, performance measures, architectures and an endless stream of time consuming schemes. In part, this is because White House and OMB officials, without their own staff, have for years rounded up CIO and GSA personnel to devote endless hours planning and implementing their latest government-wide processes such as capital asset planning, earned value management and the e-government scorecard. These were indirectly useful in government-wide IT management, but drove CIOs further into process management.

New initiatives such as Agile Development (modular development), Analytics and Big Data are priorities in all organizations worldwide. However, in the federal government, the unwillingness of agencies to share data across boundaries limits the possibilities of these technologies.

Recent Priorities of CIOs

In 2014, TechAmerica and Grant Thornton International conducted an annual survey of CIOs and Chief Information Security Officers (CISOs) to identify their current priorities.[187] Each year, some 85 industry officials working in individual interview teams meet with about 60 CIOs and federal program managers, where interviewees can speak freely. Since their comments are not for attribution, the CIOs generally provide candid views and opinions about their priorities and challenges.

The survey reveals continuity in the priorities of CIOs going back several years, and the 2014 priorities are quite similar to those of 2013. Recent priorities and concerns of CIOs include the following.

CIOs were adapting to rapid changes in technology, declining budgets, a smaller workforce and a noncollaborative and sometimes unqualified workforce.

The budget was a top concern of CIOs, and they were seeking creative ways to save money. Initiatives to save money for modernization programs were cloud computing, consolidating data centers, use of shared services and implementing *PortfolioStat,* a new management process from OMB.

The CIOs complained about ineffective acquisition support and long procurement lead times required by the 51 parts and 2,000 pages in the Federal Acquisition Regulation. The CIOs want a faster process, a process oriented to "buying by the drink" instead of grand designs, and they want procurement officials to work more closely with them rather than keeping them at arm's length in procurements.

Human capital remains a problem in the eyes of CIOs, who perennially caution that many government IT personnel are becoming eligible for retirement and the government personnel system. At the same time, Republican Party attacks on the workforce, along with wage freezes, put a damper on recruiting.

Cyber security attacks from internal and external sources increase each year and now absorb 15 percent of government-wide IT funds. The FY 2015 budget request to improve cyber security and to pay for continuous monitoring diagnostic technologies was $13 billion. In addition, the CIOs recommended that Congress update or delete the 11-year-old Federal Information Security Management Act (FISMA) to focus on risk rather than on checklists.

The explosion of mobility inside the workforce, driven mainly by smart phones, is a major opportunity and a major problem for CIOs in every organization worldwide. In addition, as with all technologies, especially new ones, security is an issue.

In addition, there are two other priorities:

- Modernizing/transforming IT operations emphasizing Agile techniques
- Managing the migration to the cloud in response to OMB's "Cloud First" policy

ALTERNATIVE ROADMAPS FOR CIOs

In August 2011, Jacob J. Lew, the Director of OMB, sent a policy memo to heads of agencies outlining a future roadmap for CIOs.[188] He noted that too many federal IT projects are late, exceed budget, do not deliver capabilities as intended and waste taxpayer dollars. Henceforth, he said CIOs will lower operational costs, cancel or fix troubled systems, deliver results faster, and improve the security of information systems.

He highlighted four areas in which CIOs would have a lead role: Governance, Commodity IT management, Program management, and Information security. After one year, it was evident that Lew's approach to elevate the stature of CIOs was ineffective.

Late in 2014, Darrell Issa (R-Calif.) and Gerry Connolly (D-Va.) sponsored new legislation, the Federal Information Technology Reform Act, included in the National Defense Authorization Act (NDAA).

The legislation provides the CIO with new authority to approve the agency IT budget before the CFO sends it to OMB. In addition, the CIO or his delegate must sign off on any new contracts before award. The Obama administration was lukewarm about this bill. Paul Brubaker, an author of the earlier Clinger-Cohen Act, observed, "My guess is that it [the Act] will make some incremental improvements, but achieving information age outcomes in this construct is not going to happen."

Dave McClure, an old hand in government, observed that, as always, CIOs need the cooperation of program managers and the Chief Financial Officers to be successful.[189] FITARA did not address these truisms. In addition, Issa-Connolly wanted presidential appointees to fill agency level CIO jobs, a mandate that would continue to place some unqualified campaign supporters in these important jobs.

The big challenge for CIOs is to find solutions that will work across agencies, even across the entire government. CIOs able to deliver these solutions will be in demand and will sit with the inner circle running each agency. Can CIOs lead the charge to future possibilities?

Legislation has uniquely positioned CIOs to be the key

orchestrators to transform government, because they are able to take a holistic view of the agency's programs. Individually, in their agencies, they sit high on a lonely hill under a clear, cold night sky and can see from north to south and east to west and all in between. With this visibility, they have the opportunity to develop a vision and plan and develop and implement the next generation of E-government in their agency or in the government as a whole.

Despite the difficulties associated with the CIO position, some CIOs already operate at a higher level, embracing a holistic view. They are aware of the broader role the legislators have chartered them to play, and they strive to lead in the transformation of their organization. They are committed to integrated horizontalism with its whole-of-government and cross-government goals.

In time, additional well-rounded CIOs likely will emerge, able to operate as Paul Brubaker hoped when he drafted the Clinger-Cohen Act and as Reps. Issa and Connolly envision in their new legislation. These future CIO managers will have technical, business and financial acumen and be agents of change (perhaps titled chief transformation officers), comfortable with trial-and-error pilot programs, dedicated to simplify and realign business processes, willing to collaborate outside their agency and share, and able to sell the need to integrate related programs.

CIOs able to perform in these roles can become future agency heads, or CEOs, of their institutions.

Today, 20 years after the Clinger-Cohen Act, it is clear that the CIO job has evolved, but the future is murky. The job is difficult and becomes more so with each passing year. One former CIO spoke of what she called the futility of the CIO role. Linda Cureton, formerly at NASA, said that in the current situation CIOs are slightly more effective than no CIO at all.[190]

The trade media hangs on every word of CIOs, treating them as demigods while inviting them to speak at fancy conferences, often after being on the job only a few weeks. Yet, the politically appointed CIO remains on the job an average of only 19 months. Career CIOs remain 32 months. So why do they leave so soon? If the jobs were good, you would think they would want the jobs for life, like African dictators.

One reason they leave early is that the jobs are difficult.

Also, sometimes the CIO position seems to exist to meet the government's need for a point man, someone to hammer on when agency records are hacked and when major systems are late and over budget.

The opportunities to make meaningful contributions are high in CIO jobs, but, especially for agency-level CIO jobs, they exist alongside the prospect for serious frustration.

Advice to Brian

Three levels of CIOs will be involved in your work. Congress and the OMB have placed them in what is essentially an oversight role. Several congressional committees and the President's Office of Management and Budget want them to be successful and steer new authorities to them to grow their influence. Therefore, CIOs are influential.

You will need to keep them informed with periodic briefings and provide them with substantial amounts of information, especially during the developmental period of your program. Under the new legislation, they will sign off on your budget request for new systems, and they will sign off on new or extending contracts before award. Although you may develop good relationships over time, recognize that if your program draws attention because of schedule slippages and cost overruns, they will become auditors because Congress and elected officials will demand answers.

42
Technologies Do Not Advance Rapidly, Some Not at All.

Frank,

As we plan our project, we are beginning to discuss the state of technologies available now or likely to become available soon. I am worried that technology changes so quickly, we will be stuck with obsolete equipment before we ever go live. How should I be thinking about and planning for this?

To protect your program from being trapped with old solutions while newer, better and cheaper ones emerge during the life of your program, recognize that switching to newer technology may have cost implications; and be sure that a clause similar to the following is included in the contact: *During the life of the contract as new technologies emerge, the government, after consultation with the contractor, may require that the new technologies be adopted. Alternatively, the contractor, after consultation with the government, may propose adopting newer technology.*

However, there is a larger issue associated with new technologies. Beware of the technology bandwagon often ballyhooed as the solution to every major problem. Before I get into the cautions, let's review some exciting developments in consumer technology.

THERE ARE TWO TYPES OF TECHNOLOGY:

- Consumer technology
- Big-systems technology needed to run governments and large corporations

Consumer Technology

Today, stories describing technology moving rapidly normally refer to consumer technology.

When technology catches on, prices fall, usually dramatically. Salt, a table ingredient, had enormous value at one time. Today, thanks to modern mining techniques, it has almost no value. Consider aluminum. In Napoleon's day, he gave the highest-ranking guests at his banquets aluminum plates as mementoes; he gave lesser nobles gold plates.

In 2002, United Airlines had me comfortably seated in business class with my wife, Mary Alice, on the way from Dulles Airport in Virginia to Singapore. Diagonally across the aisle were two preteen girls, sharing a portable DVD player with separate headphones, watching movies of their choice. The rest of us were watching the usual sterile, made-for-children airline movies.

When we returned to the US, I learned that the price of portable DVD players was about $1,100—too expensive to justify for our personal use.

Just four years later in 2006, during the Christmas buying season, I checked the prices again and discovered some were selling for as little as $49. A few months later, I saw a DVD player with no recognizable brand name for sale at Staples for $29. Portable DVD players became disposable technology in just five years. Buy it, use it, and if it develops a problem, toss it in the recycling container and buy another.

There are many similar examples. The price of 50-inch high definition digital TVs declined 90 percent from $5,000 to $499 in ten years even as TV technology became more advanced and reliable.

The price of Blue-ray players fell 75 percent in just two years as 20 percent of households adopted the newer technology.

When a Best Buy, Office Depot, Costco type of consumer electronics technology achieves mass-market acceptance—adopted by about 30 percent of consumers—the price falls quickly. Consumer electronics have relatively simple software, build on the previous versions and require few manufacturing changes. The conventional wisdom claiming that technology changes fast and drops in price even faster is a perception based largely on such products.

Continued development of microprocessors has made cell phones tiny, and lithium ion batteries allow them to run longer, providing portability and enticing customers to buy 1,000 devices each minute in recent years.

The Internet is a great invention on par in terms of impact with the wheel, plow, steam engines and the printing press. It provides access to all of the world's non-classified information in an instant. It is also the world's greatest public forum, connecting most people in the world, and its use and consequences continue to explode. Soon, computers will be in 16 trillion devices with Internet access and even in clothing. We can see the end of desktop and laptop computers as we have known them since the 1980s.

Despite these remarkable advances, some technologies advance gradually, especially the technology that governments and corporations need in their major operational systems.

Big-systems Technology is Needed by Government and Corporations

It is one thing to use technology to query the internet download music, play games and send text messages. It is quite another thing to try to use technology to integrate systems composed of thousands of subsystems and millions of lines of computer code designed to service the many and dissimilar needs of 250 million people.

The technologies needed by major organizations advance slowly, though steadily, over time. In addition, many technologies suitable for small pilot projects are not ready for the scale of major government systems.

The FAA and IRS have spent 25 years and vast sums of money with high quality firms adopting the latest technologies to modernize their systems and have seen only marginal improvements in actual performance, although IRS did have an important breakthrough in 2012, as we will discuss later.

Claims about Fast-Moving Technologies Are Often Myths

Even the Internet, which many people think is an example of rapidly advancing technology, is not as it seems. The Internet did not suddenly burst on the scene in the early 1990s; it really began in 1969. For 22 years, the federal government supplied money for research through the Defense Advanced Research Projects Agency (DARPA, the central research and development organization for the Department of Defense), nurturing the development of the program before releasing it to the public in 1991. Then, it took two years for the Internet to reach 2 percent of the population and seven more years until half of all Americans had access.[191]

When Facebook, Twitter and other social networking programs married the existing technologies of wireless communications and the Internet, they made it possible to link all people in the world for instant communication and allow them to access all non- classified information. Governments generally use these technologies to deliver information and push their messages out to the public and to its contractors. While they are technically creative and important, social networking technologies have a limited role in helping government officials to develop the systems that run the daily operations of government.

Emphasizing that technology does not move fast, Bob Seidensticker, in his book *Futurehype,* argues that new technology products do not arrive any faster now than they ever did. It takes an average of 23 years from the earliest laboratory stage until a product reaches mainstream usage in the population.

Bill Halal, emeritus at George Washington University, has identified thousands of new products, hyped for a short time in the media. However, most never reach mainstream acceptance by reaching 30 percent of the population.[192]

Sometimes technology seems to be moving fast because the new things are unfamiliar, while the technological advances of earlier ages seem commonplace. As Seidensticker says, "Live in the woods for a week and see if you miss your laptop the most." The technologies that matter the most to us, he says, are the older ones such as the automobile, agriculture, antibiotics, concrete, electricity, jet engines, telephones and textiles.

GENERALLY, EMERGING TECHNOLOGIES ARE NOT READY FOR PRIME TIME

David Walker, former Comptroller General, reported that developmental programs with immature technology experience cost overruns of 35 percent compared to programs with mature technology, which average only 5 percent in cost overruns.[193]

The Army's Future Combat System is one example where emerging technology proved to be an expensive disappointment. FCS was the Army's main modernization program from 2003 to 2009, when the DOD cancelled it after numerous problems. The goal had been to create field brigades with new manned and unmanned vehicles, all linked to the individual soldier in combat by a fast, flexible battlefield network. Cancelling the failed system proved difficult because the lead integrators, Boeing and Science Applications International Corporation (SAIC) coordinated more than 550 contractors and subcontractors in 41 states, and Congress rarely allows the government to cancel programs employing jobs in their districts. [194]

In this case, the Department of the Army and its contractors pushed ahead with a number of FCS programs when the needed technology, design and production knowledge were lacking, causing delivery milestones and cost predictions to be significantly underestimated.

In Walker's definition, this $128 billion program, the Army's principal modernization program in the first decade of the new millennium, had only one mature technology among its 49 crucial technologies eight years after the Pentagon began the program. In April and May 2009, with criticism coming from all points, including the new Obama White House, and after fighting the good fight for years to retain the failing system, Pentagon and Army officials announced they would cancel the Future Combat System vehicle-development program. Some parts of the failing FCS effort had promise, so they planned to sweep those remains into a new, pan-Army program called Army Brigade Combat.

Of the thousands of government contracts using technology, many work well. However, the most expensive and complex programs are often train wrecks. Let's look at another of the many available examples.

In May 2006, President George W. Bush announced the Secure Border Initiative (SBInet). He called it "the most technologically advanced border security initiative in American history." The first step was a 28-mile virtual fence called "Project 28." The idea was to use emerging technologies, including some adapted from the military, to find people trying to cross the border illegally.

A BIT OF HISTORY ABOUT BORDER SECURITY IS REVEALING

In 15 years since 1995, spending on border security increased tenfold from $1.2 billion to $12.7 billion, and the number of Border Patrol agents more than quadrupled from 5,000 to 21,000 (2010). Yet the number of illegal immigrants in the United States jumped from 5 million to more than 11.[195][196]

"There has been a huge amount of money poured into the border . . . but the performance of these technologies is disappointing," said Doris Meissner, a former Commissioner of the Immigration and Naturalization Service.[197]

Proceeding with President Bush's SBInet, the government hired the legendary Boeing Co. as its prime contractor. Boeing, as a company, succeeds in part with generous support from the federal government, including the federal government's Export Import Bank, sometimes called "Boeing's Bank" because, for example, it provided financing for the purchase of 634 Boeing aircraft between 2005 and 2010 by foreign countries.[198]

Boeing is an economic powerhouse in the State of Washington, where it is manufacturing its 777X 406-seat plane seating up to 451 passengers competing with the giant Airbus A350 aircraft. Fearing that Boeing might move production to South Carolina, the State granted Boeing $8.7 billion in tax breaks, which Airbus said exceed the cost of developing the 777X aircraft. Airbus suggested that Boeing is getting a new aircraft fully funded by the U.S. taxpayer. These tax breaks amount to the largest government subsidy to a company in American history. Washington State in this case, is paying $155,357 for each job to keep 56,000 employees in the state and working for Boeing.[199]

In addition, federal government programs support the famous American company with more than $18 billion in FY2014 contract awards, combined with the $457 million in federal grants and $64 billion in federal loans and loan guarantees between 2000 and 2014.[200] [201]

Boeing is an American icon and a legendary aircraft manufacturer, providing reliable long-haul aircraft for its commercial and military customers. In 2011, at the window of the international terminal in Tokyo's Narita's airport, I observed 20 Boeing 777 heavy jets lined up in a row with ANA (All Nippon Airways) and United (United Airways) proudly painted on their wide bodies, a majestic 21st century sight as they waited to carry some 6,000 passengers across oceans and great distances to the four corners of the world.

Yet Boeing, for all of its skills and contributions to society, has had limited success in managing complex information technology systems. This suggests caution to government program managers of complex systems. Even the biggest and the best companies stumble with the complex systems needed to run modern government. Program managers should moderate their ambitions for the most advanced solutions and scale back their requirements.

When the government was evaluating proposals, including Boeing's, for the prime contractor role in SBInet, Boeing was having its own difficulties. It admitted that it had gone too far in outsourcing its new and very advanced Dreamliner 787 aircraft because the program was three years late, costing the company millions in penalties for late delivery of the revolutionary aircraft. Boeing's chief, W. James McNerney Jr., conceded that Boeing lost control of the process by farming out more design and production work than ever and not keeping track of suppliers.[202]

Yet the government considered that Boeing was the best

company to integrate dozens of companies, including their managers, infrastructure, technology and rapid response technologies to secure the northern and southern land borders of the U.S.. This would be perhaps the most complex program in the government outside of the FAA's systems that control 87,000 aircraft in the skies each day.

Boeing's plan was to construct a necklace of 1,800 towers equipped with cameras, sensors and links to sophisticated computers, eventually stretching along the nation's 2,000-mile border with Mexico.

Boeing assembled a team of 100 subcontractors to build the Project 28 "virtual fence" beginning near Nogales, Arizona. Boeing committed to complete the $20 million project of sensor towers and advanced mobile communications by mid-2007, but software and technical problems delayed the project.

Boeing's plan rested heavily on adapting military technology from the battlefield and transferring it to the border. The company considered, for instance, flying a camera-equipped, 10-pound drone called Skylark, used by Israeli and Australian forces to track suspects.

Boeing also proposed a variety of ground-based sensors, including the underground seismic sensors, tower-mounted motion and heat detectors used by the U.S. military in Iraq and Afghanistan.

Congressional backers and military experts expressed confidence that technologies devised to detect troop movements and tank formations could be adapted for homeland security and, by extension, to detect illegals crossing the border.

Gervasio Prado, founder of SenTech Inc., a sensor maker, part of two unsuccessful bidding teams, said SBInet is good for his industry but is not likely to work.

"I don't think you'll make a dent really," because of the difficulty of managing information from 6,000 miles of sensors and the economic incentives for illegal migrants and their smugglers, he said. "I'd love to say that if you install thousands of sensors, you could really solve the problem. But I think the help is going to be minimal."

Homeland Security officials wanted contractors to fully deploy their equipment in four years, and ambitiously, Boeing said it could be done in three.

Gregory J. Pottie, a UCLA engineering professor specializing in sensor technology, testified to the House of Representatives in November 2006, "If we want to solve this in three years, it could cost us a fortune, and we're going to make a lot of mistakes." By February 2008, his prediction had become fact.

On February 22, 2008, Homeland Security Secretary Michael Chertoff reported the high-tech "virtual fence" on a section of the U.S. border with Mexico was finally ready for service, and he promised the technology could fight illegal crossings all along the frontier.

Six days later, Homeland Security confessed the system did not work as planned and did not meet the needs of the U.S. Border Patrol. It also cost 15 times the initial $2 billion estimate, according to the DHS inspector general.

In a series of investigative reports, GAO investigators and Homeland Security's Inspector General reported that SBInet software could not process large amounts of sensor data. Operators in the Tucson Command Center 65 miles away found it difficult to lock cameras onto the targets. This is often a problem with technology. Successful small pilot projects often fail with a full-scale workload.

DHS's Inspector General also found fault with the work of L-3 Communications, one of the dozens of Boeing subcontractors on SBInet, reporting that L-3 cameras deployed for border security as part of the Integrated Surveillance Intelligence System malfunctioned when exposed to severe cold or heat, common in the desert.

The GAO reported that the cameras had trouble resolving images at five kilometers when Boeing had promised they would work at ten. In addition, rain triggered the radar systems, sending up alarms when no illegals were in the area. Rain also blurred sensor images like water on a windshield, according to officials.

Even on the relatively short 28-mile slice of the border, cameras had difficulty with automatic-focus software. Radar systems needed continual fine-tuning to declutter their returns for the cameras. The wild region's deep canyons and thick vegetation further complicated the cameras' performance, as well as the towers' power supply and communications.

With 100 contractors working under Boeing, a major concern was the pyramid-like management structure that critics charged led to cost overruns and poor quality in other programs. The multiple contracting tiers allowed Boeing to exact a cut at every turn, increasing their income while creating a conflict of interest because the company also oversees the same subcontractors.

"The last time I saw this type of model for managing a project was the *Big Dig* in Boston," said Massachusetts Democratic Congressman Steven Lynch—quoted in *The Washington Post* on March 21, 2010—referring to a highway-rerouting mega project, including a 3.5-mile long tunnel under Boston that was estimated at $3 billion but actually cost $22 billion. This is exactly what they did. They fused the oversight function with the engineering and construction function. Everybody was in the same tent. Nobody was watching out for the owner, in this case the American taxpayer. This is a terrible model and I see a lot of it, because it is a model favored by systems integrators.[203]

GAO concluded the failure of SBInet to meet the needs of its users was at least partly because Boeing developed the system with "minimal input" from border patrol agents.[204]

In hindsight, DHS officials could have anticipated some of these problems if they had paid attention to recent history. According to their inspector general in 2005, two earlier failed border surveillance programs cost taxpayers $429 million between 1998 and 2005. After several years, the contractor had installed only half of the required 489 cameras. The Homeland Security Inspector General reported in December 2007 that agents never investigated sixty percent of sensor alerts, and 90 percent of the others were false alarms. Only one percent of the sensor alerts resulted in arrests.

Rep. Bennie Thompson, a Mississippi Democrat heading the House Homeland Security Committee, was harshly critical, saying Boeing and DHS officials actively blocked border patrol agents from pointing out obvious flaws in the new system. You see, Brian, the border patrol had already experienced failure trying to use emerging technologies, but Department officials above them forged ahead with SBInet without considering their experience.[205]

In April 2008, the government scrapped the $20 million prototype of the highly touted "virtual fence" along a 28-mile section of border southwest of Tucson on the Arizona-Mexico border, because the system failed to adequately alert border patrol agents to illegal crossings, officials said. The move came just two months after Homeland Security Secretary Michael Chertoff announced his approval of the fence built by Boeing.

In a new initiative, Boeing committed to replace the so-called Project 28 prototype with a series of towers equipped with communications systems, new cameras and new radar capability. Actually, these capabilities were close to those in Boeing's first contract.

In 2010, with $1 billion spent and about 53 miles of the targeted 2,000-mile border completed, Homeland Security halted new work on the SBInet and diverted $50 million of its funding to other uses. In January 2011, the Secretary of Homeland Security cancelled the remainder of SBInet after a yearlong assessment, stating that the 53-mile segment will remain in operation in Arizona while the agency considers alternatives for the remaining 1,947 miles along the remainder of the southern border.

Then, following the practice of other agencies responsible for failed systems, the agency released a Request for Information for a new and better system called Integrated Fixed Towers with essentially the same goals as the failed SBInet.

In March 2014, the Customs and Border Protection (CBP) awarded the Integrated Fixed Towers (IFT) contract to Elbit Systems Ltd.[206]

The award was for $145 million to detect, track, identify and classify items of interest across the southwest border through a series of fixed sensor towers and command and control center equipment that displays information on a common operating picture. The award is the first phase to install one tower and support facilities of what may become five towers or more and support facilities. [207]

People experienced with massive system failures could provide a cautionary voice, but they rarely have the opportunity to do so. In-house government technology officials are willing to take on any challenge, however dubious, while at the same time, company officials never lack a proposal for whatever government officials dream up.

Making better technology investment decisions is difficult for governments.

Years of experience demonstrate that it is difficult to make good predictions about which technologies will be successful in the market place and in governments no matter how highly placed the predictor may be.

Bill Gates said the Internet would not be important. IBM's legendary Tom Watson said three computers are all that the world needs. If these technology tycoons heading major technology firms forecast the future so poorly, how can government officials exercise better judgment?

We can learn from the past by considering the evolution of the Internet, which has been on a 40-year journey. While some think that the Internet dropped out of the sky fully formed at the turn of the century, work began on what we know as the Internet in 1969 in the DOD, which funded its development in partnerships with universities. In the early 1990s the White House decided to make the product available to the public.

The point about this and other technologies is that they take about 30 years to reach mainstream usage, which the Internet reached in the 1990s. "Do not jump too quickly" is a lesson from the past. "If you take a leap and make a costly mistake, fail fast," says Peter Bruce of Canada. Grand designs take the opposite approach and fail slowly, over years, with escalating costs.

Advice to Brian

Recognize that 80 percent of promising technologies, always highly touted by the media, never reach critical mass usage and fade into oblivion, to be remembered only by the few technology historians

Politicians and your colleagues will often rush to seek a technology-based solution for a tough political problem. Sometimes they are right to do so, but more often than not, ballyhooed technology solutions collapse in few years, sometimes at great expense to the taxpayer. As a program manager, you must determine whether the technology proposed to you is mature or not. There are several sources, including the Gartner Group and

Bill Halal's Techcast Group (that can help you determine whether the touted technology class is ready to meet your requirements.[208]

In addition to being skeptical, check with sources in other governments domestically and worldwide to see if technology that your colleagues or contractors are proposing has worked successfully in any sector. See if it worked, not that there is a plan. Existence of a plan is not a good barometer of future success. A couple planning a springtime garden wedding down to the smallest detail including a three tier white cake with images of themselves standing brightly on top is a good beginning; but who knows whether their hopes and plans will materialize during their years-long journey together?

The CIO Council in the federal government, NASCIO for state governments in the United States, and the International Council for Technology in Government Administration and their executives are sources of information about what works and does not work

From certain perspectives, even a failed project may serve two purposes.

It allows political appointees and elected officials to demonstrate that they recognized the problem and took action.

As in the Secure Freight Initiative, a failed program reveals to government and industry officials how the technology needs to improve to meet a vital, current requirement.

So do not fear failure, but take your chances in a pilot program, not the entire program where the costs of failure will be extravagant.

I hope I have convinced you to question advice and resist pressure to use new technology as the first and best solution to any problem. If you do engage in technology hype, be sure to keep your resume up-to-date and make tracks to another job before reality sets in.

In summary, fifty years of jumping on the new technology bandwagon have delivered some successes. Unfortunately, it also delivered many costly failures and will continue to do so in the future. While the perennial optimists in government and industry confidently claim that they and new technology can do anything government leaders dream up, experience proves otherwise. Do not be one of the early jumpers!

43

SHARING IN SAVINGS
WHEN MONEY IS SCARCE.

Dear Frank,
Please explain share-in-savings contracts,
sometimes called self-funded or risk sharing contracts
in the United States. Are they good alternatives when
the need exists and money does not? Internationally,
other countries call these arrangements Public Private
Partnership Programs (PPPP's).

Simply put, the contractor uses the company's own money to build the system, and the government pays the contractor a fee for each transaction the system processes. The contractor, therefore, shares in the revenue generated or money saved, hence the name Share in Savings.

Under the right conditions, they are a great tool to modernize a system without a major investment of government money. Twenty-six state and local governments use the SiS approach, especially for systems that process transactions, such as applications for licenses, permits, renewals and payments.[209]

Each year, Chicago collected only 10 percent of the fines it levied for parking violations. To improve the collection rate, the city hired EDS to install the latest in technology—document scanning equipment, client-server networks and wireless hardware—and to reorganize the way drivers contested tickets and paid the fines. EDS invested $26 million of its own money, agreeing to share in the revenue produced by the new system.

The deal turned out to be a huge winner for both parties. After one year, Chicago collected $336 million in parking fines, and EDS earned $50 million, with more to come. Not a bad return on its investment.

Soon after Chicago and a few additional successes elsewhere, other state governments signed share-in-savings contracts requiring private firms to make upfront investments in technology in return for a share of the savings, or a cut of the revenue.

Both parties benefit. The state obtains a system with little, if any, upfront investment, and equally important, the contractor has built-in incentives to do well. Potentially, the contractor gets a bigger payday than might have been possible under traditional fixed-price or cost-plus contracting.

Federal agencies tested the share-in-savings waters, and while it had its proponents such as Ken Buck, formerly with GSA, and Steve Kelman at Harvard's Kennedy School, the method has not taken hold as it has in other governments. Buck summarized three main reasons for the lack of take-up.[210]

Termination liability funding: the E-Government Act of 2002 that authorized SiS, essentially trumped the Anti-deficiency Act and allowed the government to enter into contracts without appropriated funds. However, the E-Gov Act required the government to set aside funds to cover any termination costs should the government terminate the contract for its convenience. Because this "insurance policy" added costs to the contract, the Office of Management and Budget "scored" these costs, which raised the cost of proposed SiS programs and discouraged many agencies from considering SiS as a viable option.

Budget Surpluses: in the early 2000s, government agencies received ample funding from Congress and were not motivated to innovate to stretch their funds.

Unreliable Cost Baselines: during this period, business intelligence data was in its infancy. As such, it was difficult to develop reliable baselines to identify the total cost of ownership for a system. Today, there is much greater reliability on total program-related life cycle cost estimates.

In addition, contractors and some agencies expressed concern about the quality of the outcome and the cost-effectiveness of such deals for government. In addition, OMB officials discouraged the contracts, which place project funding somewhat beyond their control. At the same time, industry prefers contracts in which the government regularly pays its bills and awards bonuses regardless of how well the companies perform. With OMB opposition and industry generally opposed, share-in-savings contracts in the U.S. federal government are as difficult as selling dogs to cat lovers, despite the proven merits of the Share in Savings approach.

States Make the Case

In other governments, share-in-savings projects have flourished, benefitting governments and companies alike. The California Franchise Tax Board initiative from the early 1990s is probably the granddaddy of them all. Access Indiana and Texas Online are examples of statewide portals in which the risk and reward were shared by government and industry using industry funding. Kansas and Virginia launched similar programs. The Arizona Department of Revenue's Integrated Tax System, the North Carolina Central Procurement System and Iowa's Child Welfare System are other examples.

The Texas-Online Portal provides a typical example of how these systems work. The Texas state legislature directed its Department of Information Resources to create an E-government portal for use by all government agencies. Built without using the state's general revenue funds, Texas-Online is a self-supporting model using a private partner. BearingPoint paid for the portal infrastructure costs, estimated at $26 million. It recovered its investment through a combination of user fees, subscription fees and premium service fees. Initially, the state received 10 percent of the gross revenue generated by applications. After Bearing Point recovered its initial investment, the state government's share jumped to 60 percent of net revenues.

Three International Examples

Internationally, Share-in-Savings procurements are increasing common as governments and industry become more comfortable with the model. SiS programs bring different issues to the forefront. These sit on top of the traditional challenges of complex IT systems management. One key is to learn from previous travelers of the same road able to tell you what lies around the next corner.

Singapore, always a leader in managing public sector information technology, provides three SiS examples.

In the Integrated Land Information Service, the government and its industry partner co-share investment of capital and recurring costs. Singapore pays for the development, maintenance and enhancement of the application software, and it owns the data, applications software and intellectual property rights. The industry partner pays for hosting the application, marketing to generate demand and operating the system.

To recover its costs, the government receives royalties from the industry partner for data sold. The partner recovers its costs from transactions processed and from a fee for maintaining the application software.

In the second example from Singapore, the National E-Payment Hub System arrangement allowed the private sector company two choices. Either bid to participate in a joint venture with an equity stake or bid as an outsourcing service. In either case, the winning bidder had to meet performance targets, including the number of consumers and billing organizations signed up, the number of active consumers, and the number of bills paid and presented within the first five and eight years. The private sector company receives revenue by charging a fee for each payment transacted through the Hub system.

In the third example, in its Integrated Platform for Trade and Logistics Program, Singapore pays for the software applications and owns the software, the business processing rules, the designs and data. The private sector partner, under a 10-year contract, is responsible for the costs of all operations, maintenance,and the acquisition of all required hardware and infrastructure. The fee paid to the private sector partner consists of fixed and variable components, which the contracting officer awards based on measurable performance.

Strong IT management is required. Most of the studies and literature on share-in-savings contracts—or public-private partnerships in general—highlight the benefits of using such partnerships in government work. Nevertheless, as in any new venture, there are fresh issues to consider.

FIVE SHARE-IN-SAVINGS TIPS

Realistic milestones are necessary. Some innovative contracting methods, such as design-build—where the government combines two usually separate services into a single share-in-savings contract—can create a schedule so compressed, and pressure to meet it, that the contractor delivers a lower quality outcome than promised. Allow the contractor reasonable time to develop the system.

Anticipate that the government managers may need to allocate extra time to manage the contract after award. State governments using the SiS approach experienced a sharp increase in workload adapting to the special requirements. Virginia, for example, experienced a noticeable increase in the time senior officials spent on projects built under the Public-Private Transportation Act of 1995.

Nail everything down before signing the contract. Wu Choy Peng, Singapore's former CIO and vice chair of the International Council for Technology in Government Administration (ICA), has a keen understanding of how and why certain share-in-savings contracts succeed. Singapore identifies any adverse circumstances that could occur after award and factors them into the terms and conditions of the contract to protect the government's interests. We manage the projects closely, providing performance scores each month, she said. "Depending on the conditions, penalties may be assigned monthly, although we only do this in severe cases."

Projected revenues must be realistic. Share-in-savings programs may collapse after award because the government' design team was too optimistic when they predicted the future use of the system. There needs to be some guarantee the agencies will actually use the system and generate the transactions necessary to produce the predicted revenue. The best assurance is legislation requiring the agencies to use the system after implementation. One example is Canada's ill-fated Marketplace Program. IBM requested and received a government-wide policy requiring agencies to use the system as a condition of the contract.

Windfall profits will stir public debate. Be wary when contractors earn exceptionally large profits, because these will draw the attention of auditors and the media. Even if the government considers the project a great success, there will be criticism if the public views the contractor's profit as excessive. In Ontario, Canada, Accenture invested about $50 million to develop the Welfare Reform Re-engineering Program to aid the province in distributing social benefits. The government capped the company's return on its investment at $180 million. The operational program was a success, but auditors, the press and subsequently the public questioned Accenture's 360 percent profit from its investment.

Private partners need deep pockets. Few companies are willing to invest millions of dollars in a bid and then wait two years without income, hoping for a possible contract award. Because of the long delay, the government sometimes makes a sole source award because only one bidder remains in the competition. After award, in some scenarios, the contractor needs to work for a few years before receiving any income. Because of these factors, be careful when you initiate a share-in-savings acquisition; you will be dealing with mega contractors and their lawyers, and you must read every line in the contract before your contracting officer signs it. You must anticipate possible vendor performance problems down the road and incorporate protections for eventualities before the government signs the contract.

In summary, the Share-in-Savings approach promises progress and profit, allowing government and industry to join forces and develop the advanced systems needed to operate the government. There is no single best approach to meeting the respective needs of government and industry. As we saw in the Singapore examples, there are many variations for sharing the risk and reward. Everything is negotiable. The only limitation is the imagination of government and the officials of interested companies.

While the federal sector has almost no experience in using this approach, state and local governments and other national governments have been active in SiS for more than a decade. If asked, they can teach federal CIOs and systems managers how to organize these specialized procurements and manage them after contract award.

When funds are not available traditionally, large contractors can be a source of funds to build a system. Finally, recall that Singapore will pay for some of the development costs, sharing the financing burden with the contractor in a modified Share in Savings example. Today, this approach may have merit in the U.S. and in other governments.

In recent years, private sector companies and governments have become more tightly integrated. Share in Savings is but one additional step in the integration process between the parties.

44
FORECAST THE FUTURE FOR SUCCESS

Frank,
Navigating the swiftly changing digital world and
advancing technology is challenging. How can I work
with my staff and others to analyze the possible effects
of new legislation, a new boss or new technology?

Technology continues to advance as it has since the beginning of time. Government managers should ensure that the opportunities of the future are recognized, adopted and implemented, while protecting the rights of citizens. Will you be one of those few seizing the future?

Forecasters, anticipators of the future, often look ahead as a full-time job while employing various methodologies from their toolkit to improve the accuracy of their predictions.

WE FORECAST FOR SEVERAL REASONS

Guide policy
Shape strategy
Get ahead personally
Detect adverse conditions

Anticipate unexpected events
Adapt to a changing environment
Explore new markets, products and services
Access collective intelligence and crowdsourcing

Obviously, as a full-time program manager working on billion-dollar programs, you will not be able to devote large chunks of time studying the future and the effects it will have on your program.

Basic Forecasting 101 Employs Three Steps

What might happen? = What are our options?
What changes will we make? = What are our choices?
What will we do? = What action will we take?

Advice for Brian

To help you to forecast for the near future of 5–10 years, I suggest three courses of action.

First, monitor the macro trends, trends that are going to evolve no matter what governments want. To do this, you should join the World Future Society, read their several publications each year and attend one of their annual conferences every two years.

In addition, follow the work of Bill Halal and his 100 forecasters in his speeches, on his web site (techcast.org) and in his book, "Technologies Promise," and if possible, sign up for full access to TechCast forecasts. Not all of his interests will be relevant to your program, but his vision of the future will help you see the big picture likely to evolve, and when.

PricewaterhouseCoopers provides helpful technology forecasts. Also, Gartner has been providing technology forecasts for several decades. You may want to attend their annual conference every two years. In addition, after their annual conference others will summarize the major trends predicted by Gartner. For example, the 2014 Gartner forecasts were summarized by Forbes at this site: ***http://www.forbes.com/sites/peterhigh/2013/10/14/gartner-top-10-strategic-technology-trends-for-2014/***

Second, organize three brainstorming groups. Ask five

people with different skills, job experiences and backgrounds to join you. The rules for a good brainstorming session are these.

After describing the goal of the session and the process (described below), ask the group to close their eyes, relax, meditate, and focus only on the goal.

Then for 10 minutes, ask the group to write what their memory reveals relative to the goal.

A crucial item here is that group members not stop the flow from their brains (people know more than they think they do) and allow one side of their brain to argue with the other side saying this idea is not a good idea (all ideas are good in brainstorming).

Then ask each person to discuss one of their ideas, while you, as the leader, continue to emphasize there are no wrong answers. Write each idea on flip chart paper or on connected computers, so all can see the consensus that is evolving. After you circle the room a few times, you will observe some people with three or four ideas, while others have nine or ten. In addition, there will be duplicates. At some point, you will want to end the process, allowing those with remaining ideas to present them if they are materially different from those already reported.

Now it is up to you to summarize what you have learned from the work group and what you plan to do with it.

Also, promise to issue a short document sharing the group's insights.

Then take them to a celebratory lunch.

45

TAKING A JOURNEY: YOUR NEXT JOB AFTER GOVERNMENT

Frank,

Your thoughts on the future are exciting, but already I wonder how long I can realistically expect to work in the government. Can I stay for 20 years, until my kids are through college? What are my job prospects when my time in government is up? Are there jobs in the Washington metropolitan area for former government officials? Do they pay well?

Not that I am planning to leave anytime soon, but eventually I know I probably will. What can I expect when I leave government?

As you leave government, you will be a wiser man, perhaps humbled as well. The experience will have opened your eyes to power and complexity. You will understand the internal dynamics of government, how high level officials make decisions, how they manage policy and regulatory issues, and much more.

First, know that the decision to leave government may not be yours to make. If you had taken a political appointment, you are already a short timer. After the next presidential election, as we have already discussed—even if the incumbent wins—political appointees must submit their resignations, and in all likelihood, the president will accept them.

This often shocks individuals deeply dedicated to their job and accustomed to working long hours. A boss of mine was assistant secretary for management in the Treasury Department. He was dedicated, and he made a real difference. After an election, the White House changed hands, and the new administration moved him from his elegant office overlooking the White House to a basement cubbyhole with no windows and gave him three weeks to find a new job in the private sector and leave. He and we, his managers, were shocked at the rough treatment of such a dedicated official.

Other times, you can choose when to leave. The motivation for change ordinarily creeps in gradually over time. You will know when it is time to leave the challenges of government. Your inner soul slowly awakens you to the fact that is time to go. There can be many reasons, including exhaustion, burnout, boredom, desire for more money, a general dislike of the job and the environment, or you may feel the need for greater challenge or more independence.

In addition, some career officials decide to retire after an election if they have already been through a few presidential transitions. They dread educating what may be yet another marginally qualified political appointee.

After deciding to leave, do eight things

Selecting the right time is only fair to your boss and staff. You may choose to leave after your contracting officer signs a major contract for your program and before the contractor begins work. Alternatively, you may leave after a major lawsuit is resolved. The idea is to pick a milestone, which provides a clear demarcation and a logical place for your successor to take over. Obviously, never leave in the middle of a public relations mess.

Tie up loose ends. Finish what you can before you leave. Create a list of pending tasks and review them with your manager for his use with your replacement.

Examine your own financial situation. Are you fairly well off, maybe independently wealthy? Can you wait several years for a big payoff from stock options received from a startup or do you need money right now for things like tuition? Depending on your answer, define your objectives and develop a plan to achieve them.

In the job search, try to create opportunities rather than waiting for them to appear. Then, update your address files, e-mail addresses and telephone number lists.

Be sure your home e-mail, voicemail services and social networking sites are up-to-date. Use these, not your office facilities, for your job search activities.

Write an article for *The Washington Post* or the trade papers to position your ideas and yourself in the public eye.

In addition, accept any speaking opportunities that responsible organizations offer while you are still in your government job.

Seek "advice" luncheons with friendly, former government executives that have done well in the private sector. They will understand the need for discretion; and they can give you good advice on where there may be opportunities for your skills and knowledge. In addition, they might offer you a job, or they might pass your name quietly on to executives in other companies.

Almost everyone leaving government and seeking employment will find work with contractors in Washington and its suburbs.

With recent government experience and contacts at high levels, companies will see you as an individual able to give them an edge in procurements and help them sell to the government. You are marketable because you have current knowledge about how things work and contacts to provide insights into current directions. You can expect to earn a high salary, up to $250,000 a year, maybe more, for a few years. Eventually, you will have to move from an advisory role and prove yourself capable of a high-level job in the company, because your contact list will become less and less useful and your insights about government priorities and business opportunities will soon be outdated.

When planning your exit, consider whether you want to work for a small firm or a large company. There are some important differences.

In a small company, you can meet with the boss every day. In a large company, you will be far down in the hierarchy and may have a top boss located across the country in California, one you will never see except on an annual DVD cheerleader-type presentation.

A large company will have mature management processes and a broader and deeper base of skills to draw upon when needed. In addition, there will be full-time marketing pros, allowing you to spend more time on your customer's requirements.

In a small company, you will have to do more for yourself. You will not have a secretary as you did in your government job to manage your calendar, schedule and reschedule your appointments, fill out your travel expense reimbursement forms, and the many other things secretaries do to free up time for government officials.

In small companies, the processes are often immature, so there are many internal meetings to try to hold things together. Likely, everyone will be overloaded. There can be constant pressure to get it all done. Everyone works far more than 40 hours per week.

In addition to internal coordination and process meetings, expect to call in weekly from your telecommuting workplace, probably your kitchen, your car, Panini's or Starbucks, to discuss the revenue "pipeline" with current contracts and possible new business. In addition, there will be regularly scheduled voice conferences to discuss which opportunities to bid because bids are costly.

You should also expect the owners of a small or medium-size company to sell the business at some point. Usually, they have a target for annual sales, and once they reach it, they will seek a buyer. This leaves the employees who helped the company grow suddenly vulnerable and alone because the new people have no awareness of the good work each employee did in the past.

After Government, Allocating Your Time is Different

In large and small companies, expect to spend at least 20 percent of your time—sometimes as much as half—on internal company politics.

You will soon learn your main job is to protect your piece of the organization and its resources by demonstrating the value of your program and its ability to increase revenue.

The more senior you are, the more time you will spend on internal company political conflicts. There will be battles to determine which group has jurisdiction over a policy issue or a business line, and you will want to win these skirmishes because they provide new revenue opportunities.

You will also spend a lot of time on personnel matters, especially when you or your company wins a new contract and the search begins to find qualified people to work it. Suppose you helped to win the contract and the company asks you to build the team and manage the program. If you cannot find the right people in the company, you will have to hire from the outside. Recruiting, interviews and negotiations with new hires are time consuming.

If security clearances are required, building your team is more complicated. Once you find qualified employees, it could take nine months or more before the government's investigators grant security clearances. In the interim, as the manager, you will need to find unclassified work for the new employees to keep them busy and earning income to cover their salaries. At the same time, you need to meet the milestones on the newly won classified contract, even though you do not yet have a full staff.

You will spend another 20 percent of your time in internal meetings to discuss important issues—and some not so important—with the company's management.

Obtaining new or follow-on business is the singular goal and can occupy a third of your time. To win new business, you need to refresh your network of personal and business contacts. Arranging appointments including breakfasts, lunches, and dinners, attending events, and being out and about take time. A lunch is not an hour; it can take half a day once you include travel time, clearing security in a government building, and allowing ample time for the kind of bonding that may help you to identify new business possibilities.

As in the government, expect a blurring of your personal and business life in either a large or a small company. Anticipate being available at all hours on your smart phone, and spending evenings, even Sundays, reviewing and answering emails. When proposals are due, expect to review them at the last minute just before your company delivers them to the government agency.

Meanwhile, you may look back fondly on the intellectually stimulating work you enjoyed in the government. Unfortunately, you probably will spend less than 10 percent of your time in the private sector on anything similar. Your bosses want you to bring in revenue or solve specific problems associated with the contract; they are not interested in your big-picture, thought-provoking ideas.

Many managers may spend about 40% of their time directly managing work for their clients. In addition, the following table summarizes the likely remaining time distribution of the average manager.

ACTIVITY	TIME DISTRIBUTION %
Internal politics	12
Personnel matters	12
Internal meetings	12
Seeking new business	18
Intellectually stimulating work	6
Total	60 percent

Jobs in Industry for Former Government Officials

The jobs frequently offered by large companies to former government officials are door-opener jobs. These come with many titles, but if this is your function, your new employer expects you to reach out to your government contacts and introduce company officials to government officials. These meetings can be useful because each party can share practical planning information.

Recall the ethical dilemma you face as a government official trying to do business with friends or the problems you will face if you seem to favor one contractor over another. When you move to the private sector, you will be on the other side of the equation, asking your previous colleagues to meet with you and your new bosses. It is like asking to meet your former sweetheart when she is in town with her new husband. Your former government colleagues may meet with you, but there will be some tension and they will be careful to provide similar meeting opportunities with other companies to avoid charges that you, as a former colleague, received preferential treatment.

You should recognize door-opener jobs for what they are. One company had several retired Army and Air Force generals lined up in adjacent offices. They did little other than to arrange meetings and accompany marketing officials to meetings in the Pentagon.

Door-opener employment is not satisfying, but the money is good for a short time. These jobs have a life span of about two years because by then your high-level contacts will themselves have left government.

Project management jobs are another option. This type of work may be available in small companies. However, a large company rarely would assign a recent hire from the government to a project management role. The former government official would require years to learn a company's elaborate human resources, financial, program management processes, and the corporate culture in order to represent the company to the government.

Working independently as a consultant is a road with potholes, a bumpy trip. It is difficult for one person to do high-caliber work for current clients and simultaneously be on the prowl for new business. Eventually, one's knowledge becomes stale, contacts drift out of government, and the business dries up. Nevertheless, some few individuals manage to stay current and active and succeed for years as independent consultants. Bob Guerra and Phil Kiviat are examples of two individuals who successfully helped clients for almost three decades. The disadvantage of this approach is that at the end of the day, the principals have nothing to sell. Better that they started a company, hired people, grew it to $50 million in sales and then sold it.

There is a variation on the independent consultant option. Some former government employees work independently but maintain loose ties to a collaboration group. In this alternative, independent consultants use each other to round out a team during a proposal or after an award.

One CIO joined a company that wanted to sell to his former agency. To entice him, the company offered stock options. When he sold the company, the former CIO cashed in his options and prospered.

Still another possibility after leaving the government is seek appointments as a Board Member for emerging companies that have not yet gone public. Mega contractors supporting government tend to buy out emerging companies, allowing Board members to cash out their stock options.

How to Make Real Money

My recommendation is to go for the gold and start your own company. Sure, you will need $2 million or so to start up, but not to worry, there are people willing to help you to raise the money. Of course, they will want something in return—perhaps 51 percent of your new company. In addition, small investors, friends and family members may kick in some of the required funds in the hopes that you are a new version of Bill Gates.

After you have the initial funding, you need to think about how to compete with established companies, both large and small. Fortunately, the government has programs to help small start-ups. If you are willing to settle for a minority ownership position in the company you are creating, seek a partner eligible for one of the Small Business Administration's special set-aside programs, and you will find it much easier to win contracts, particularly in the early days when your company lacks a record of accomplishment.

If you go for the gold as I advise, plan to spend about 10 years steadily increasing the company's revenues, perhaps to the $50 million level. Then you can sell and retire to whatever life of luxury you want to pursue, possibly including a 12,000-square foot mansion on a five-acre horse farm with an antique car collection in Great Falls, Virginia, a favorite choice of some who have followed this model.

FINAL THOUGHTS FOR BRIAN

In closing, Brian, these discussions have been interesting. I am happy to have helped you in your journey to *understand and enjoy success in your high-level government job.*

As Winston Churchill said, "Now . . . is not the end. It is not even the beginning of the end. But, it is, perhaps, the end of the beginning."

Each one of us arrives full of ideas and ambition and a bit of hostility for the old ways and the old guard. We leave wiser, decidedly less hostile, slightly awed by the scale of the federal government, holding vague ideas about returning someday. We even know the job we would like to have next time.

What caused the change? Was it a "good ole boss," kindly, helpful, supportive, and a good lunch partner? Was it a victory against a dubious, resistant, White House or Congress, or was it success versus a poorly performing contractor in a long and stressful court battle?

Was it something else? Was it because you became one with your staff striving to move your program ahead, and together you did so against formidable odds and opponents in and out of the government? On the other hand, as you leave, did you change because of newfound respect for the institution, the complexity of the government's missions, and because you knew you had achieved some success in the major leagues of government?

For each person, the change always occurs, but the reasons vary. What will change you, Brian?

SHORT BIO

Frank McDonough enjoyed more than 40 years of federal service and held senior executive positions in four U.S. government organizations: the Department of Health, Education and Welfare, the Department of the Navy, the Department of the Treasury, and the General Services Administration (GSA). In addition, he worked in management positions with IBM.

He led GSA's Information Technology Policy Office for sixteen years, providing government-wide policy and oversight for all federal agencies when they acquired $300 billion in IT resources.

In addition, he represented the United States in many international discussions with the G8-Government On-line Working Council, OECD, World Bank, the International Council for Technology in Public Administration (ICA) and other international forums.

In retirement, he authors short articles on electronic government and teaches graduate-level classes emphasizing future government in the digital society.

Frank makes his home in Potomac, Maryland with his wife Mary Alice.

ENDNOTES

1   Paulo Coelho, Warrior of the Light, An *Imprint* of Harper Collins *Publishers*, First Harper mass market International printing, New York, New York, July 2011.

2   http://www.fema.gov/news-release/2014/05/22/closeout-process-begins-new-jersey-public-assistance-projects

3   *https://answers.yahoo.com/question/index?qid=200 80922165827AAR0WCu* (Number of Postal Service employees)

4   Al Karmen, *The Washington Post*, March 26, 2014, page A17.

5   Carol D. Leonnig and David Nakamaura, "Presidential travel, kingly sums," *The Washington Post*, June 14, 2013, p. A1.

6   "Security Entourage Earning Epic Reputation Ahead of Obama India Visit," *FoxNews.com*, November 5, 2010.

7   Doug Conway, "Bush has a backup or two for his jumbo," *New Zealand Herald News*, September 5, 2007.

[8]   "Bush's Travelling Entourage," Posted by Mark Frauenfelder, *BoingBoing.net,* November 29, 2007.

[9]   Kellie Lunney, "Firing Federal Employees Isn't Easy, But It Can Be Done," *Government Executive,* May 29, 2014

[10]   Max Stier, "5 Myths about federal workers," *The Washington Post,* December 5, 2010, p. B3.

[11]   *http://en.wikiquote.org/wiki/William_Howard_Taft*

[12]   Philip K. Howard, "What Broke Washington," *The Washington Post,* May 25, 2014, p. A17

[13]   Ibid.

6. Get to Know Your Ethics Officer

[14]   Adam Liptak, "Right and Left Join to Challenge United States on Criminal Justice," *The New York Times,* November 24, 2009.

[15]   Lillian Cunningham, "The fast fall of a Washington career," *The Washington Post,* April 27, 2014, p.G1.

[16]   Jerry Markon and Carol D. Leonnig, "Blagojevich is convicted on just 1 count of 24," *The Washington Post,* August 18, 2010, p. A1.

8. Do Not Be the Fall Guy!

[17]   Bill Bransford, "When it Comes to Oversight, Be Prepared, Be Careful, and Tell the Truth," *Action (Senior Executives Newsletter),* February 2007, p. 4.

[18]   Jim Snyder, "Solyndra Decisions Mine, Chu Tells Inquiry," *Bloomberg.com,* November 17, 2011.

12. Learning From Senior Officials in Other Countries

[19]   *http://ec.europa.eu/information_society/index_en.htm*

[20]   ICA-it.org

[21] Organization for Economic Co-operation and Development (*OECD*)

14. Accepting the Influence of Government Unions

[22] Editorial, "Eight Years is More Than Enough," *The New York Times*, November 23, 2008.

[23] Juliet Eilperin and Carol D. Leonnig mentioned actions in the Interior Department and the Justice Department, *The Washington Post*, November 18, 2008, p. A1.

15. Observing the Modern Day "Spoils System"

[24] Questia, Civil Service Section, *http://www.questia.com/ library/encyclopedia/civil_service.jsp*

[25] Bill Bransford, "Legislative Update, A New Year, and a New Congress May Bring More Action on Federal Employee Issues" *Action (Senior Executive Association Newsletter)*, January 2007.

16. Managing Personnel, Often an Oxymoron

[26] Stier, "5 Myths," p. B3.

17. Recovering When "They" Go after You

[27] Kim Eisner, "Better Get Brendan," *Washingtonian Magazine*, June 2010, p. 35 ff.

[28] Dana Milbank, "In Debt to an Arlington Whistleblower," *The Washington Post*, June 20, 2010.

[29] Calvin Woodward, Associated Press Writer, "Nixon dug deep for dirt on Ted Kennedy," *Yahoo News*, August 28, 2009. His reference was Luke Nichter, professor at Texas A&M University, and Nichter's web site, nixontapes.org

[30] "The Increasingly Uncomfortable 'catch -22' of the Career Senior Executive, *Action (Senior Executive Association Newsletter)*, January 2011.

19. Rationalizing How the Public May View You

[31] oncologist
HYPERLINK *"http://en.wikipedia.org/wiki/Medical_ researcher"* \o
AIDS
National Cancer Institute
HYPERLINK "http://en.wikipedia.org/wiki/Arthur_S._ Flemming_Award" \o

[32] Catherine Rampell, "Cutting off the hand that pays," *The Washington Post*, December 16, 2014.

[33] The IRS's disconnect with the public," *The Washington Post*, January 7, 2010, p. A12.

[34] Harold Myerson, "End slacker-state subsidies," *The Washington Post*, May 18, 2011, p A-17, which quoted from a 2007 Tax Foundation study that compared federal spending in each state to each state's contribution in federal taxes.

20. Using Political Spin and Manipulation

[35] *https://en.wikipedia.org/wiki/Committee_on_Public_ Information*

[36] John Maxwell Hamilton, "How our information wars began in World War I," *The Washington Post*, August 3, 2014, Page B2.

[37] *http://www.propagandacritic.com/articles/ww1.cpi. html*

[38] See: Christian Davenport, "At Arlington graves, a pain beyond words," *The Washington Post*, October 12, 2010, page B1.

[39]   Chelsea Manning, "The Fog Machine of War," *The New York Times*, Sunday Review, June 14, 2014.

[40]   Ibid.

[41]   Reuters, "Study: Cancer uses fructose to multiply," *The Washington Post*, August 3, 2010, p. A4.

[42]   "Restoring Honor rally," Wikipedia.

[43]   "Sizing up a Crowd," *The Washingtonian*, May 2012, page 24.

[44]   *http://www.motherjones.com/news/feature/1996/05/alterman.html*

[45]   Walter Updegrave, "What you need to know about Social Security," *Money on CNN*, September 17, 2009.

[46]   Cay Johnston, a Pulitzer Prize-winning journalist, *The New York Times*, "Social Security is not going broke," *http://blogs.reuters.com/david-cay-johnston/2012/05/04/social-security-is-not-going-broke/*.

[47]   Dana Milbank, "The Clinton campaign puts the 'moron' into oxymoron, *The Washington Post*, September 11, 2015.

[48]   Kenneth T. Walsh, "Brand Hillary Tries a Makeover," *U.S. News*, Feb. 25, 2014.

[49]   Dana Hedgepeth, "Boeing Loses Bid to Build Tankers to its Rival," *The Washington Post*, March 1, 2008, p. D1.

[50]   "Air Force stuns Boeing on tankers," *thenewstribune. com*, March 2, 2008.

[51]   Dana Hedgepeth, "Boeing Loses Bid," *The Washington Post*, March 1, 2008,

[52]   Karen West, MSNBC Contributor, "How Boeing Transformed the Aviation Industry," *msnbc.msn.com/ is/19421415*. July 2, 2007.

[53]   Gretchen Morgenson, "Repaying Taxpayers with Their Own Money," *The New York Times*, April 30, 2010.

54 "Dick Cheney and the ploy of the political memoir," *washingtonpost.com*, August 31, 2011.

Changes after World War II Led Us to Today with its Benefits and Problems

55 http://en.wikipedia.org/wiki/Federal_Government_of_the_United_States

56 http://en.wikipedia.org/wiki/1955

57 http://en.wikipedia.org/wiki/June_12

58 http://en.wikipedia.org/wiki/1949

59 See Wikipedia for more information on the Hoover Commissions.

60 Elizabeth Newell Jochum, "Homeland Security contractors outnumber civilian employees," *Government Executive*, February 24, 2010.

61 Gideon Rachman, "Declare victory, and end the 'global war on terror," *The Financial Times*, May 31, 2011, p. 13.

62 Interview with Matt Rose, "Rebuilding Roads and Rails," *Fortune Magazine*, November 21, 2011, p. 26.

22. The First Insight, Once You Are on the Job

63 "The Medical Revolution," editorial, *The Evening Star*, July 15, 1969, p. A-12.

23. A Single Member of Congress Can Change the Government

64 http://en.wikipedia.org/wiki/Jo_Moore
http://en.wikipedia.org/wiki/Paraphrase
http://en.wikipedia.org/wiki/Misquote
http://en.wikipedia.org/wiki/September_11%2C_2001_attacks
http://en.wikipedia.org/wiki/2001

[65]   Simon Brody, "GAO Report Says Bid Protests Declined in 2013," National Association of Government Contractors, *http:// web.governmentcontractors.org/content/news/GAO_report. aspx*, January 10, 2014.

[66]   Lindsay Simmons, "Time Is On My Side: Protests Extend Incumbency," Jackson Kelly, *Government Contracts Monitor*, August 19, 2013

[67]   Kathleen Miller of Bloomberg Government, "As government contracts dwindle, more failed bidders are filing protests," *The Washington Post*, April 30, 2012, page A10.

[68]   Kim Hart and Renee Merle, "As Military Contracts Grow, So Do Protests," *The Washington Post*, February 27, 2007, p. D1.

24. Tracking New Legislation is Part of Your Job

[69]   See the complete Clinger-Cohen Act at: *http://www. cio.gov/Documents/it_management_reform_act_Feb_1996. html*

25. Observing How the White House Gets Its Way

[70]   Paul Singer, "Bush and the bureaucracy: a crusade for control," *Government Executive*, March 25, 2005.

[71]   http://www.washingtonpost.com/wp-08070103071_ pf.html" \t "_blank

[72]   Carrie Johnson, "Whistle-Blower Suits Languish at Justice," *The Washington Post*, July 2, 2008.

26. Protecting Your Boss

[73]   "GSA Gives up on Computer System," *The Washington Times*, July 14, 1988.

[74]   "GSA Finds [ed. System] Out of Step," *Federal Computer Week*, July 4, 1988.

75 "GSA Razes $100 Million PBS Data Project," *Federal Computer Week*, July 18, 1988.

76 "Local Companies Linked to GSA Info Systems Snafus," *Washington Technology*, June 23-July 6, 1988.

77 https://en.wikipedia.org/wiki/Business_process_reengineering

27. Reorganizing Your Shop

78 Ed O'Keefe, "Government reorganizations aren't easy, history shows," *The Federal Eye*, posted 01/13/2012.

28. Probing the World of Political Appointees

79 David E. Lewis and Gabe Horton, "Obama's Presidential Appointments to Date: The Other Part of the Story," Vanderbilt University, undated.

80 Thom Shanker, "Despite the Slump, the United States Role as Top Arms Supplier Grows," *The New York Times*, September 6, 2009.

81 Al Kamen, "The USDA on Iraq: Everything's Coming Up Rosy," *The Washington Post*, In the Loop, May 8, 2006, page A 17.

82 Keith Cowing, "George Deutsch Daily Update," *nasawatch.com*, February 10, 2006.

83 Andrew C. Revkin, "Ex-Press Aide for NASA Offers Defense," *The New York Times*, February 10, 2006.

84 *http://www.govexec.com/management/2015/10/white-house-creates-new-leadership-group-help-execute-final-agency-goals/122798/?oref=govexec_today_pm_nl*

29. Can Political Appointees Run the Government?

85 Lewis and Horton.

[86] See the following site for one view of the top 15 of the worst George W. Bush appointments; *http://www.metafilter.com/45735/The-15-most-imcompetent-Bush-appointments*

Also, *http://www.motherjones.com/news/outfront/2007/09/how-to-succeed-in-dc-without-really-trying.html*

[87] Erin Dian Dumbacher, "Senior executives give low marks to Obama appointees," *Government Executive*, May 27, 2010.

[88] *http://www.theocracywatch.org/bush_cronyism_bloomberg_sept30_05.htm*

Also, Bloomberg, posted on Truthout, "Bush Cronyism Weakens Government Agencies," *Bloomberg.com*, September 30, 2006.

[89] Paul Light, "Placing the Call to Service: How Past and Future Presidential Appointees View the Appointment Process," *The Brookings Review*, Spring 2001, Vol. 19 No. 2, pp. 44–47.

30. Seizing the Opportunities after a Presidential Election

[90] Wikipedia, Laurita Doane

[91] Robert O'Harrow Jr. and Scott Higham, "Doane Ends Her Stormy Career as GSA Chief," The Washington Post, May 1, 2008, online Business Section.

31. Winning While Outsourcing

[92] *https://acquisition.gov/far/current/html/Subpart%20 7_5.html* (Subpart 7.5 Inherently Government Functions)

[93] Paul Light, *A Government Ill-Executed*, Harvard University Press, 2009.

[94] "The Best Allies Money Can Buy," *The New York Times*, November 4, 2009.

[95] Richard Powers, "What is Artificial Intelligence," *The New York Times*, February 5, 2011,

96 "Statement of the Honorable Daniel I. Gordon, Administrator for Federal Procurement Policy, Office of Management and Budget" before the Subcommittee on Oversight of Government Management, United States Senate, May 20, 2010.

97 Moshe Schwartz, "Department of Defense Contractors in Iraq and Afghanistan: Background and Analysis," *Congressional Research Service*, September 21, 2009.

98 Allison Stanger, author of "One Nation Under Contract," *http://www.youtube.com/watch?v=LR5RAZuiGoA*

99 Govcon Daily, September 29, 2010.

100 *Government Executive*'s 2010 "Top 200 Federal Contractors," *http://www.govexec.com/features/0810–15/0810–15s1s1.htm*

101 http://www.bga-aeroweb.com/Lockheed-Martin.html

102 *http://www.forbes.com/lists/2012/12/ceo-compensation-12_Robert-J-Stevens_RIMI.html*

103 Annie Gowen, "Great Falls Reflects Big Windfall," *The Washington Post*, August 16, 2011.

104 "Cisco to invest in more new ideas," *The Washington Post* (quoting *Bloomberg News*) May 12, 2014, Page A9.

105 "Top 50 Systems Integrators," *FCW*, September 30, 2015, page 26.

106 Scott Shane and Ron Nixon, "In Washington, Contractors Take on Biggest Role Ever," *The New York Times*, February 4, 2007.

107 Ibid.

108 Ibid.

109 "Report Details Misbehavior by Kabul Embassy Guards," *The Washington Post*, September 2, 2009, p. A11.

[110] Emma Brown, "Sued United States defense contractor in Iraq," *The Washington Post*, September 24, 2010, p. B6.

[111] Frank McDonough, "The Imbalance That Favors Government Contractors," *The Washington Post*, May 28, 2007, p. A16.

[112] "Mission Accomplished," *Taipei Times*, October 14, 2011, p. 6.

[113] Robert L. Grenier, <u>88 Days to Kandahar, A CIA Diary</u>, Simon and Schuster, New York, NY, 2015

[114] *http://www.nytimes.com/2011/02/06/opinion/06powers.html?pagewanted=1&nl=todaysheadlines &emc=tha212*

[115] Arnold Brown, "'Not with a Bang': Civilization's Accelerating Challenge," *The Futurist*, Sep-Oct 2007.

[116] Martin Ford, "The Lights in the Tunnel," (Acculant Publishing), 2009.

[117] "Study on privatizing government functions," *The New York Times*, December 27, 1994.

32. Working with Congress.

[118] "Distrust, Discontent, Anger, and Partisan Rancor," The Pew Research Center, April 18, 2010. See also, http://www.pewresearch.org/fact-tank/2013/09/03/current-congress-is-not-the-least-productive-in-recent-history-but-close/

[119] See: James Joyner, "Congress' Approval Even Lower than Bush's," Outside the Beltway, May 15, 2007. *http://www.outsidethebeltway.com/archives/2007/05/Congress'_approval_even_lower_ than bush's/*

[120] "Few See Quick Cure for Nation's Political Divisions," PEW Research Center, U.S. Politics & Policy, December 11, 2014

[121] Lori Montgomery, "For GOP, who'll make a deal," *The Washington Post,* August 9, 2013, page A1.

[122] Roger W. Johnson, "It Can Be Fixed!," Claremont Graduate University Press, Claremont, CA.) 2004. p. 102

[123] Ibid, pp. 96–97.

[124] Robert Pear, "Lawmakers Defend Social Security's Chief Actuary in Clash with the Commissioner," *The New York Times*, July 11, 2011, p18; and also July 10, 2010.

[125] GAO-12-215R, "Addressing Government Performance Issues," December 9, 2011.

33. Using Regulatory Authority to Change a Program's Direction

[126] See *http://www.access.gpo.gov/nara/cfr/cfr-table-search.html#page1* for a list of 50 areas in which government agencies write regulations with the power of law.

[127] Jonathan Turley, "The Rise of the Fourth Branch," *The Washington Post,* Outlook Section, May 26, 2013, page B.

[128] Joshua Gallu, "SEC Reviews S&P Math, Possible Leak of Rating," *Bloomberg.com*, August 13, 2011.

[129] *http://money.cnn.com/news/storysupplement/ economy/bailouttracker/index.html*

[130] For details on the housing bubble, see en.wikipedia.org/ wiki/Subprime_mortgage_crisis.

Also, Andrew Ross Sorkin, *Too Big to Fail*, Viking, 2009- for insights about the activities of federal officials and Wall Street chiefs leading up to the Lehman Brothers and Merrill Lynch collapses and the near failure of other firms.

[131] *http://www.examiner.com/populist-in-national/ finally-a-move-to-abolish-mortgage-finance-giants-fannie-mae-and-freddie-mac*

[132] William Hubbard, "Wrongly Blaming the FDA," *The Washington Post*, May 8, 2006, p. A19.

[133] Ryan Phillips and Aarti Shahani, "Safety measures at a standstill," News 2-Center for Public Integrity, *The Washington Post*, September 26, 2010, p.A1.

[134] *ucsusa.org/scientific_integrity/interference/executive-order.html*

[135] "Letter to senators regarding Susan Dudley's nomination to OIRA," Citizens for Sensible Safeguards, November 3, 2006.

[136] Karen Tumulty, "Obama criticized over 'signing statement," *The Washington Post*, June 3, 2014, p.A8.

[137] See: Wikipedia for an extensive history of Madoff

Also, "Madoff Chasers Dug for Years to No Avail," *WSJ.com*, January 6, 2009.

[138] Mark Schoeff Jr. "Schapiro: SEC budget cuts would 'dramatically 'curtail exams," *www.**investmentnews.com**/ **article/20110316/free/110319952***

35. Introducing Procurement, a Primer for Program Managers

[139] Blank

[140] Askold Boretsky, "Resource Projection Model (RPMTM) Overview," draft PowerPoint presentation, ASI Government, August 2012.

[141] Ibid.

[142] Mark Rockwell, "SEWP: An acquisition pioneer is still going strong, *Federal Computer Week*, March 15, 2015, page 24.

[143] Dana Hedgpeth, "The Man behind the Army's Monetary Might, Rebuilding a staff after 15 years of downsizing," *The Washington Post*, June 1, 2010, page B3.

[144] Joe Davidson, "Contracting work a good thing, but requires adult supervision," *The Washington Post*, July 15, 2010, page B3.

[145] Josh Rogin, "DOD policies to address contractor award concerns," *Washington Technology*, March 16, 2007.

The Bid Protest Process

[146] Robert Brodsky, "Contract disputes reach an all-time high," *Government Executive*, December 1, 2010.

Also, GAO protest cases between 1997 and 2012, *http://www.wifcon.com/protestsgaostat.htm*

[147] Nick Wakeman, "GAO hands down decision on Unisys bid protest," *Federal Computer Week*, August 2, 2010.
Fewer Competitors for Major Government Procurements.

[148] Vivek Kundra, "Kundra: 'IT cartel' holds back government efficiency," *The New York Times*, September 1, 2011.

36. Reckoning with Congress, Lobbyists, and Political Appointees during Procurements

[149] *The Washington Post*, Sept 2, 2009, page F22.

[150] Matthew Weigelt, "Political Connections, Robertson sees his role at GSA as being a conduit rather than a policy wonk," *Federal Computer Week*, August 24, 2009, page 22.

[151] "Round up the usual lobbyists," *The New York Times*, July 25, 2010.

[152] Kimberly Kindy, "Automotive industry regulators 'too cozy,'" *The Washington Post*, March 9, 2010, page A1.

[153] William Lowther, "Taiwan Spending on US Lobbyists to Push F-16C/D Sale," *The Taipei Times*, October 13, 2011, page one.

[154] *"OpenSecrets," http://www.opensecrets.org/lobby/index.php.*

[155] Dan Eggen, "Gingrich found gold in health reform," *The Washington Post*, November 18, 2011, page A1.

[156] PAC Summary: Total Raised/Total to Candidates, *http://www.opensecrets.org/pacs/index.php*.

[157] Ibid, page *29*.

[158] Ibid, page *29*.

37. Six Reasons Help Explain Why Major Programs Fail

[159] Craig Whitlock, "Zooming around the Alps in a homemade wing suit," *The Washington Post*, July 4, 2008, page A10.

[160] "At Microsoft, a Sad Software Lesson," *The Washington Post*, January 30, 2007, Page A 17.

[161] Robert W. Poole, Jr. and Chris Edwards, "Airport and Air Traffic Control," CATO Institute, June 2010.

[162] Letter to the Committee on Transportation and Infrastructure, House of Representatives, "Integration of Current Implementation Efforts with Long Term Planning for the Next Generation Air Transportation System," United States General Accountability Office, November 22, 2010.

[163] William Jackson said, "What's Keeping FAA's NextGen air traffic control on the runway?" *Government Computer News*, July 22, 2013

[164] Philip K. Howard, "What Broke Washington," *The Washington Post*, May 25, 2014, p. A17.

[165] Lisa Rein, "Cost to build digital archive could hit $1.4 billion, federal auditors say," *The Washington Post*, February 6, 2011.

[166] John Eichelberger, Letter to the Editor, "A Broken Immigration System," *The Washington Post*, March 28, 2010, Page A14.

[167] "6 keys to avoiding another 'grand design failure," *Federal Computer Week*, October 21, 2010.

[168] *http://006371b.netsolhost.com/granddesignreport. html*

[169] Richard A. Spires, "GAO brings the hammer down on IT acquisition," *Federal Computer Week*, March 15, 2015, Page 32.

[170] Ed O'Keefe, "New boss moves quickly to change sluggish Patent Office," Federal Diary, *The Washington Post*, October 20, 2009, Page 17A.

[171] Edward Cone, "The Ugly History of Tool Development at the FAA," *baselinemag.org*, April 9, 2002.

38. Managing the Hundred Million Dollar Programs

[172] See: Rossotti's response to questions from Barry Bozeman, Professor of Public Policy at Georgia Institute of Technology, "Government Management of Information Mega-Technology: Lessons Learned from the Internal Revenue Service's Tax System Modernization." funded by the PricewaterhouseCoopers Endowment for The Business of Government, December 23, 2002.

Also, Charles O. Rossotti, *Many Unhappy Returns*, Harvard Business School Press, 2005.

[173] Steven Pearlstein, "Innovation Comes from Within," *The Washington Post*, Friday March 4, 2005, Page E01.

[174] Jerry Seper, "IG report hits FBI Sentinel program: woes seen on schedule, budget," *The Washington Times*, October 20, 2010.

[175] J. Nicholas Hoover and John Foley, "FBI takes control of troubled Sentinel Project," *Information Week*, September 15, 2010.

[176] "IT Turkeys: 7 government projects worthy of a roast," *Government Computer News*, November 20, 2009.
Eight Additional Lessons

40. Respecting the Inspectors General

[177] Kymm McCabe, "Overcoming Fear of the Inspector General," *Federal Computer Week*, May 15, 2015, Page 30.

[178] Josh Hicks, "At Energy Dept., a long trained eye," *The Washington Post*, October 21, 2014, Page A Table

[179] Frank McDonough, "The Need for IGs," *Federal Computer Week*, June 4, 2007, Page 32.

[180] Matthew Weigelt, "Senate committee concerned about Doan's IG Comments," *Federal Computer Week*, February 13, 2007.

[181] *https://www.ignet.gov/sites/default/files/files/ CIGIE%202013%20Progess%20Report.pdf*

41. Understanding Chief Information Officer Jobs

[182] TechAmerica_Grant Thornton, Twenty-Fourth Annual Survey of Federal Chief Information Officers, "*CIO/CISO Insights: Achieving Results and Confronting Obstacles,*" jointly published by TechAmerica and Grant Thornton, May 2014.

[183] Judi Hasson, "CIOs want the power of the purse," *Federal Computer Week*, January 9, 2006.

[184] Colby Hochmuth, "The CIO puzzle,: 'It's not that simple,'" *Federal Computer Week*, June 5, 2015.

[185] TechAmerica

[186] "What CIOs Actually Study," *Federal Computer Week*, August 30, 2015, P20.

[187] Ibid.

[188] "Memorandum for Heads of Executive Departments and Agencies, Subject: Chief Information Officer Authorities, M-11-29," Executive Office of the President, Office of Management and Budget, August 8, 2011.

[189] Adam Mazmanian, "More effective oversight. Maybe," *Federal Computer Week*, February 2015.

[190] "Three Reasons We Don't Need Federal CIOs," *Information Week*, July 22, 2014.

41. Technologies Do Not Advance Rapidly, Some Not at All

[191] William E. Halal, "Technology's Promise," Palgrave MacMillan, 2008, p 48.

[192] Ibid.

[193] GAO report "Defense Acquisition Assessment of Major Weapons Programs," GAO 07–406SP, March 2007.http://www.gao.gov/new.items/d07406sp.pdf

[194] Boeing Company and Science Applications International Corporation (SAIC),

[195] "Post 9/11 Border Buildup," Texas Public Radio, retrieved Feb. 11, 2012, *http://www.tpr.org/news/2011/09/news1109091.html*

[196] Julia Preston, "11.2-million Illegal Immigrants in United States in 2010, Report Says; No Change from '09," *The New York Times*, February 1, 2011.

[197] *http://www.answerway.com/viewans.php?pgtitle=questions&expid=ETWolverine&category=163&msection=0&quesid=63690&ansid=297403*

[198] George F. Will, "High-flying corporate welfare," *The Washington Post*, March 18, 2012, Page A21.

[199] Tim Hepher, "EU may challenge $8.7 billion U.S. tax breaks in Boeing-Airbus trade dispute: sources," *http://www.reuters.com/article/2014/05/16/us-trade-aircraft-subsidies-idUSBREA4F0IK20140516*, May 16, 2014.

and

Justin Bachman, "Boeing Grabs Jumbo Subsidies from Washington State for 777X Jobs," *Bloomberg Business Week*, November 12, 2013.

[200] Niraj Chokshi, "Data: Boeing leads in state, local subsidy dollars," *The Washington Post*, March 22, 2015, page A2.

[201] Philip Mattera and Kasia Tarczynska, "Uncle Sam's Favorite Corporations," Good Jobs First, March 2015.

[202] *http://www.nytimes.com/2009/09/06/business/06boeing.html?pagewanted=all&_r=0*

[203] Pratap Chatterjee, "Billion-dollar Boeing Fence on U.S.-Mexico Border Canceled," Inter Press Service, North America, January 2011.

[204] Spencer S. Hsu and Dana Hedgpeth, "Bush's 'Virtual Fence' Faces Trouble, Delays," *The Washington Post*, September 26, 2007, Page A04.

[205] Spencer S. Hsu and Gruff Witte, "Plenty of Holes Seen In a 'Virtual Fence,' Border Sensors Not Enough, Experts Say," *The Washington Post*, September 21, 2006, Page A03.

[206] Elbit Systems Ltd.

[207] "Elbit Systems Wins CBP's Integrated Fixed Towers $145 Million Contract," *Jewish Business News*, March 2, 2014.

[208] *techcast.org*

43. Share in Savings When Money is Scarce

[209] Frank McDonough, "Share and Save Alike," *The Public CIO*, August 2005.

[210] Telephone call with Ken Buck, Ph.D, Executive Director for Management Integration, Department of Homeland Security, Office of the Secretary, September 30, 2015

ACKNOWLEDGMENTS

My thanks to Michael Hardy, News Editor, *Federal Computer Week*, who did the initial edit of Spring Training for the Major Leagues of Government. In addition, he introduced the Q&A format beginning each chapter when the main character poses a question for his mentor.

Thanks are also due to Lauren Markoe, national reporter and author at *Religion News Service,* who did an intermediate edit and brought the Chicago Style to Spring Training for the Major Leagues of Government.

Several people reviewed selected chapters and suggested changes or confirmed the accuracy of specific content including Dale Christensen, Renny DiPentima, Martha Dorris, Phil Kiviat, and John Sindelar.